ARCHITECTURAL DRAFTING FUNDAMENTALS

John E. Ball
Northeast Louisiana University

RESTON PUBLISHING COMPANY, INC., Reston, Virginia
A Prentice-Hall Company

Library of Congress Cataloging in Publication Data

Ball, John E.
Architectural drafting fundamentals.

1. Architectural drawing. I. Title.
NA2700.B273 720'.28'4 80-14753
ISBN 0-8359-0254-4

10 9 8 7 6 5 4 3 2 1

Printed in the United States of America.

Preface

Architectural Drafting Fundamentals is an introductory experience in architectural drafting and is designed for students who have little or no drafting experience. The text can be used in high schools, vocationa and technical schools, community colleges, and universities.

Architectural Drafting Fundamentals covers the very basic elements of architectural drafting, moving from the simple to the complex. It is designed to cover the basic instruction in the drawing of a small building. Step-by-step illustrations are used to explain details and construction procedures. A student should be encouraged to complete each assignment and work toward the completion of a complete set of plans. If a student completes each assignment, he should develop the necessary skills in architectural drafting. To complement and enrich the course, manufacture's catalogues should be made available to the student.

The basic format of the text has been tested on thousands of high school and college students and has been found to be highly successful.

Contents

Chapter 1
DRAFTING EQUIPMENT

In order to produce a quality drawing a draftsman should have some basic drafting equipment and should be quite familiar with the operation of the equipment. To obtain satisfactory work from the equipment, it should be of a good quality. A reliable dealer in drafting equipment could be an asset to the beginner in the selection of the equipment. The tools and equipment are, in most cases, precision instruments and will last a lifetime, if taken care of properly.

THE T-SQUARE

The T-square (Figure 1-1) is used to draw horizontal lines and can be used with triangles to draw vertical lines. It has a head and a blade that forms a right angle. The blade is constructed of hardwood, or it can have a transparent blade edge made of plastic. The blade of the T-square can vary in length from twelve to sixty inches, but the most popular length is twenty-four inches.

To use a T-square properly, place the head against the left edge or right edge of the drawing board and apply a small amount of pressure. If a person is right-handed, the head is placed against the left edge of the drawing board, but if a person is left-handed the head is placed against the right edge of the drawing board. The head of the T-square can then be slid up and down the drawing board. As a line is drawn, the hand should be positioned on the blade and enough pressure applied to keep the T-square in proper alignment (Figure 1-2).

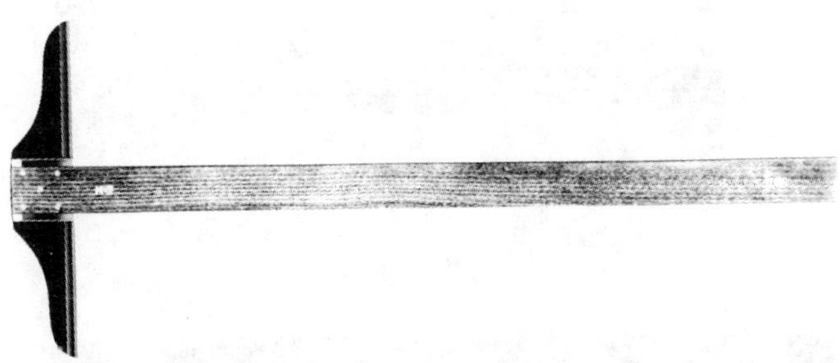

Figure 1-1
The T-square.

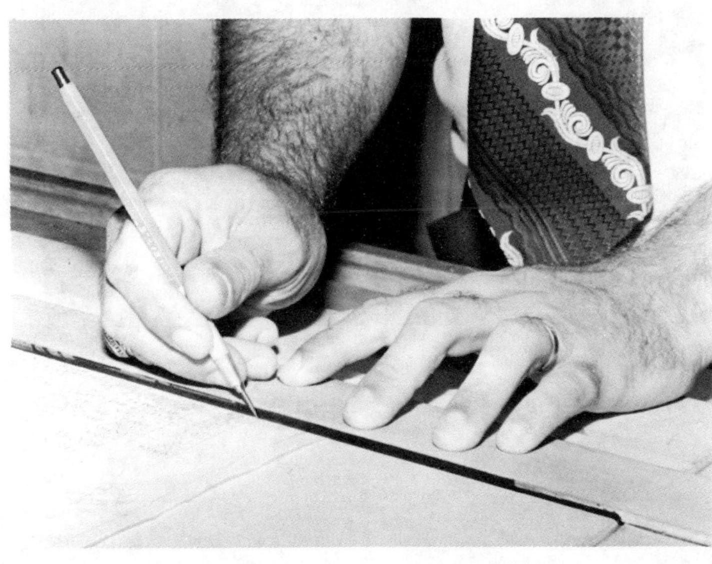

Figure 1-2
Using the T-square.

THE PARALLEL STRAIGHT-EDGE

Many architects and architectural draftsmen prefer to use a parallel straight-edge in place of a T-square (Figure 1-3). The straight-edge is available in many different lengths and can be fastened to a drawing board, or it can be mounted to a drafting table. The straight-edge has the advantage of automatically maintaining its parallel motion regardless of the amount of pressure applied (Figure 1-4). Some parallel straight-edges have small ball bearings on the underside of the blades. This allows the straight-edge to operate more freely and, in some cases, they help in keeping the drawing clean.

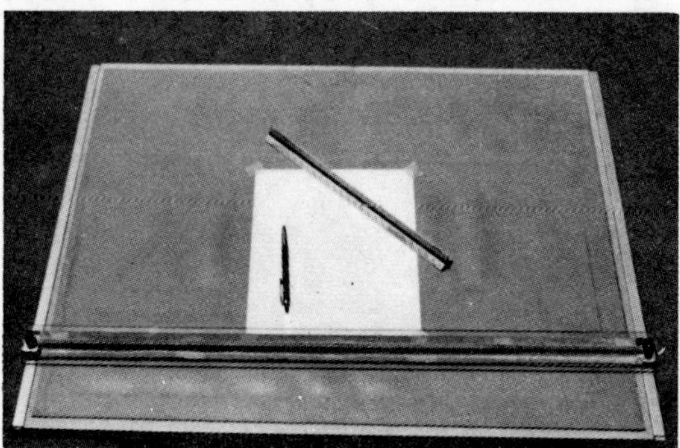

Figure 1-4
The parallel straight-edge.

Figure 1-3
Using the parallel straight-edge.

THE DRAFTING MACHINE

The drafting machine can be used in place of the parallel straight-edge or T-square (Figure 1-5). The drafting machine replaces the scale, triangles, and adjustable triangle. It can be used to draw vertical or horizontal lines, or it can be used in laying out and measuring angles. The desired angle is achieved by depressing a control button and shifting the blades to an angle on the protractor (Figure 1-6). The scale assembly can automatically be snapped into any unit multiple of 15 degrees. The blades on the drafting machine can be interchanged, using either the architect's or engineer's scale.

Figure 1-5
A drafting machine.

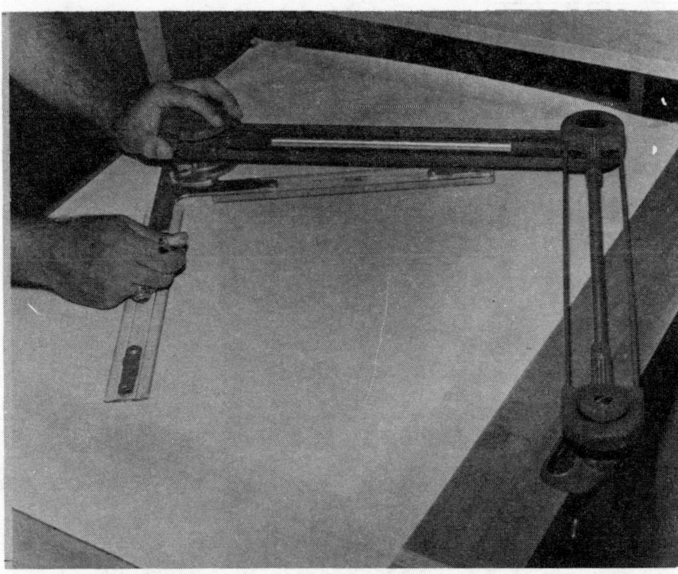

Figure 1-6
Adjusting the drafting machine.

PENCILS AND LEAD

Drawing pencils are available in a variety of shapes and sizes. Many draftsmen prefer to use a mechanical holder for their lead while some would rather use a traditional drawing pencil. The lead used can range from 9H (the hardest) to 7B (the softest). See Figure 1-7. Each lead is used for a specific purpose. The beginning draftsman should be aware of the different grades of lead, but will probably have to experiment with the leads to find one to his liking. Because the different brands of lead usually vary in hardness, it is advisable to use only one brand of lead.

The pencil should be kept sharp at all times. There are two basic ways to keep the lead sharp: a sandpaper pad (Figure 1-8) or a lead pointer (Figure 1-9). The sandpaper pad is messy and requires a certain amount of skill in sharpening a lead. The lead pointer is usually preferred by most draftsmen and is available in many different styles.

In architectural drafting there are various types of lines, each used for a specific purpose. The most common lines are shown below along with the most common leads used to draw the lines.

outline of an object (dark, thick - H or 2H)

hidden line (medium thick - H or 2H)

section line (thin - 6H)

center line (thin - 6H)

dimension line (thin - 6H)

cutting plane (extra thick - HB)

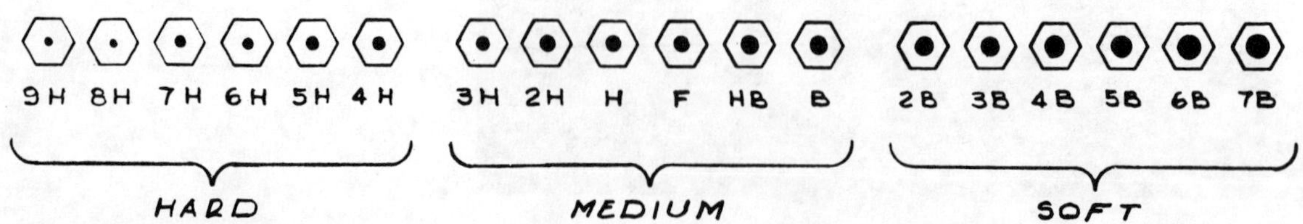

Figure 1-7
Lead grades.

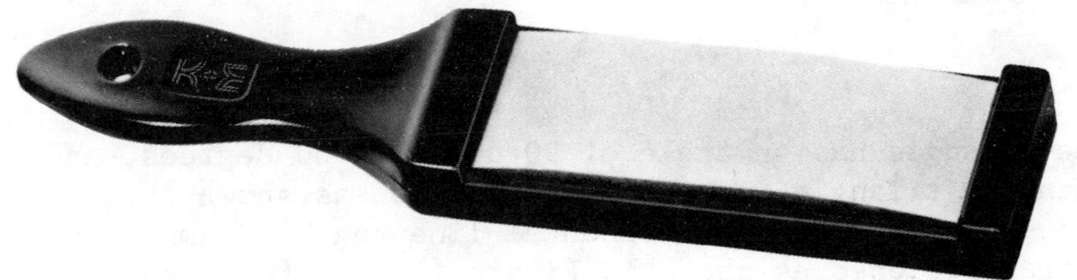

Figure 1-8
A sandpaper pad.

Figure 1-9
Pencil pointer.

THE 30-60 DEGREE TRIANGLE

The 30-60 degree triangle has an angle of 90 degrees, 30 degrees, and 60 degrees. When the triangle is held in a position as shown in Figure 1-10, a 30-degree line to a horizontal line can be drawn. If the triangle is repositioned as shown in Figure 1-11, a 60-degree line to a horizontal line can be drawn. When the line is drawn the base of the triangle should be placed on top of the blade; never place the triangle on the underside of the blade.

Figure 1-10
Using the 30-60 degree triangle.

Figure 1-11
Drawing a 60-degree line to a horizontal line.

THE 45-DEGREE TRIANGLE

To draw vertical or inclined lines, a 45-degree triangle can be used in combination with a parallel-ruling straight-edge or T-square (Figure 1-12). The 45-degree triangle has two angles of 45 degrees and one angle of 90 degrees. To properly use the 45-degree triangle, the vertical edge of the triangle should be placed to the left side of the drawing board. The pencil is then placed adjacent to the triangle and inclined in the direction to which the line will be drawn (Figure 1-13). As the pencil is drawn along the edge of the triangle, it should be slowly rotated between the thumb and forefinger. The rotation of the pencil keeps an even point on the lead.

Figure 1-12
45-degree triangle.

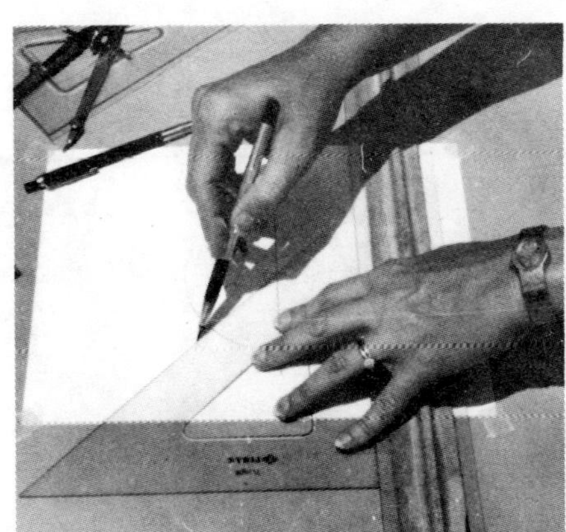

Figure 1-13
Using the 45-degree triangle.

THE ADJUSTABLE TRIANGLE

The adjustable triangle is often used as an aid in the drawing of inclined lines (Figure 1-14). The adjustable triangle has a protractor scale that will permit the measuring of an angle between 0 degrees and 90 degrees. The protractor has two rows of graduation, an outer and an inner (Figure 1-15). The outer row is used to measure angles from 0 to 45 degrees, while the inner row is used to measure angles from 45 to 90 degrees. When the adjustable arm is set in position, it is secured by a thumbscrew.

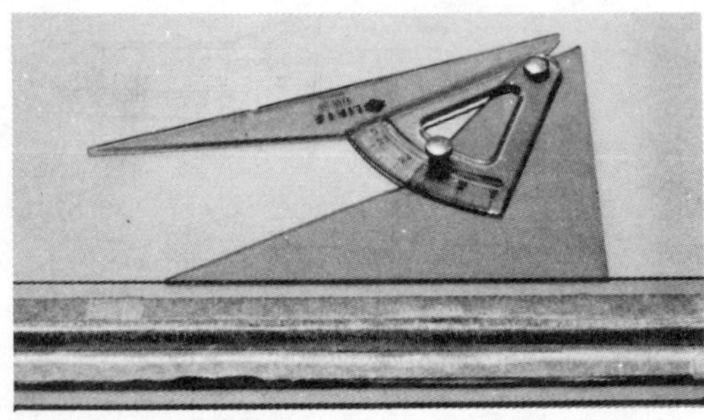

Figure 1-14
The adjustable triangle.

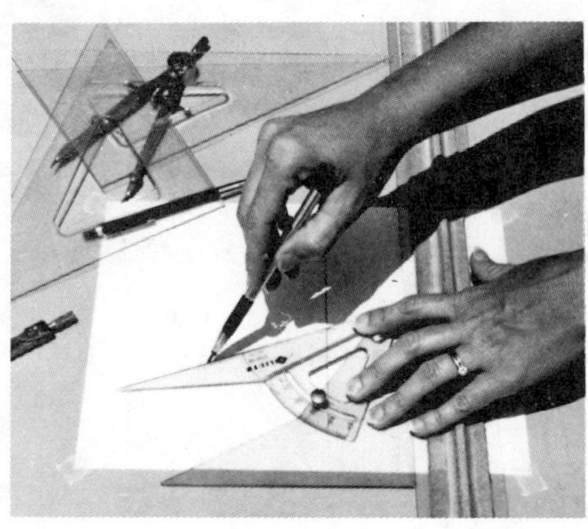

Figure 1-15
Using the adjustable triangle.

THE ARCHITECT'S SCALE

Most of the measurements of a set of plans are made with the architect's scale (Figure 1-16). The triangular scale is one of the more popular scales and has eleven different scales: full scale = 1/16" graduations; 1/8" = 1'-0"; 1/4" = 1'-0"; 3/4" = 1'-0"; 1/2" = 1'-0"; 1" = 1'-0"; 3" = 1'-0"; 3/32" = 1'-0"; 3/16" = 1'-0". Each scale has several divisions representing feet and one division at the end of the scale which is divided into inches and fractions. The dimension in feet is read from the zero out, and the dimension in inches is read from the zero in (Figure 1-17).

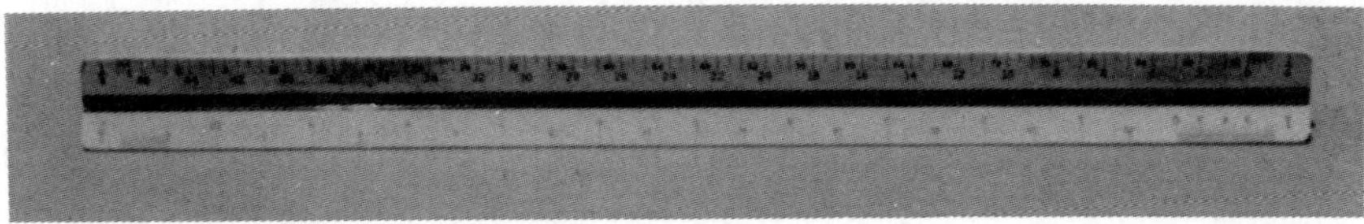

Figure 1-16
The architect's scale.

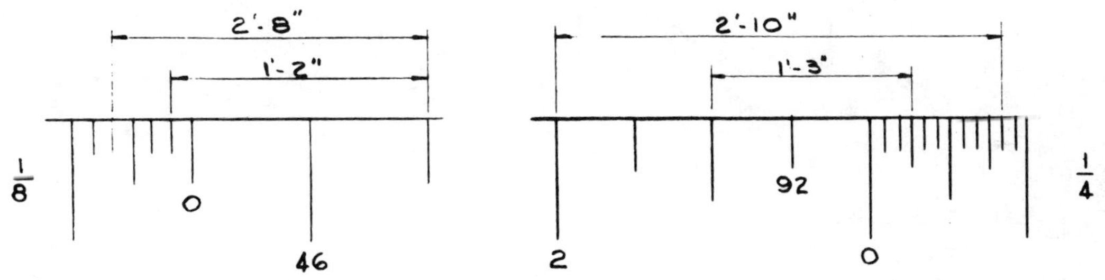

Figure 1-17
Reading the architect's scale.

THE ENGINEER'S SCALE

The engineer's scale (Figure 1-18) is used, in architectural drafting, primarily for the construction of plot plans. The engineer's scale is graduated into decimal units (Figure 1-19). There are six different scales, each representing an inch that is divided into 10, 20, 30, 40, 50, and 60 equal parts.

Figure 1-18
The engineer's scale.

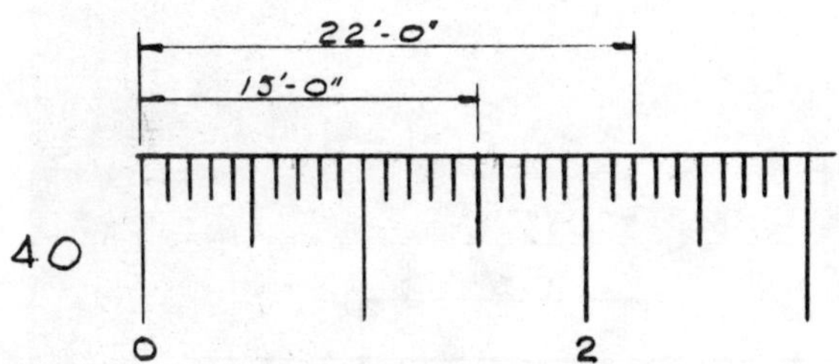

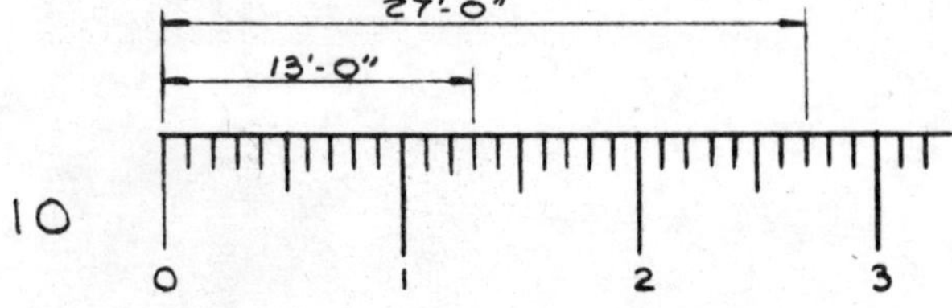

Figure 1-19
Reading the engineer's scale.

THE FRENCH CURVE

Often it is necessary to draw a curve other than a circle or arc. A French curve, or irregular curve, can be used to draw these curves, (Figure 1-20). The French curve is made of transparent plastic and has many geometric curves in its shape. To use the irregular curve properly, a series of points should first be plotted. After the points are plotted they should be connected by placing the French curve over a minimum of three points (Figure 1-21). The three points are then connected, and the curve is repositioned so that at least one of the previous points falls on the French curve, thus fairing the line in a smooth curve.

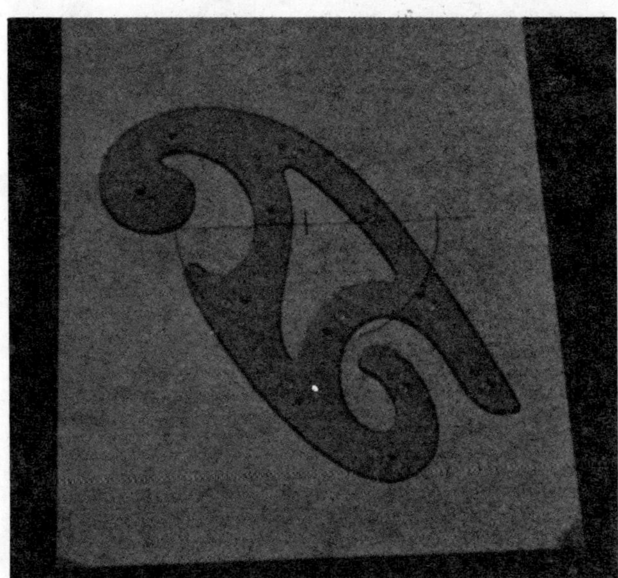

Figure 1-20
The French curve.

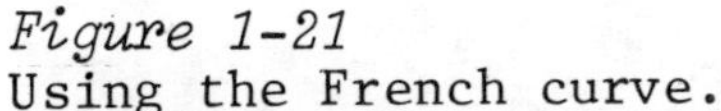

Figure 1-21
Using the French curve.

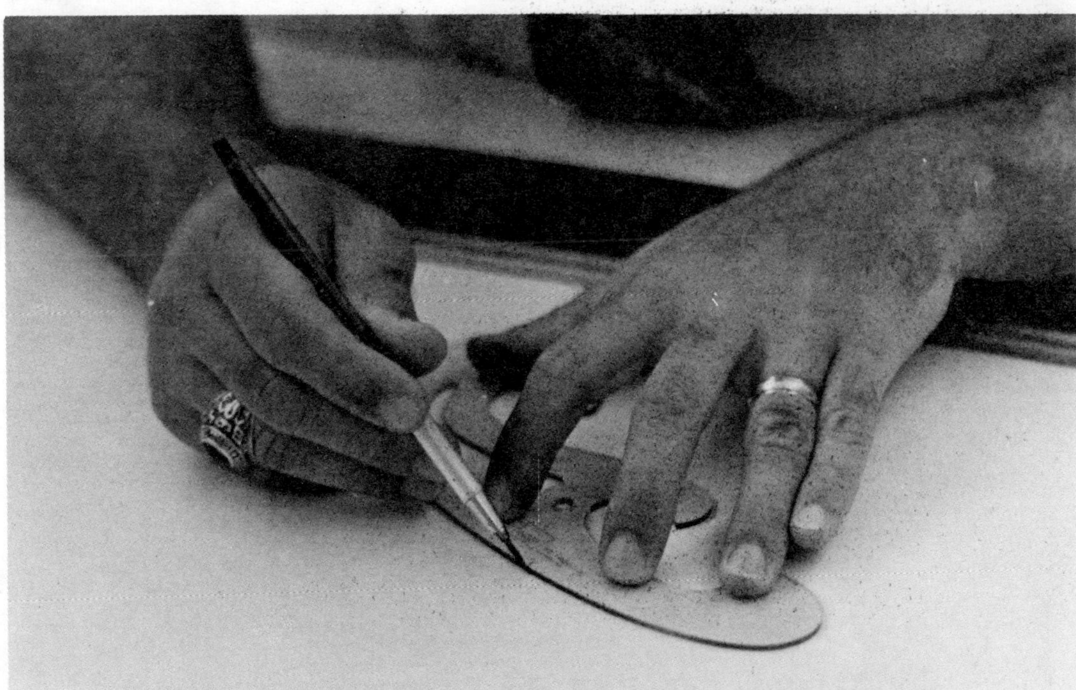

INCLINED LINES

A series of different angles can be accomplished by using the two common triangles (30-60 degree and 45 degree) or by using the two in combination (Figure 1-22). An angle of 30 degrees, 60 degrees, or 90 degrees can be achieved by using the 30-60 degree triangle. An angle of 45 degrees or 90 degrees can be accomplished by using the 45-degree triangle. The 30-60 degree triangle and 45-degree triangle can be combined to achieve angles of 15 degrees and 75 degrees.

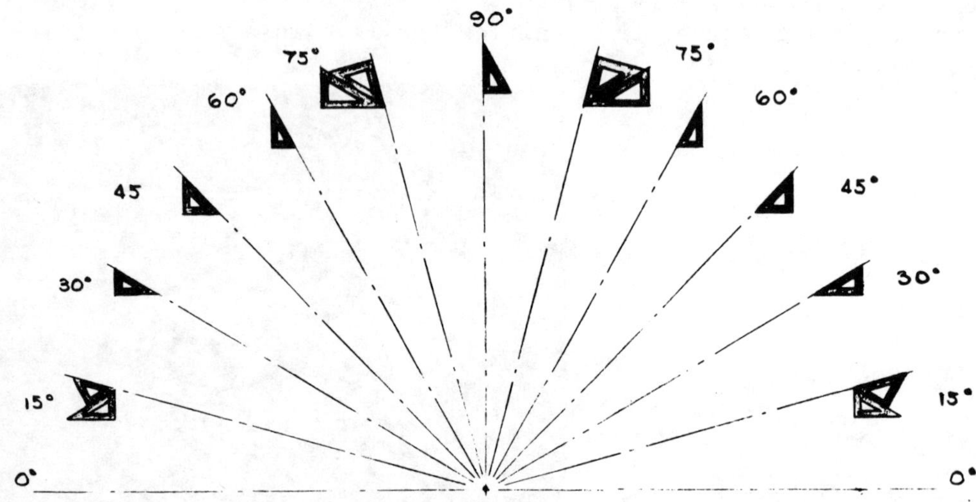

Figure 1-22
The application of the triangles.

DRAWING INSTRUMENTS

A "set" of drawing instruments, in architectural drafting, is not as popular as they once were, but some draftsmen still use them. The instruments are usually sold in a set consisting of a compass, dividers, and ruling pens.

To use the compass properly, the needle point should be adjusted so that it projects slightly past the point of the lead. The needle point should be placed at the appropriate location and the required radius set. Leaning the compass forward, a line is started in a clockwise direction, rotating the handle between thumb and forefinger (Figure 1-23).

The dividers are used for dividing a line into equal parts or for transferring measurements from one location to another. To divide a line into equal parts is largely trial and error. To use the divider properly, the handle is held between the thumb and forefinger, and the divider is rotated alternating from clockwise to counterclockwise. (Figure 1-24).

Figure 1-23
Using the compass.

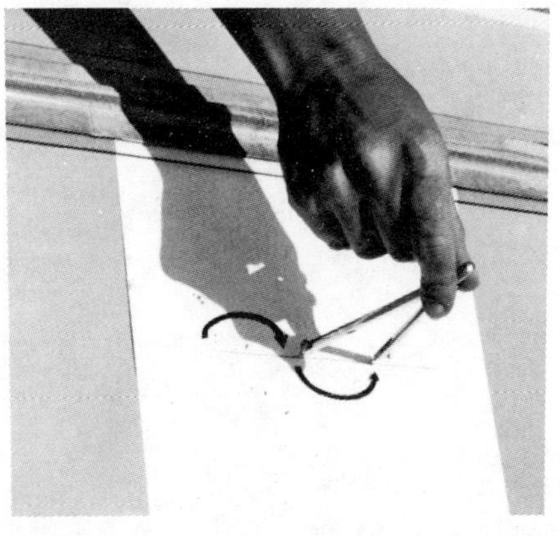

Figure 1-24
Using the dividers.

Assignment: Using the T-square, draw a series of horizontal lines.

Assignment: Using the T-square and a triangle, draw a series of vertical lines.

Assignment: Using the parallel straight-edge and a triangle, draw a two-inch square.

Assignment: Using the parallel straight-edge and a 45-degree triangle, draw a series of inclined lines.

Assignment: Using the drafting machine, divide the circle into 5-degree segments.

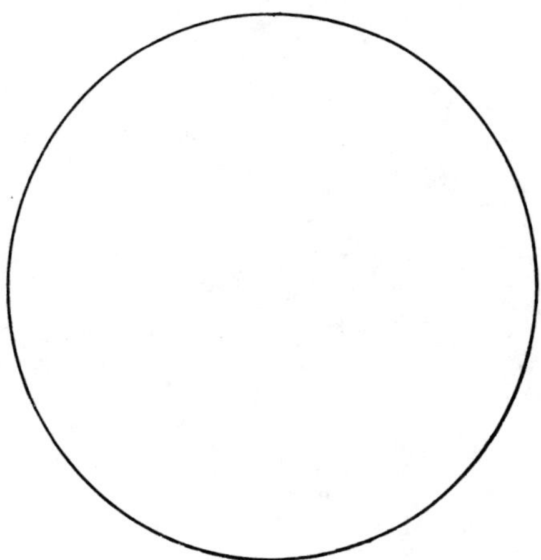

Assignment: Using the correct lead, draw the indicated lines.

hidden line

section line

center line

cutting plane line

dimension line

center line

outline of an object

Assignment: Draw a series of inclined lines at a 30-degree angle.

Assignment: Draw a series of inclined lines at a 60-degree angle.

Assignment: Draw a series of vertical lines.

Assignment: Draw a series of inclined lines at a 45-degree angle.

Assignment: **Draw a series of inclined lines, 5 degrees apart.**

Assignment: Draw an inclined line 2-1/2 degrees to the horizontal. Also draw lines that are: 26, 27-1/2, 36, 38-1/2, 46, and 73-1/2 degrees from the horizontal.

Assignment: Using the specified scale, measure the given lines.

	ft.	in.
3/8" = 1'-0"	4	4
1/2" = 1'-0"	4	6
3/32" = 1'-0"	29	0
1/8" = 1'-0"	16	0
1/4" = 1'-0"	11	0
3" = 1'-0"	4	?
1-1/2" = 1'-0"	2	?

Assignment: Using the specified scale, draw the lines to the proper length.

Length	Scale
2'-6"	3/13" = 1'-0"
9'-0"	3/32" = 1'-0"
4'-3"	1/4" = 1'-0"
8'-0"	1/8" = 1'-0"
2'-2"	1/2" = 1'-0"
3'-0"	3/4" = 1'-0"
2'-6"	1/2" = 1'-0"

Assignment: Using the specified scale, measure the given lines.

1" = 10'-0"	____ ft.	____ in.
1" = 20'-0"	____ ft.	____ in.
1" = 30'-0"	____ ft.	____ in.
1" = 40'-0"	____ ft.	____ in.
1" = 50'-0"	____ ft.	____ in.
1" = 60'-0"	____ ft.	____ in.

Assignment: Using the irregular curve, connect the plotted points.

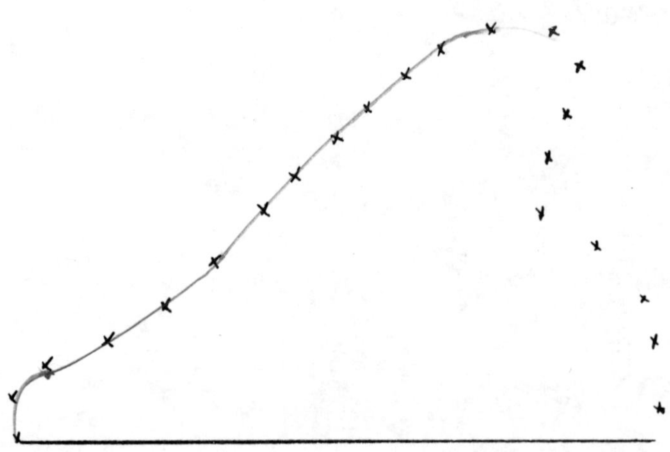

Assignment: Using the 30-60 and 45-degree triangles, draw a series of angles at: 15, 30, 45, 60, 75, and 90 degrees.

Assignment: Using a compass, draw a circle that has a diameter of 4-1/2 inches.

Assignment: Using a divider, divide the line into 5 equal parts.

UNIT END TEST

Measure the given lines, using the specified scale.

1/4" = 1'-0" ____ ft. ____ in.

3/8" = 1'-0" ____ ft. ____ in.

3/4" = 1'-0" ____ ft. ____ in.

3/16" = 1'-0" ____ ft. ____ in.

Draw inclined lines that are 5, 10, 12, 20, 30, 45, and 90 degrees to the horizontal line.

Using the French curve, connect the plotted points.

Chapter 2
LETTERING

The lettering found on architectural drawings is extremely important, for without legible notes and dimensions the plans are useless. Lettering is used to convey a message on a drawing that cannot be shown by graphic shapes and symbols. The lettering on a drawing can and should complement the graphic shapes, or it can be done in "poor taste" and make the drawing difficult to read.

LETTERING

The style of lettering that most draftsmen use is called single stroke gothic. In using the single stroke gothic technique, a 2H or H pencil is held at an approximate angle of 45 degrees, and each letter is made with a series of strokes (Figure 2-1). To aid in the lettering process, light guidelines 1/8 inch to 3/16 inch are used.

ABCDEFGHIJ
KLMNOPQRS
TUVWXYZ

Figure 2-1
Single stroke gothic lettering.

ARCHITECTURAL LETTERING

Although many architects prefer the single stroke gothic style of lettering, some draftsmen and architectural firms have developed their own style of lettering (Figure 2-2). It is often difficult for a beginning student to develop a distinctive style of lettering. To develop a style of lettering, there are certain points to remember: (1) keep the area between the letters equal (it is not necessary to measure the distance, but correct spacing is important); (2) the space between words should equal the space of a letter; (3) *always* use guidelines (Figure 2-3); (4) make the letters uniform in height; (5) make the letters stable, so that they do not appear top heavy.

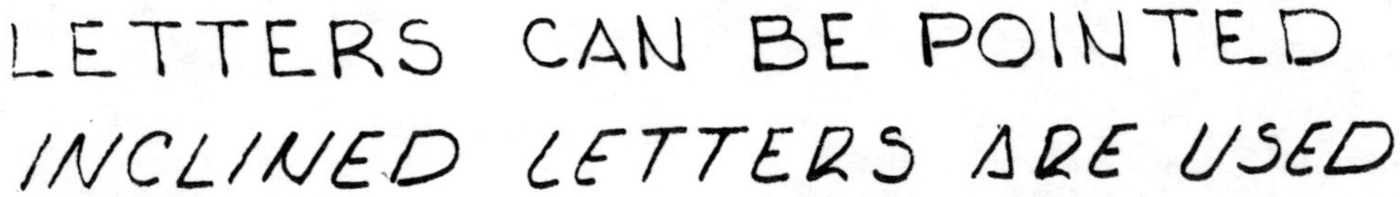

LETTERS CAN BE POINTED
INCLINED LETTERS ARE USED

Figure 2-2
Various lettering styles.

GUIDE LINES ARE LIGHT,
DRAW WITH A 6H, AND
ARE USUALLY 1/8 TO 3/16
IN HEIGHT. A LETTERING GUIDE
CAN BE USED TO ACHIEVE
UNIFORM GUIDE LINES.

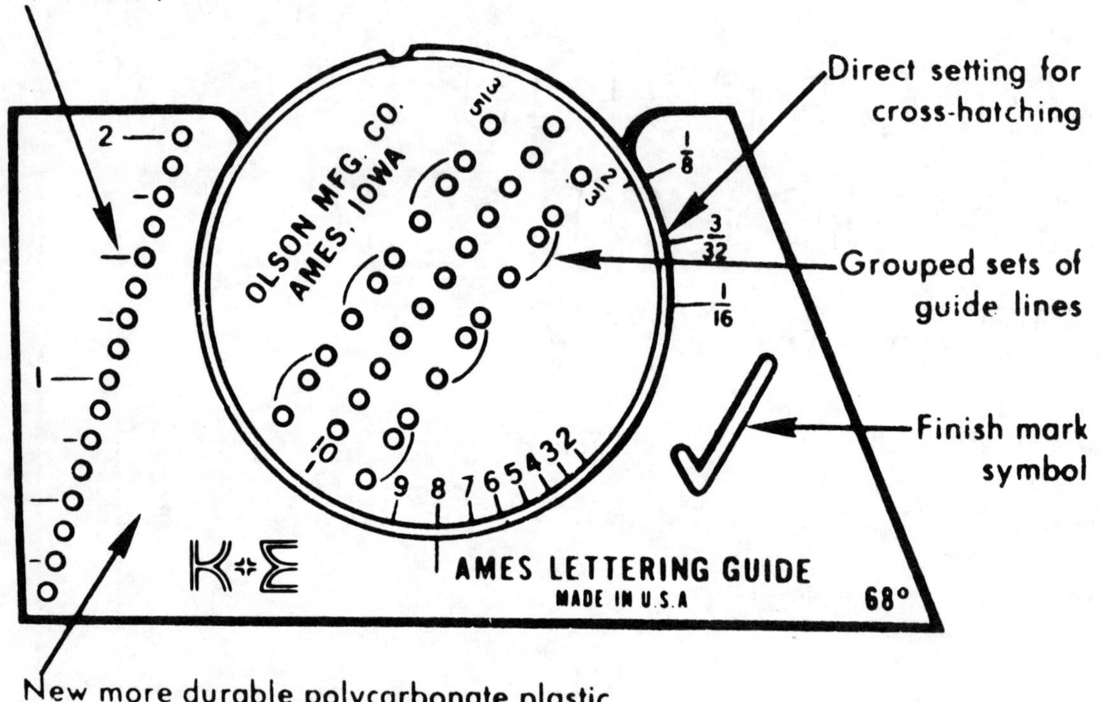

Figure 2-3
Guidelines.

TITLE BLOCKS

A title block or title strip should always accompany a drawing. The title block should be easy to read and contain certain information. It should have the name of the architectural firm and their address, the date, sheet number, the draftsman's name, scale, and the title of the sheet.

Some firms use a rectangular title block (Figure 2-4), placed in the lower right-hand corner of the sheet, while other firms use a title strip that extends across the bottom or the end of the sheet (Figure 2-5).

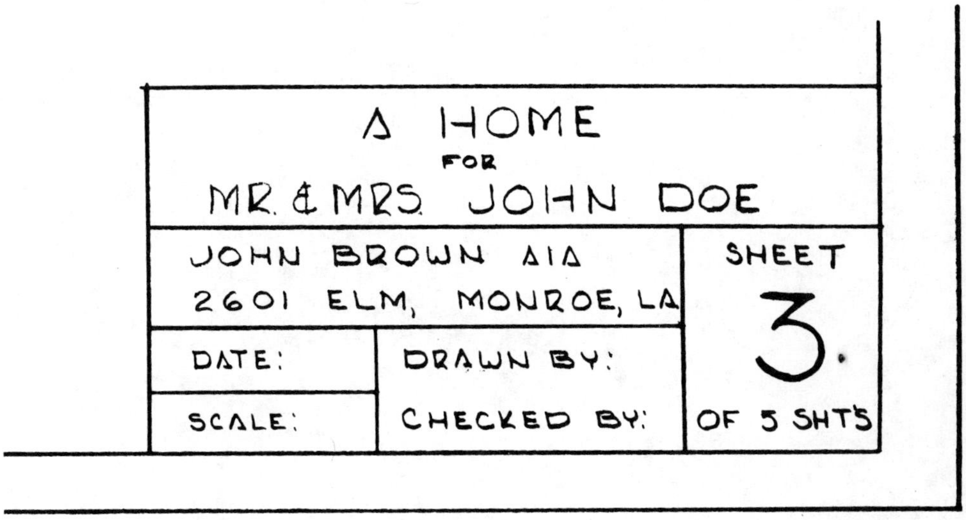

Figure 2-4
Title block.

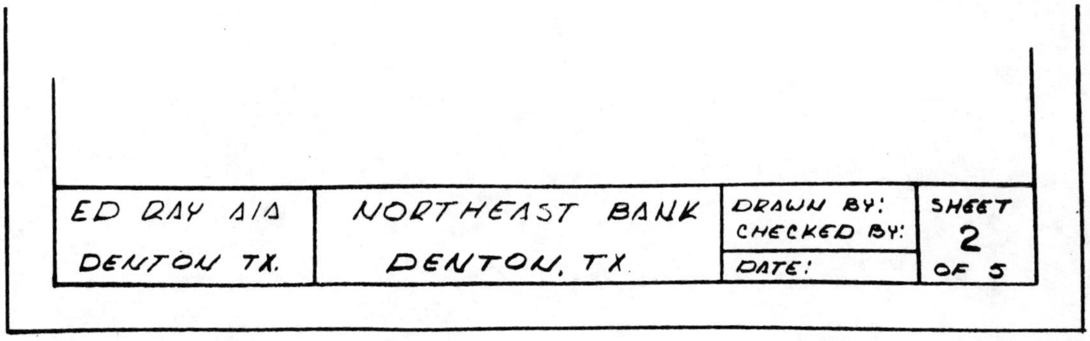

Figure 2-5
Title strip.

Assignment: Using the letters in the left-hand margin as a guide, practice the single stroke gothic lettering technique.

A

B

C

D

E

F

G

H

I

J

K

L

M

N

O

P

Q

R

S

T

U

V

W

X

Y

Z

1

2

3

4

5

6

7

8

9

Assignment: Draw a series of guidelines, and practice your lettering.

Assignment: Design a title block or title strip.

UNIT END TEST

Using an approved style of lettering, discuss the points to remember when developing a style of lettering. PRACTICE *YOUR* STYLE OF LETTERING!

Chapter 3
REVIEW OF BASIC TECHNICAL DRAWINGS

A draftsman without an understanding of technical drawing has difficulty in architectural drawing. Geometric construction, orthographic projection, sectioning, and pictorial drawings are fundamental to architectural drafting. Geometric construction is used in the formulation of general shapes and line intersections; orthographic projection is a universal technique used to show the principal views of an object; sectioning is used for a wide variety of details; and pictorial drawings are used for the untrained eye to see a particular structure or detail in pictorial form.

ANGLES

There are five basic types of angles. They are: right angles, acute angles, straight angles, obtuse angles, and reflex angles. A right angle has an angle of 90 degrees (Figure 3-1). An acute angle is an angle that has less than 90 degrees (Figure 3-2). A straight angle contains 180 degrees and is drawn as a straight line (Figure 3-3). An obtuse angle is greater than a right angle but less than a straight angle (Figure 3-4). A reflex angle is an angle that is larger than a straight angle (Figure 3-5).

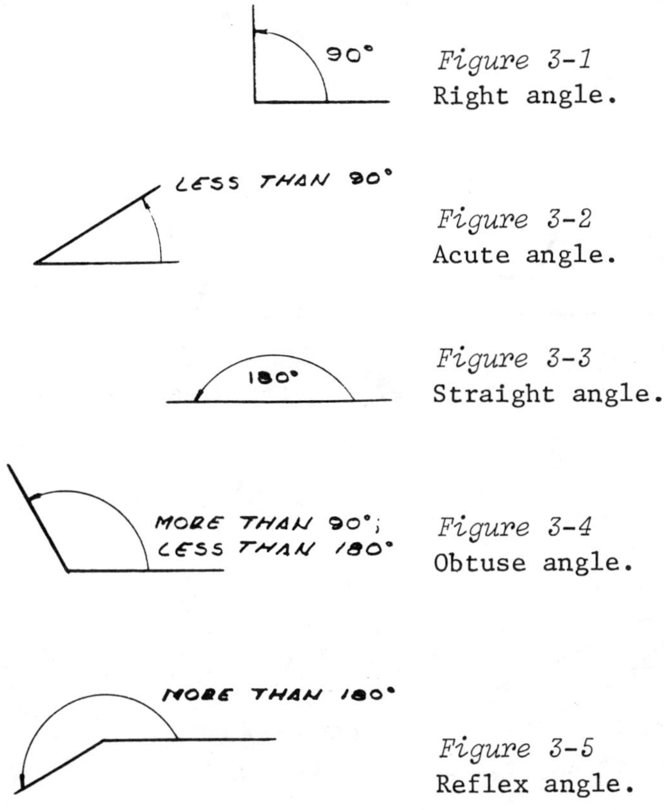

Figure 3-1
Right angle.

Figure 3-2
Acute angle.

Figure 3-3
Straight angle.

Figure 3-4
Obtuse angle.

Figure 3-5
Reflex angle.

TRIANGLES

Triangles are classified as: scalene triangles, isosceles triangles, or equilateral triangles. A scalene triangle has no two sides that are equal (Figure 3-6). If all three sides of a triangle are equal, it is an equilateral triangle (Figure 3-7). If the triangle has two equal sides, it is called isosceles triangle (Figure 3-8).

Triangles may also be classified according to their angles. A right triangle has one angle of 90 degrees and two acute angles (Figure 3-9). An obtuse triangle has one angle greater than 90 degrees and two acute angles (Figure 3-10). An acute triangle has three angles less than 90 degrees (Figure 3-11).

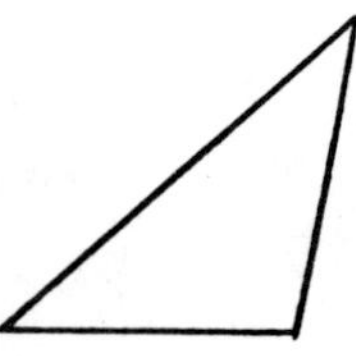

Figure 3-6
Scalene triangle.

Figure 3-7
Equilateral triangle.

Figure 3-8
Isosceles triangle.

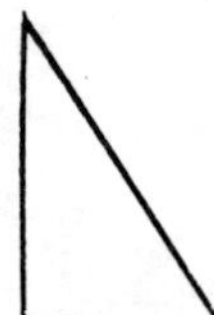

Figure 3-9
Right triangle.

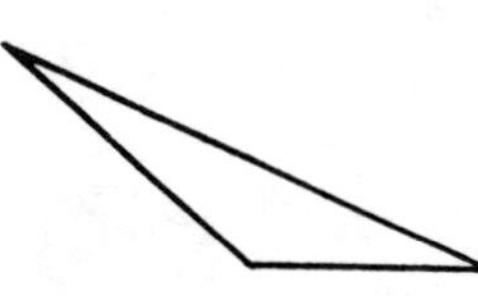

Figure 3-10
Obtuse triangle.

Figure 3-11
Acute triangle.

DIVISION OF A LINE INTO EQUAL PARTS

Frequently a line must be divided into equal parts. One of the easiest techniques used in the equal division of a line can best be described in a series of steps.

1. Draw a vertical line at the end of the line that is to be divided (Figure 3-12).

2. Place a scale at the end of the line and adjust the scale to the perpendicular line so the required divisions fall between the end of the line and the perpendicular line (Figure 3-13).

3. At each equal interval, mark the division (Figure 3-14).

4. Draw a vertical line from each division line (Figure 3-15). Equal divisions are created where the vertical lines intersect the horizontal line.

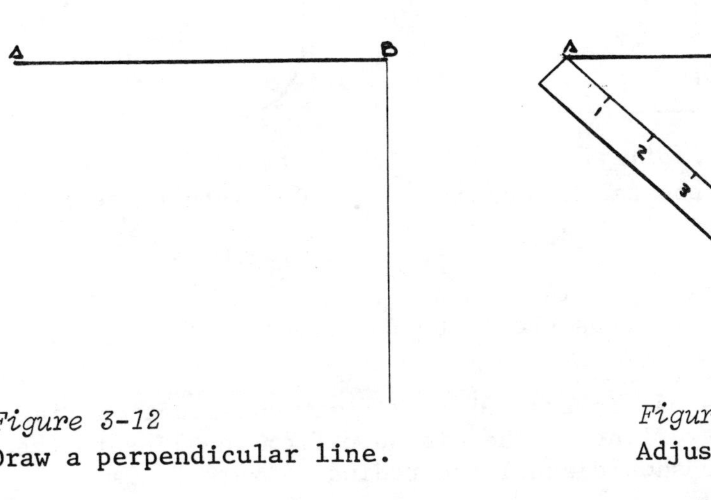

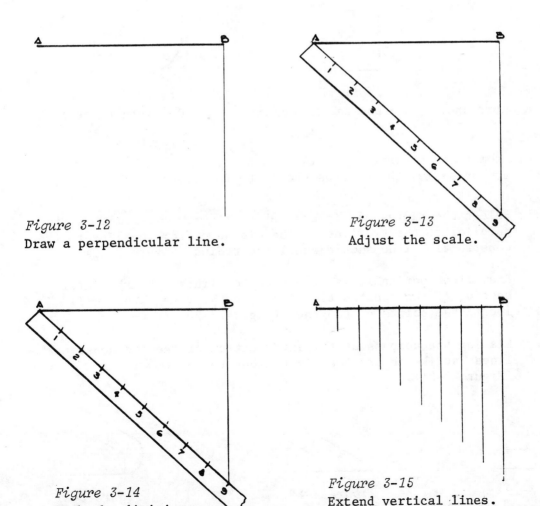

Figure 3-12
Draw a perpendicular line.

Figure 3-13
Adjust the scale.

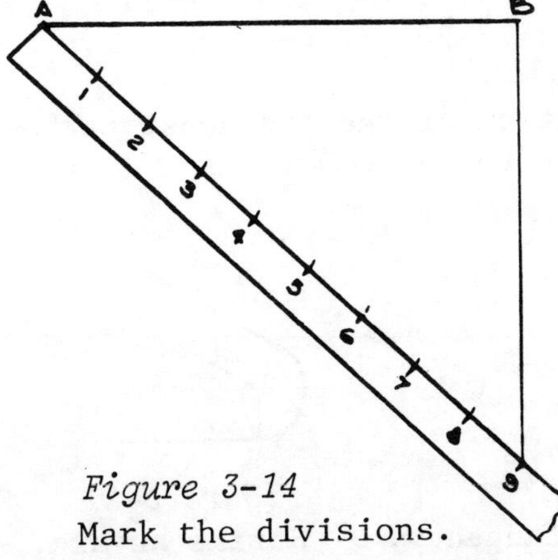

Figure 3-14
Mark the divisions.

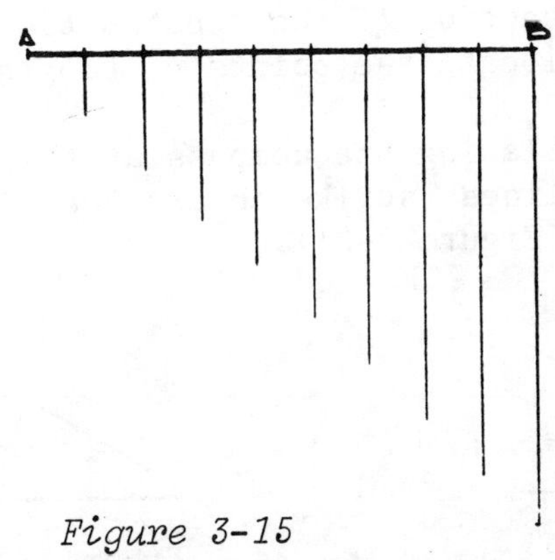

Figure 3-15
Extend vertical lines.

ARC

When a rounded corner is desired, it is necessary to draw an arc tangent to perpendicular lines. To achieve the desired round, these steps should be followed:

1. Set the compass on the radius of the round.
2. Place the point of the compass at the intersection of the two perpendicular lines and strike a short arc on each line (Figure 3-16).
3. Place the point of the compass on each of the short arcs and strike two intersecting arcs to locate the center of the rounded corner (Figure 3-17).
4. Placing the compass at the intersection of the two arcs, strike an arc that is tangent to the perpendicular lines (Figure 3-18).

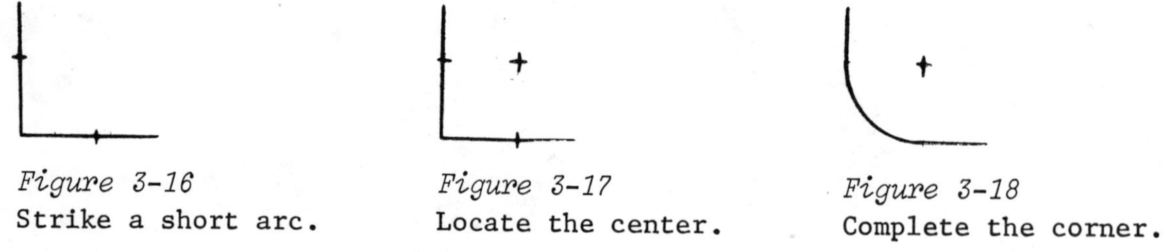

Figure 3-16
Strike a short arc.

Figure 3-17
Locate the center.

Figure 3-18
Complete the corner.

It is sometimes necessary to place an arc tangent to two lines. To place the arc properly, these steps should be followed:

1. Select the radius of the arc and draw light construction lines parallel to the two lines. The distance from the line to the construction line should equal the radius (Figure 3-19).
2. Draw light perpendicular construction lines from the intersection of the construction lines to the line. This will locate the points of tangency (Figure 3-20).
3. Placing the compass at the intersection of the two construction lines, strike an arc that is tangent to the two lines (Figure 3-21).

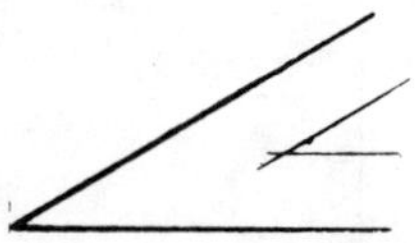

Figure 3-19
Draw construction lines.

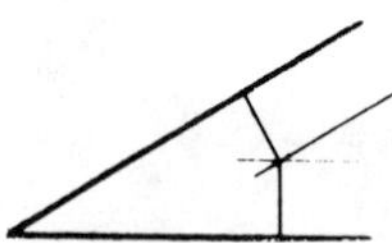

Figure 3-20
Locate points of tangency.

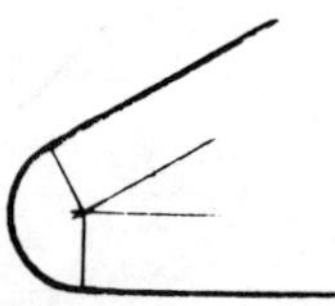

Figure 3-21
Strike an arc.

POLYGONS

A polygon is a plane figure that has several angles and sides. The more common types of polygons are: triangles, squares, hexagons, and octagons.

An equilateral triangle can be drawn by first drawing a horizontal line. The triangle is completed by drawing two 60-degree angles on the horizontal line (Figure 3-22).

A square can be drawn by first drawing a circle and then drawing 45-degree tangents. The diameter of the circle should equal the length of one side (Figure 3-23).

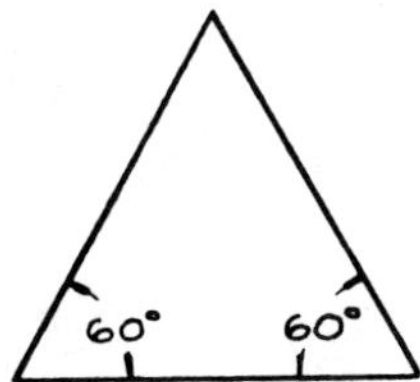

Figure 3-22
Equilateral triangle.

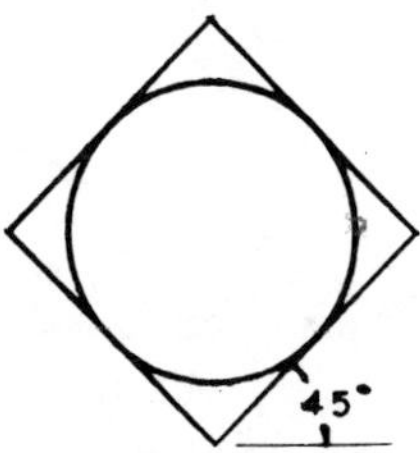

Figure 3-23
Square.

OCTAGON

An octagon can be inscribed in a circle or a square. To inscribe an octagon within a circle, draw center lines through the circle and then draw 45-degree diagonals through the center point (Figure 3-24). To complete the octagon, lines are drawn from the intersection of the center lines and the circumference of the circle (Figure 3-26).

If an octagon is inscribed within a square, a compass is placed on each corner and an arc is passed through the center of the square (Figure 3-26). The sides of the octagon are then drawn by connecting the intersection of the two arcs (Figure 3-27).

Figure 3-24
Draw center lines.

Figure 3-25
Complete the octagon.

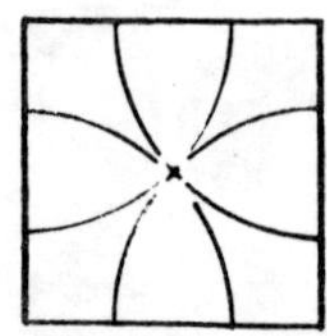

Figure 3-26
Strike four arcs.

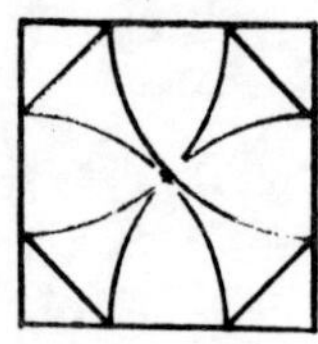

Figure 3-27
Complete the octagon.

HEXAGON

A hexagon can be drawn inside a circle or it can be drawn outside of a circle. If a hexagon is drawn inside a circle, a 30-60 degree triangle is used. The first angle of the hexagon is drawn from the intersection of the vertical center line and the circumference of the circle. Using the vertical center line as a reference line, three other angles are drawn. The vertical sides of the hexagon are then drawn in at the intersection of the angle and circle (Figure 3-28).

To draw a hexagon on the outside of a circle, a top and bottom line are drawn tangent to the circle. The 30-60 degree triangle is then used to draw four sides that are tangent to the circle (Figure 3-29).

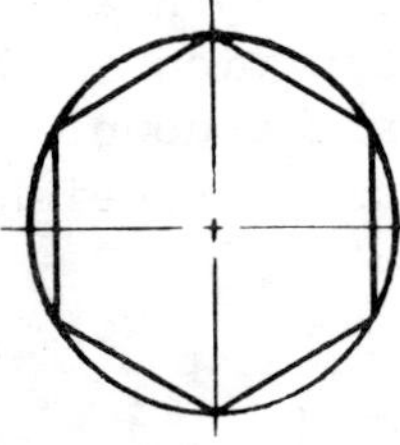

Figure 3-28
Hexagon inside a circle.

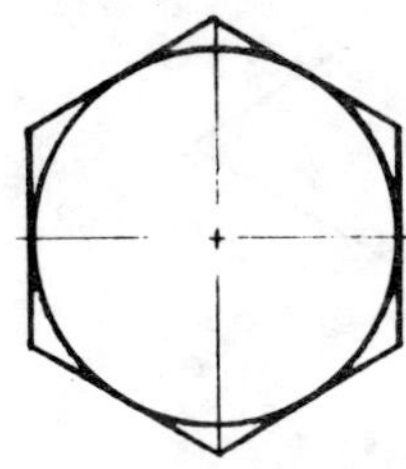

Figure 3-29
Hexagon outside a circle.

ORTHOGRAPHIC PROJECTION

There are six possible views that can be used in technical drawing: top or plan, front, right side, bottom, back or rear, and left side view. Although there are six possible views, usually only three basic views are used in technical drawing: top, front, and right side view (Figure 3-30). The use of these three views is based on the principles of orthographic projection. In its simplest form, orthographic projection means that two or more views of an object can be drawn by projecting lines from one view to another.

The front view of an object appears as if you were looking directly at the front of the object. The front view shows the dimension of height and width but does not show depth.

The right side or profile view has the dimension of depth and height but does not show the dimension of width. The top view is drawn as if you were directly over an object and looking straight down. It has the dimensions of depth and width but not the dimesion of height.

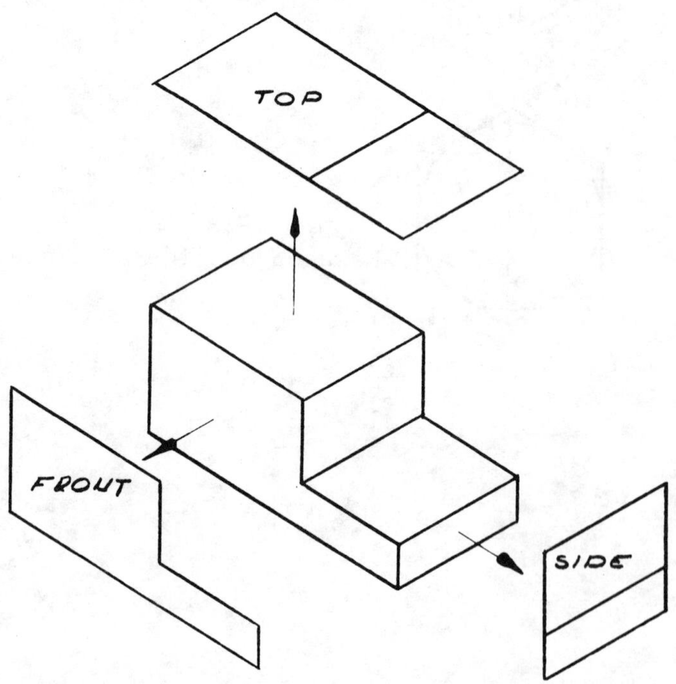

Figure 3-30
The three basic views.

PLACEMENT OF VIEWS

One of the worst mistakes made in technical drawing is the improper placement of the different views. All of the views must line up with each other. The top view is directly over the front view, and the right side view is projected from the front view (Figure 3-31). To align the top and right side views properly, light construction lines are projected from the front view.

The three principal dimensions are height, width, and depth, with only two of the dimensions being common to one view. Since the dimensions are common, they can be projected from one view to another. For example, the front view of an object has the dimension of width that can be projected to the top view.

Note: If a surface makes an abrupt change in direction, a line will occur on two of the views.

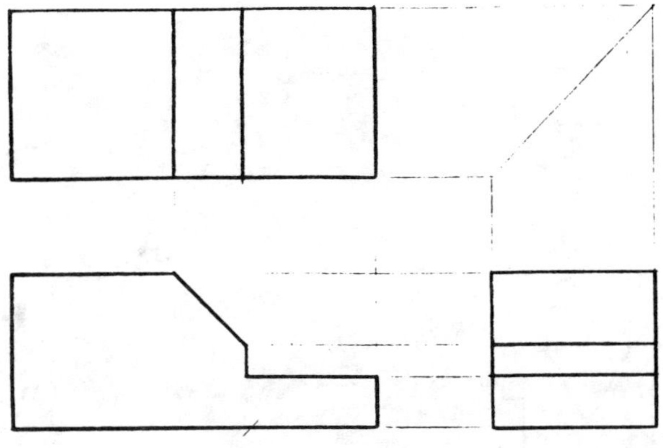

Figure 3-31
Correct placement of the views.

HIDDEN SURFACES

In some cases a surface cannot be seen in one of the principal views, but for clarity the surface should be shown. The surfaces that cannot be seen are represented by hidden lines (Figure 3-32). A hidden line is composed of short dashes approximately 1/8 inch in length with a 1/32-inch gap between the dashes.

There are several rules that should be followed when using hidden lines. They are:

1. The first dash should touch the object line.
2. Hidden lines should touch at corners.
3. If a hidden line is a continuation of an object line, there should be space between the two lines.
4. The hidden line for an arc starts at the end of the tangent points.

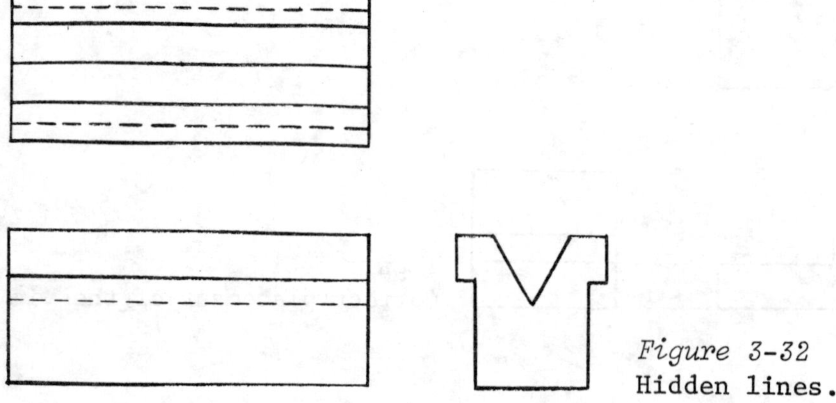

Figure 3-32
Hidden lines.

CURVED SURFACES

Cylinders and cones are represented by a circle in one view and a straight line in another view (Figure 3-33). If the surface of the cylinder is parallel to a plane of projection, the surface will be projected as a circle. If the axis to the cylinder is parallel to a plane of projection, the surface of the cylinder will be projected as a straight line. A sphere, however, will be viewed as a circle in any view (Figure 3-34).

Machine parts often have rounded internal and external corners. A rounded internal corner is called a fillet, and a rounded external corner is called a round (Figure 3-35).

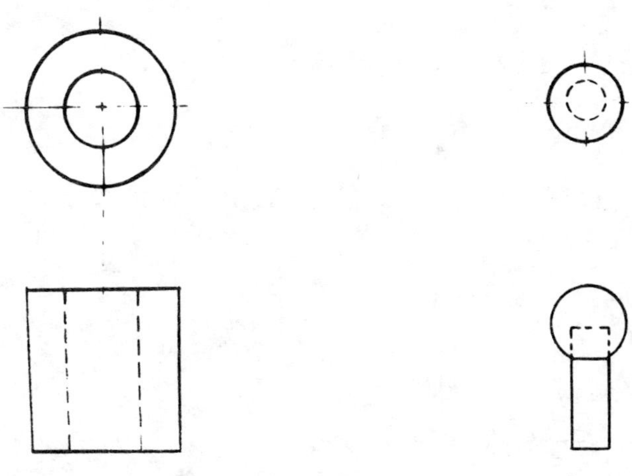

Figure 3-33
Two views of a cylinder.

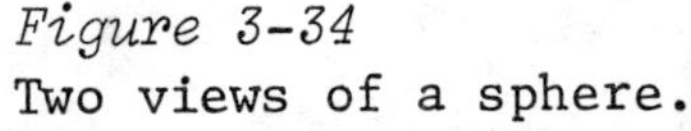

Figure 3-34
Two views of a sphere.

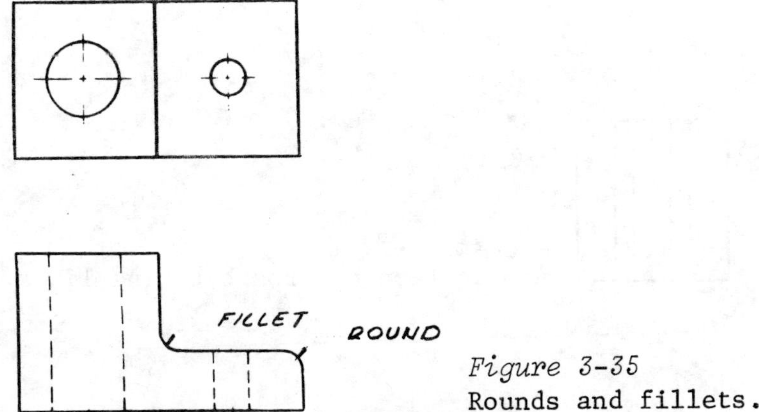

Figure 3-35
Rounds and fillets.

SECTIONS

Sections are used to show hidden details. If the interior of an object is relatively simple, hidden lines are sufficient; if the object has several parts, the hidden lines are sometimes confusing. For this reason an imaginary portion of the object is removed, and the interior of the object is revealed. The portion to be removed is indicated by an imaginary cutting plane (Figure 3-36). After a portion of the object is removed and the interior is revealed, the portion of the object that was touched by the imaginary cutting plane is crosshatched (Figure 3-37). The crosshatching lines are drawn with a 6H lead, at a 45-degree angle, and they are spaced 1/8 inch apart.

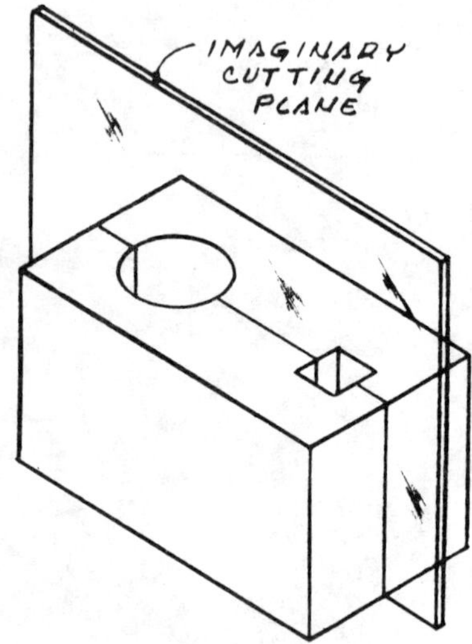

Figure 3-36
Use of a cutting plane.

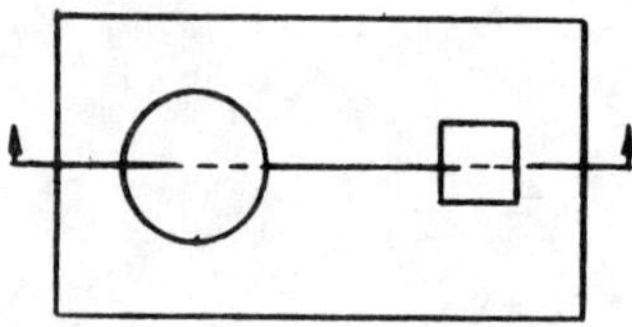

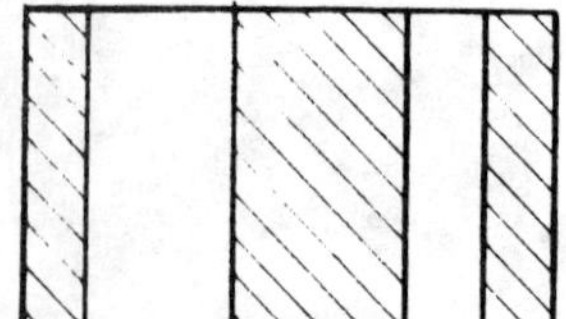

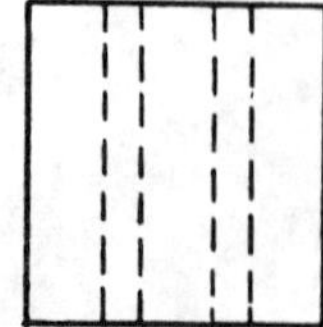

Figure 3-37
Application of crosshatching lines.

HALF SECTIONS

If the cutting plane passes through only half of an object and a quarter of the object is removed, the section is called a half section (Figure 3-38). In most cases the object is symmetrical, and through the use of a half section, both the inside and outside of an objedt can be shown (Figure 3-39). To indicate the direction of sight, the cutting plane line is terminated by only one arrowhead (Figure 3-40). Unless hidden lines are needed for clarity, they are usually omitted.

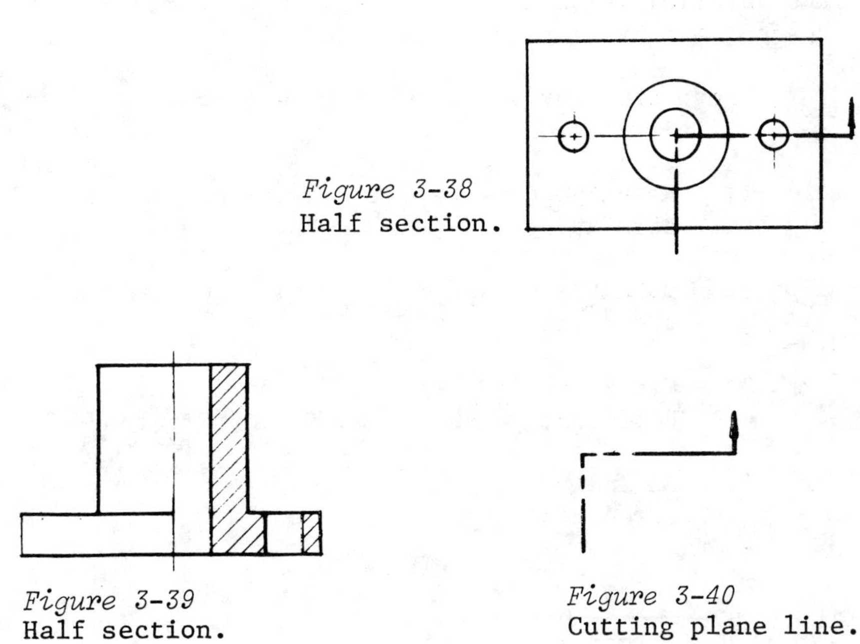

Figure 3-38
Half section.

Figure 3-39
Half section.

Figure 3-40
Cutting plane line.

FULL SECTIONS

There are several different types of sections. One of the most common is a full section. A full section is drawn when the cutting plane line passes entirely across and through the object and the front half of the object is removed (Figure 3-41). The cutting plane line is dark and is composed of a series of dashed lines (Figure 3-42). The arrowheads on the end of the cutting plane line indicates the direction in which the observer is looking at the object. The crosshatching lines not only show where the object was cut, but it also indicates the type of material that the object is made of. If the lines are uniformly spaced, the material is usually cast iron, but if two of the lines are closely spaced, the symbol indicates steel.

There are four basic rules in sectioning. They are:

1. Keep the crosshatching lines uniform and, if possible, draw them at a 45-degree angle.

2. Make the crosshatching lines contrast with the outline of the object.

3. Crosshatching lines in different directions indicate different parts of an object (Figure 3-43).

4. An individual part of an object must be crosshatched in one direction.

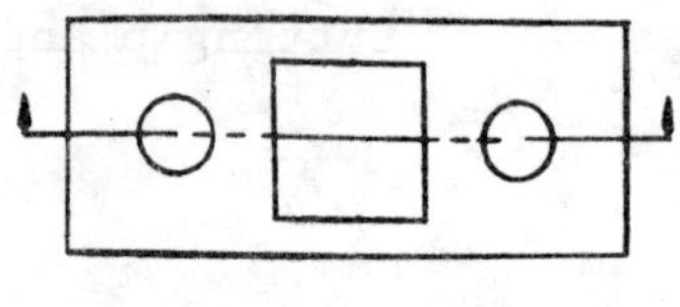

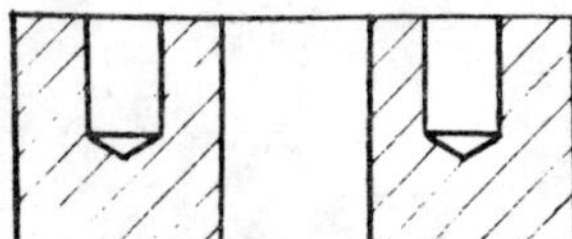

Figure 3-41
Full section.

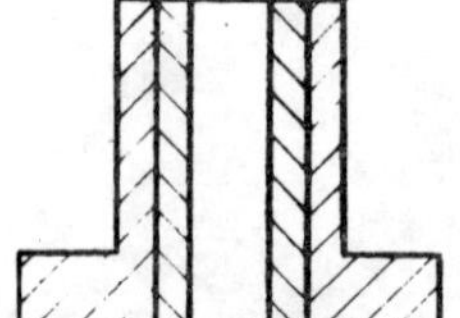

Figure 3-42
Cutting plane line.

Figure 3-43
Adjacent pieces in section.

REMOVED SECTIONS

A removed section is a section that is removed from the object and is placed at a convenient location on the drafting paper (Figure 3-44). It is used to clarify a particular detail and may be drawn to a larger scale. The removed section differs from a revolved section in that the lines in a removed section are parallel to the lines as they would appear in a normal position. Since a portion of the object is removed, it is necessary to label the cutting plane line or lines (Figure 3-45). The cutting plane line is usually labeled A-A, B-B, C-C, etc., and the removed section is labeled as Section A-A, Section B-B, Section C-C, etc.

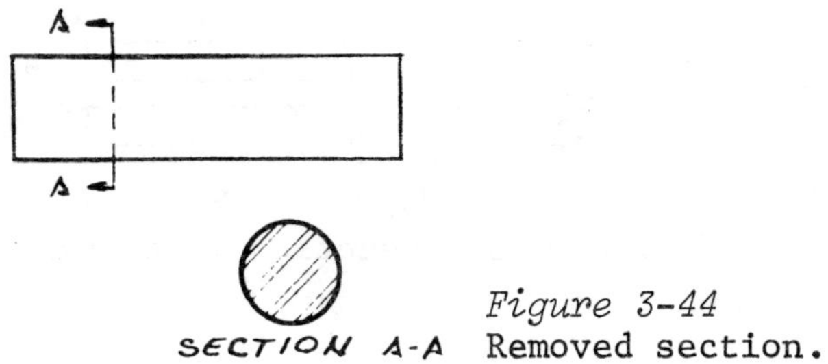

Figure 3-44
Removed section.

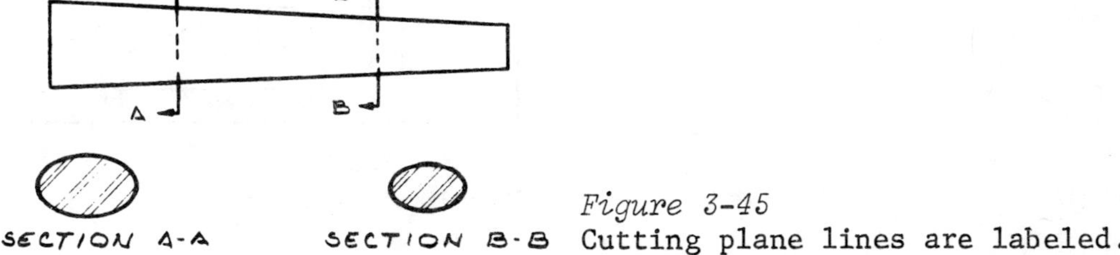

Figure 3-45
Cutting plane lines are labeled.

REVOLVED SECTIONS

If a profile view of an object tends to be confusing, a revolved section is used to show the profile shape (Figure 3-46). The section is drawn by passing a cutting plane through the object at a 90-degree angle. The section is then revolved 90 degrees on a vertical axis. The revolved section can be placed between two break lines (Figure 3-47), or it can be revolved to fit directly on the elevation (Figure 3-48). If break lines are used, the object can be shortened, but the full length should be indicated by the correct dimension.

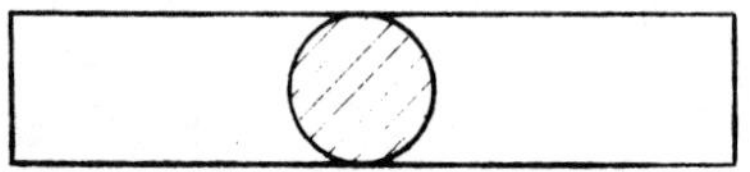

Figure 3-46
Revolved section.

Figure 3-47
Revolved section with brake line.

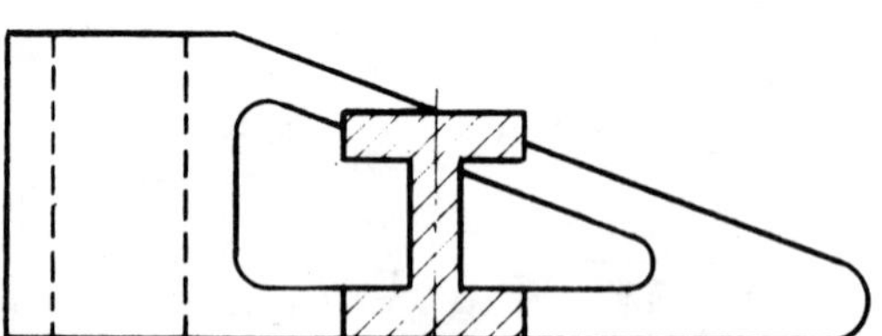

Figure 3-48
Revolved section.

OBLIQUE DRAWING

An oblique drawing is a form of a pictorial drawing. It has one surface parallel to the frontal plane of projection. The other sides of the object are drawn at an angle to the frontal plane. The longest side of an object, or the side of the object that has the most irregular shapes, should be placed parallel to the frontal plane (Figure 3-49). An oblique drawing is built around a skeleton of three lines: two of the axes form a right angle, and the other angle is drawn at any convenient angle (Figure 3-50).

The procedure for making an oblique box is:

1. Draw an oblique axis.

2. Select the longest dimension or the side that is the most irregularly shaped.

3. Determine the height, width, and depth on the three axes.

4. Draw the front view of the oblique.

5. Complete the oblique.

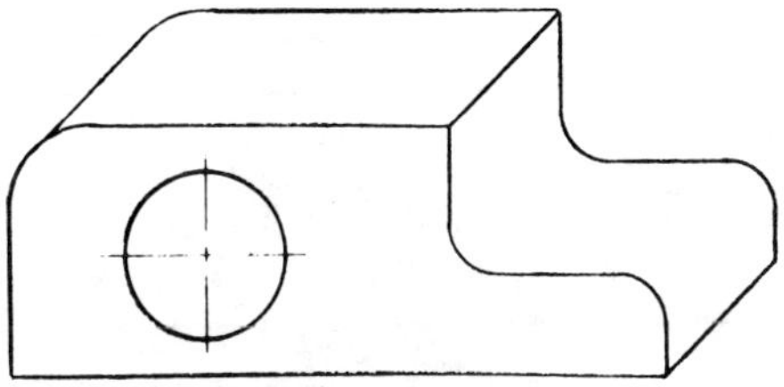

Figure 3-49
Oblique drawing.

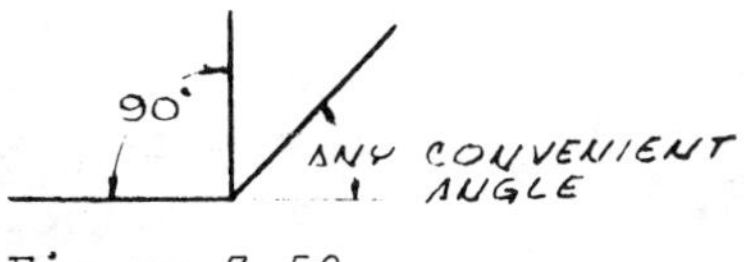

Figure 3-50
Oblique axis.

ISOMETRIC DRAWING

An isometric drawing is also a type of pictorial drawing. The isometric shows the three principal dimensions -- height, width, and depth -- in a single view (Figure 3-51). Isometric drawing is based on the theory of revolution. The object is rotated about a vertical axis 45 degrees and is tilted forward 35 degrees and 16 minutes.

To properly develop an isometric, an isometric axis is laid out. One of the axes is vertical, and the other two are drawn 30 degrees to the horizontal (Figure 3-52).

The procedure for making an isometric box is:

1. Draw an isometric axis.
2. Determine the height, width, and depth on the three axes.
3. Complete the isometric box by drawing the lines parallel to one of the three axes. If a line is not parallel to one of the three axes, the line is called a non-isometric line (Figure 3-53).

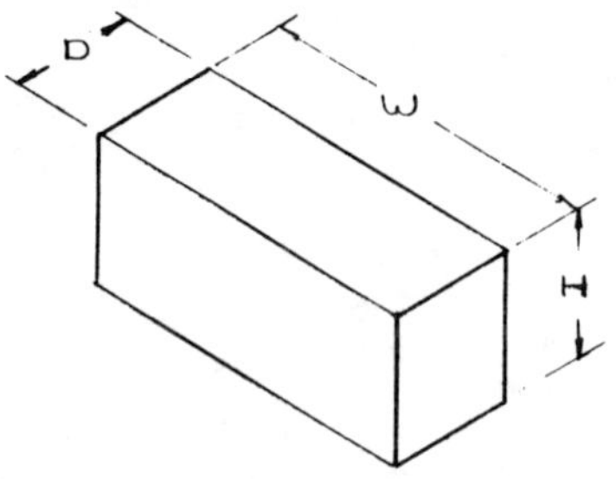

Figure 3-51
The principal dimensions.

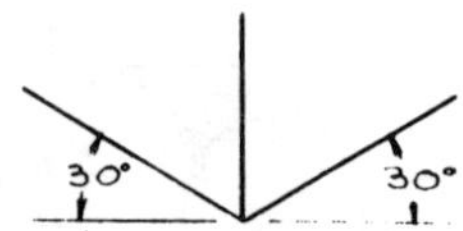

Figure 3-52
Isometric axis.

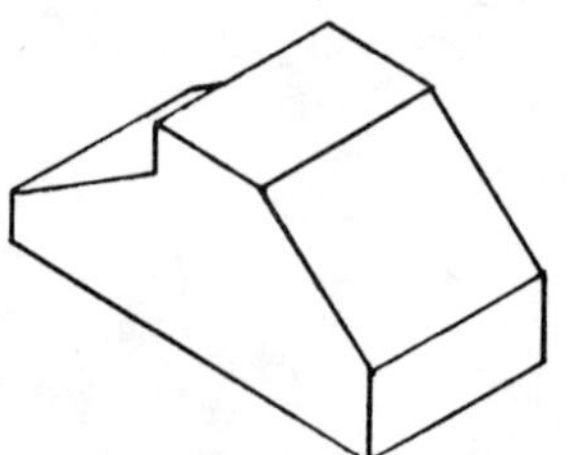

Figure 3-53
Non-isometric lines.

Assignment: Draw an acute angle and a right angle. Label each angle.

Assignment: Draw a reflex angle and an obtuse angle. Label each angle.

Assignment: Draw a scalene, right, and isosceles triangle.

Assignment: Draw an equilateral, obtuse, and acute triangle.

Assignment: Divide the line into 3 equal parts.

Assignment: Divide the line into 5 equal parts.

Assignment: Draw an arc tangent to the two lines.

Assignment: Draw a rounded corner on the patio.

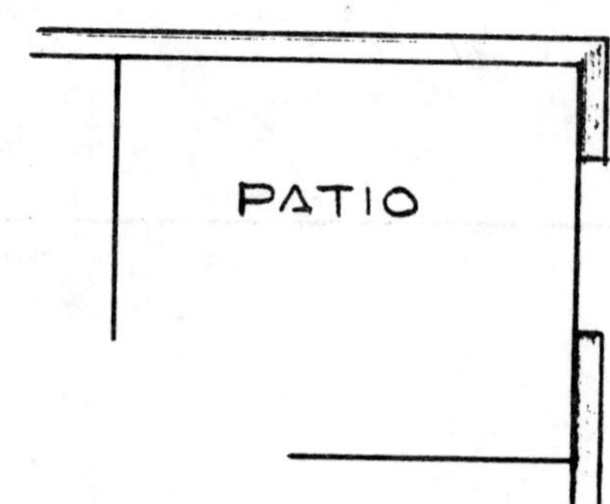

Assignment: Draw an arc tangent to the two lines.

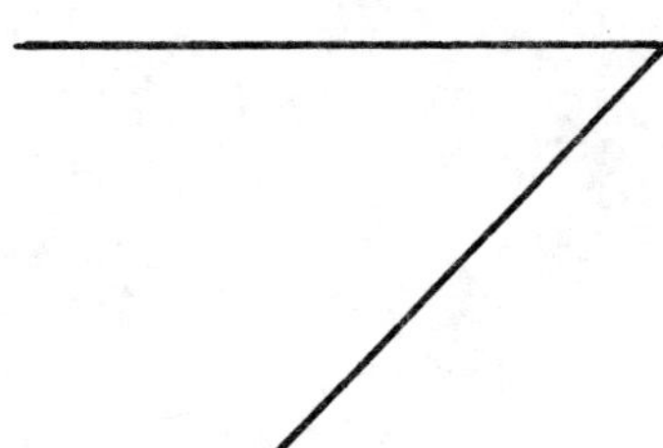

Assignment: Draw a rounded corner on the two intersecting lines.

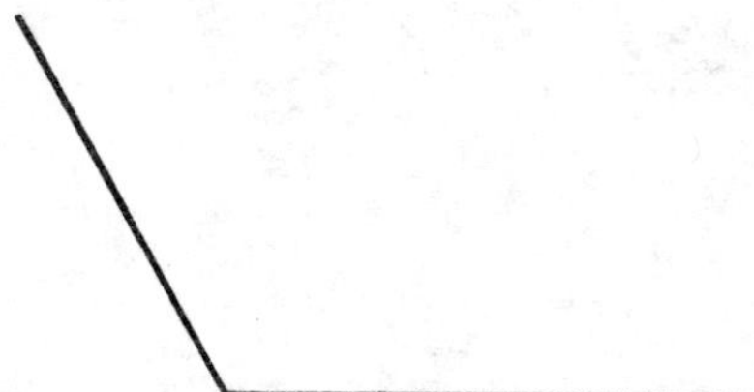

Assignment: Draw an equilateral triangle that has a base of 2 inches.

Assignment: Draw a square that has 4 two-inch sides.

Assignment: Inscribe an octagon within the circle.

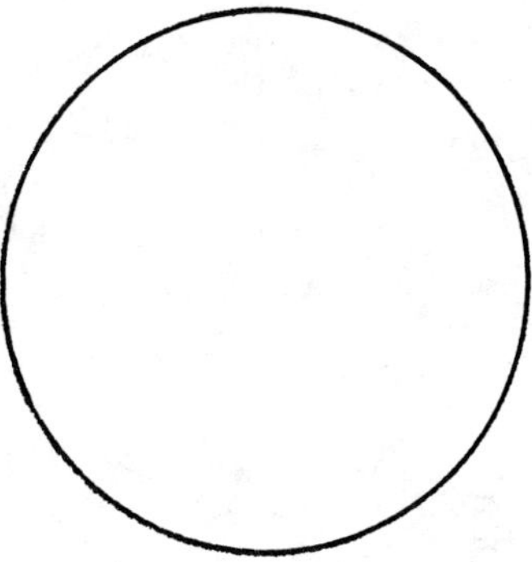

Assignment: Inscribe an octagon within the square.

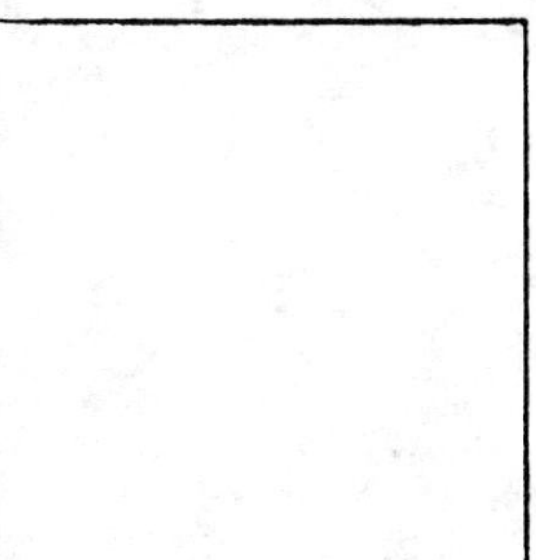

Assignment: Draw a hexagon in the circle.

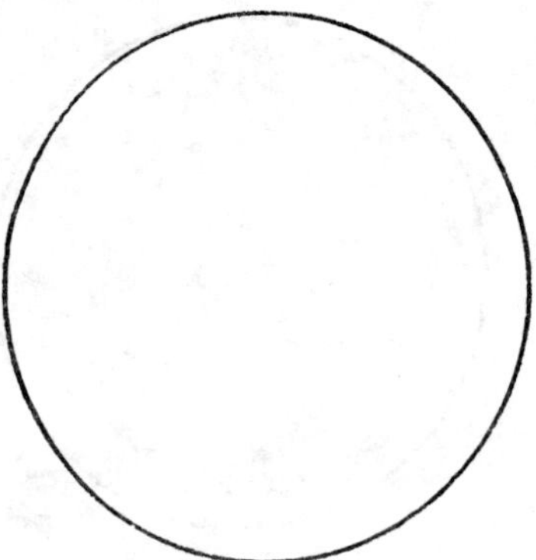

Assignment: Draw a hexagon on the outside of the circle.

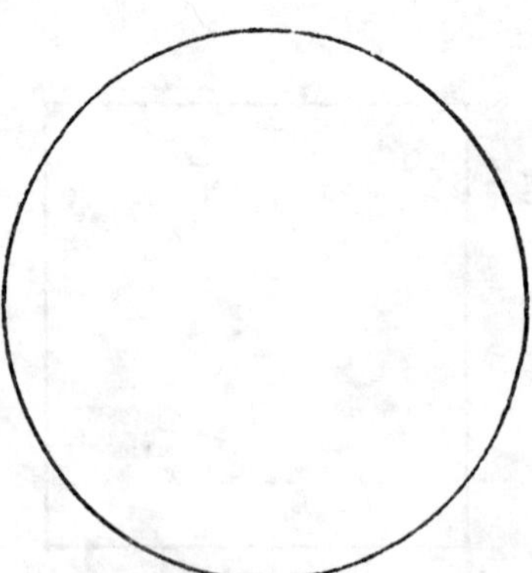

Assignment: Label the three views.

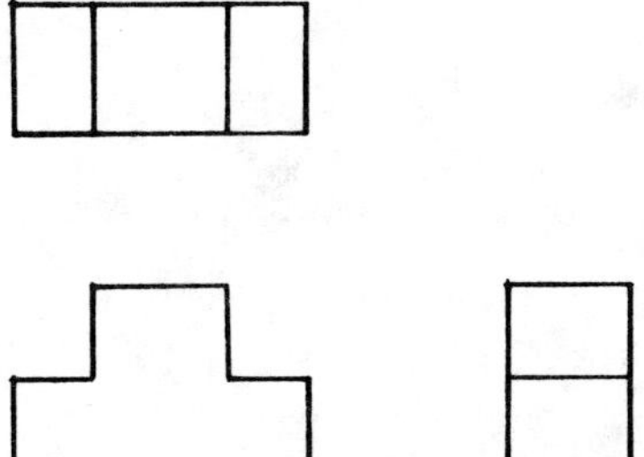

Assignment: Indicate the correct dimensions on each view.

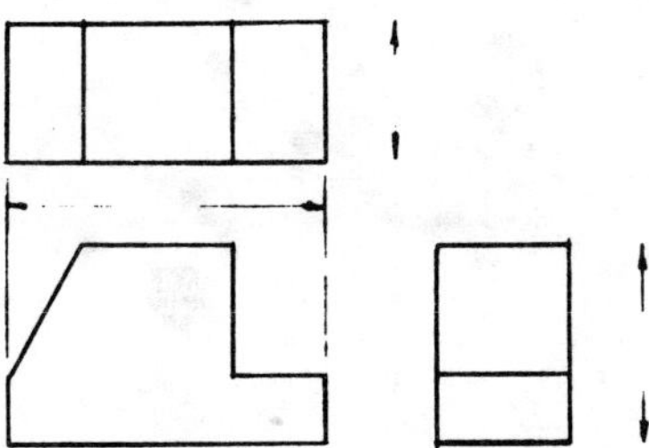

Assignment: Draw the top view.

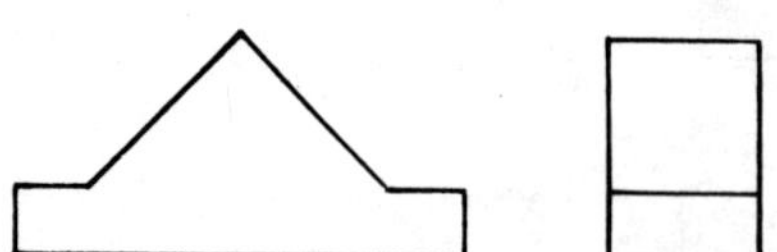

Assignment: Draw the right side view.

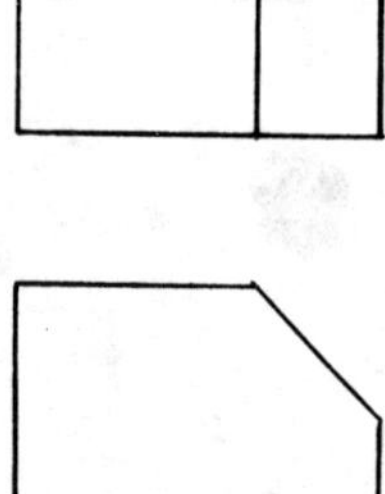

Assignment: Add all the missing lines.

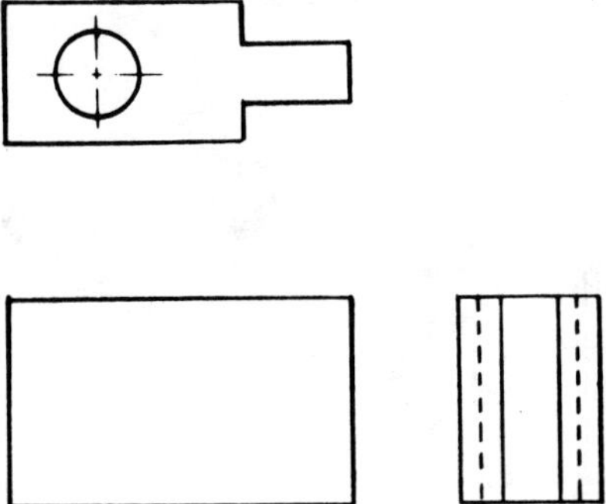

Assignment: Add the missing view.

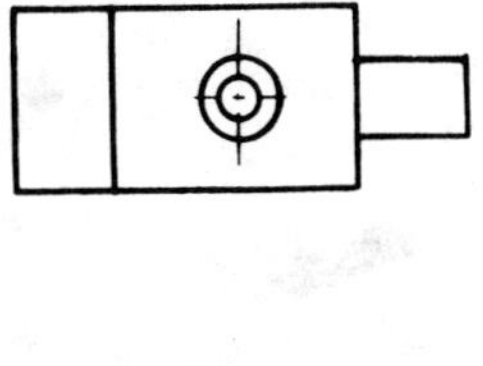

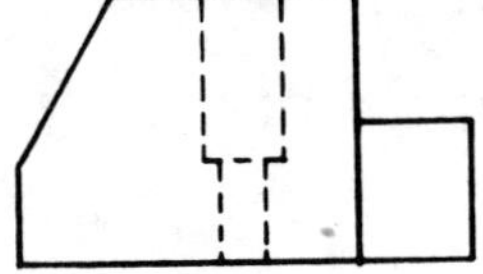

Assignment: Complete the three views.

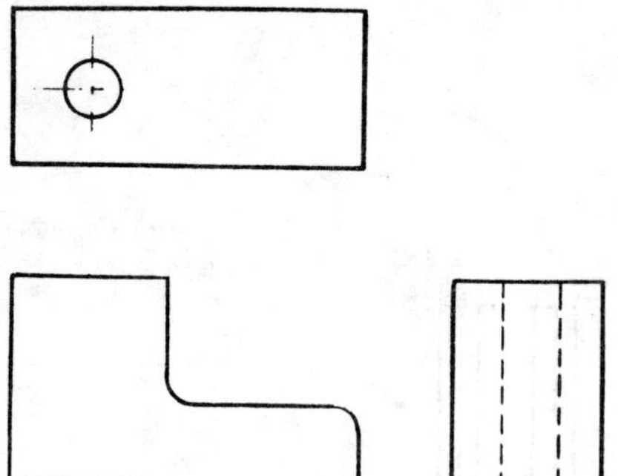

Assignment: Complete the three views.

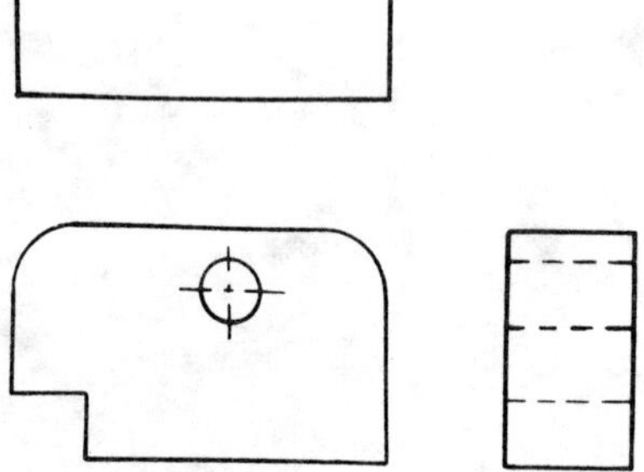

Assignment: Add the missing view.

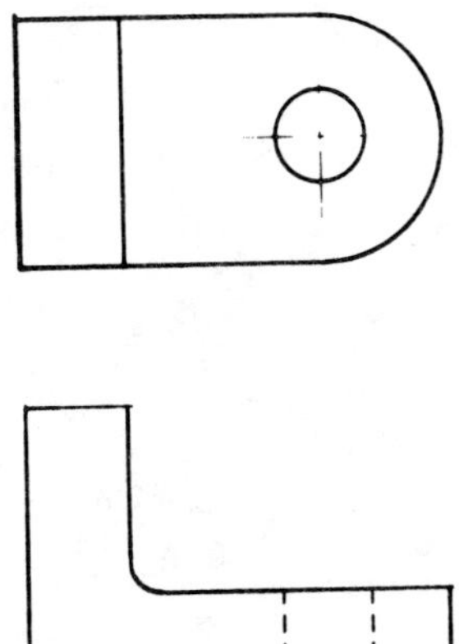

Assignment: Add the missing view.

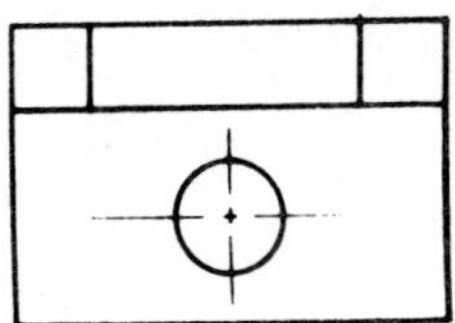

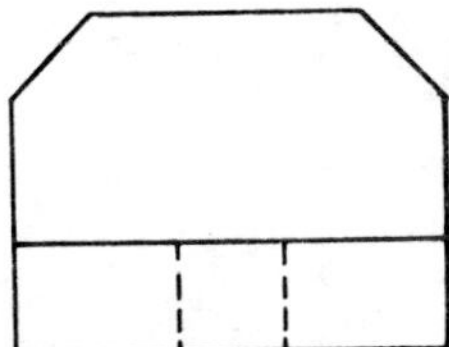

Assignment: Add the missing view.

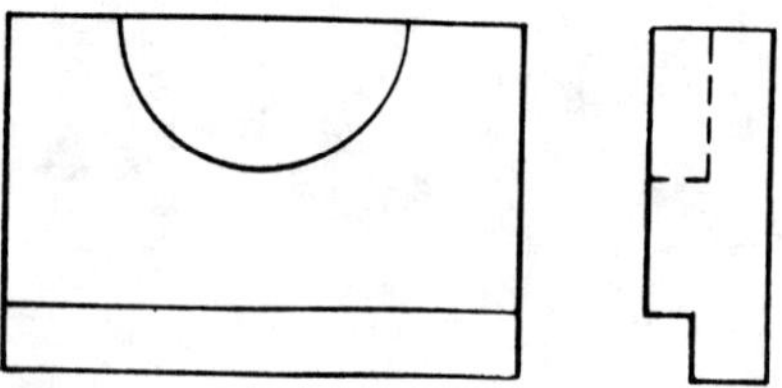

Assignment: Add the missing view.

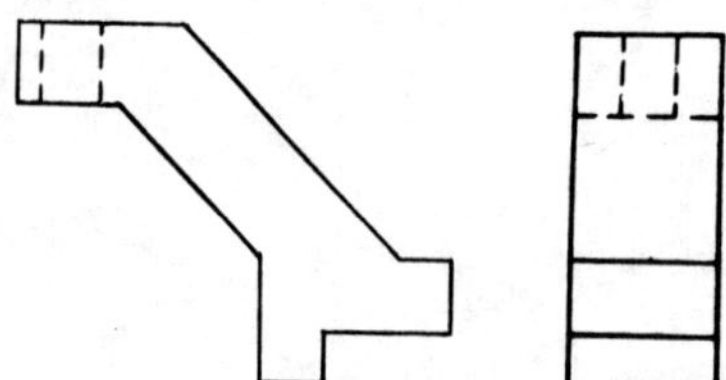

Assignment: Add the missing lines.

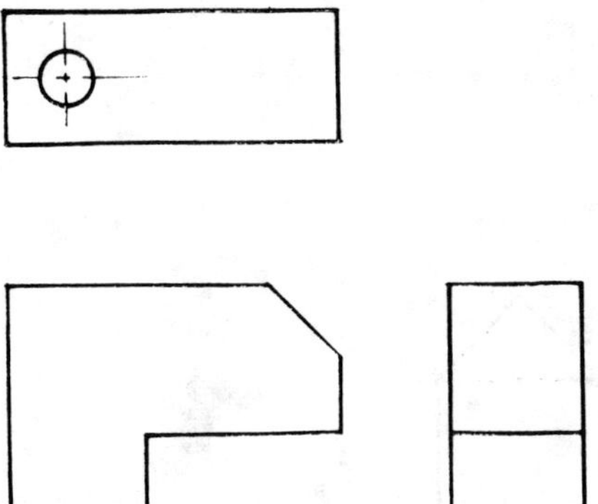

Assignment: Add the missing lines.

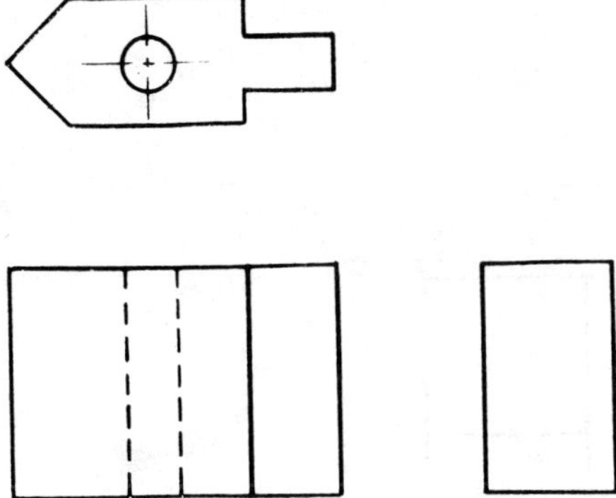

Assignment: Add the missing lines.

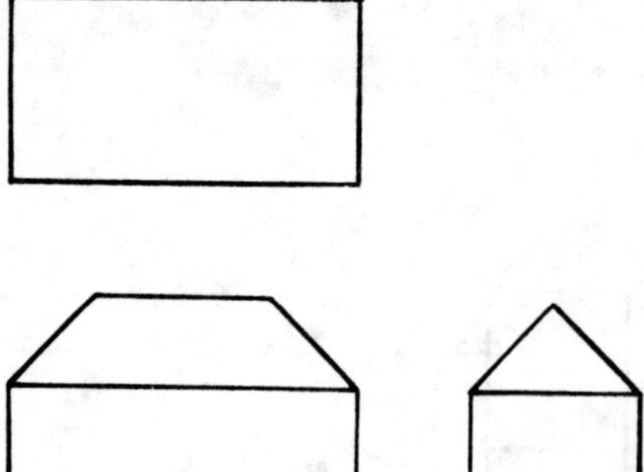

Assignment: Add the missing lines.

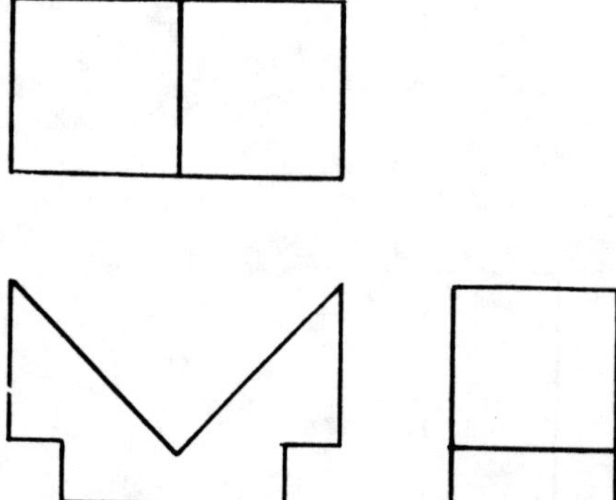

Assignment: Complete the front view.

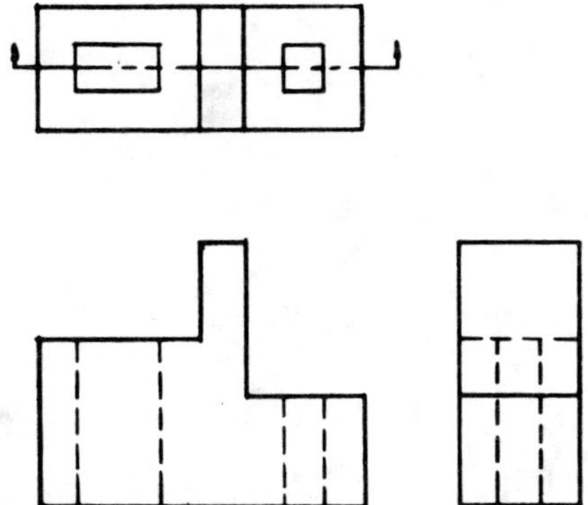

Assignment: Complete the front view.

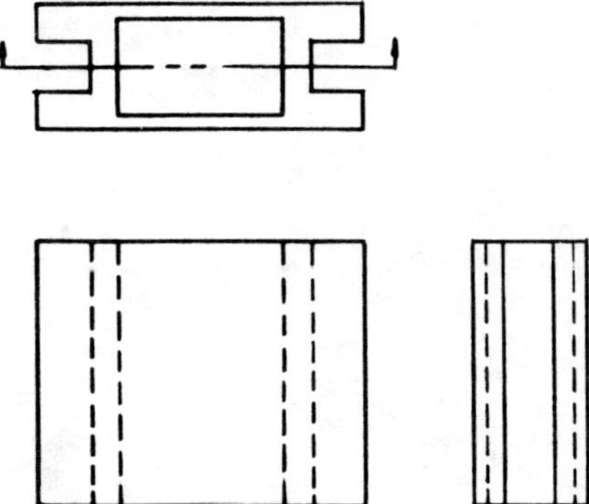

Assignment: Complete the front view.

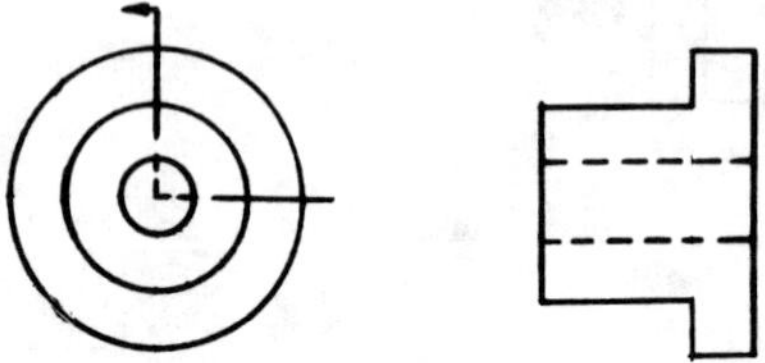

Assignment: Complete the front view.

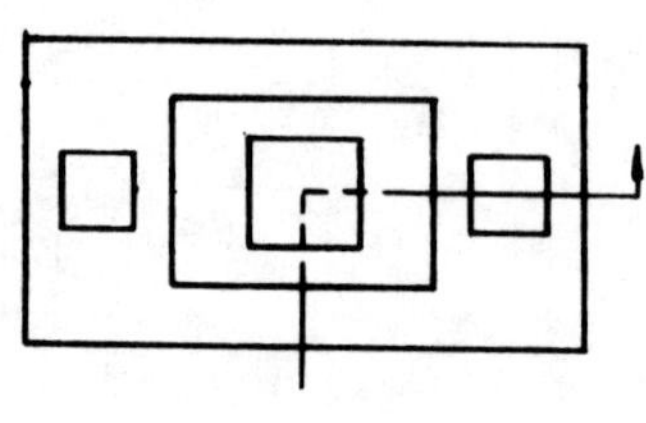

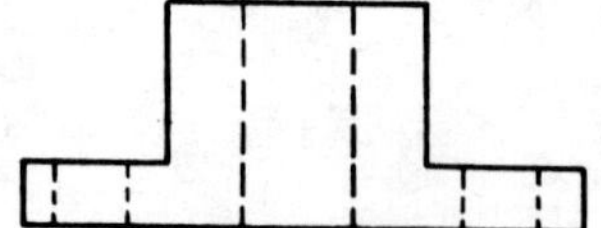

Assignment: Complete the front view.

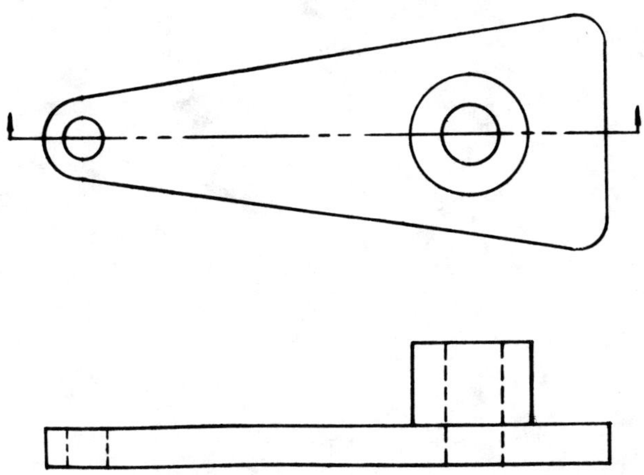

Assignment: Draw a removed section of the steel rod.

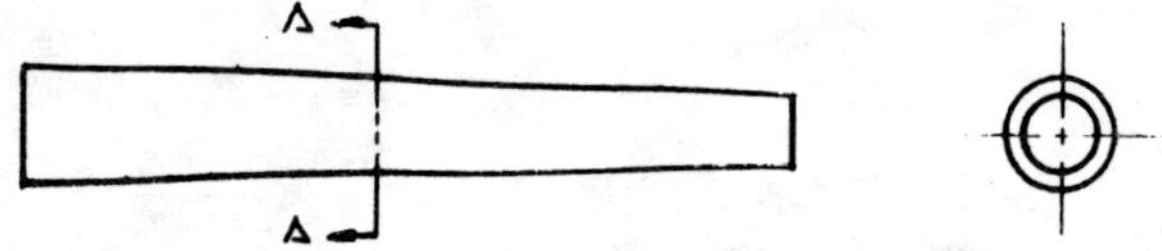

Assignment: Draw a removed section of a drafting pencil.

Assignment: Draw a front view and a revolved section.

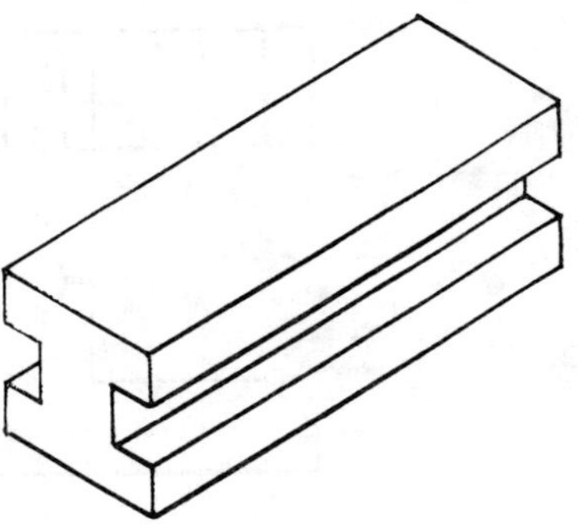

Assignment: Draw a revolved section.

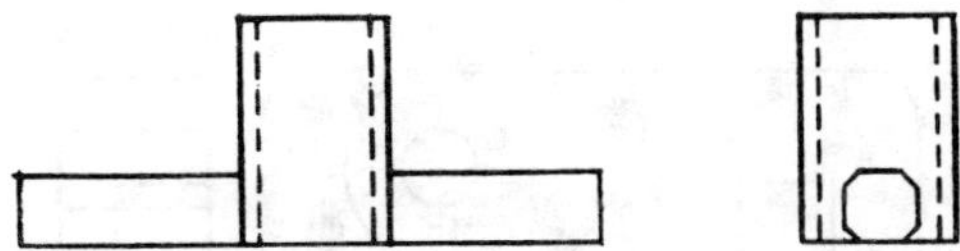

Assignment: Draw an oblique from the three view drawing.

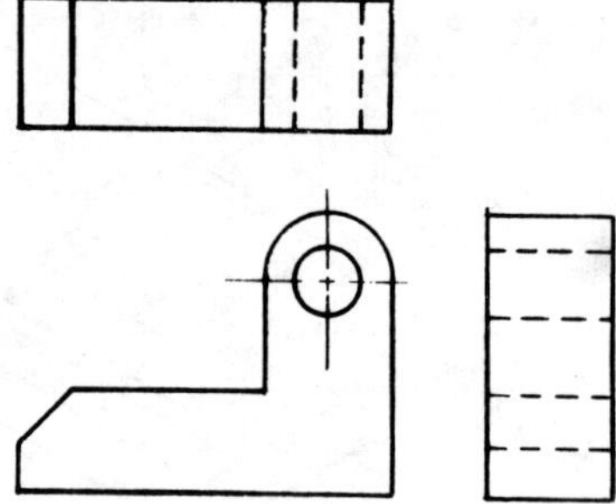

Assignment: Draw an oblique from the three view drawing.

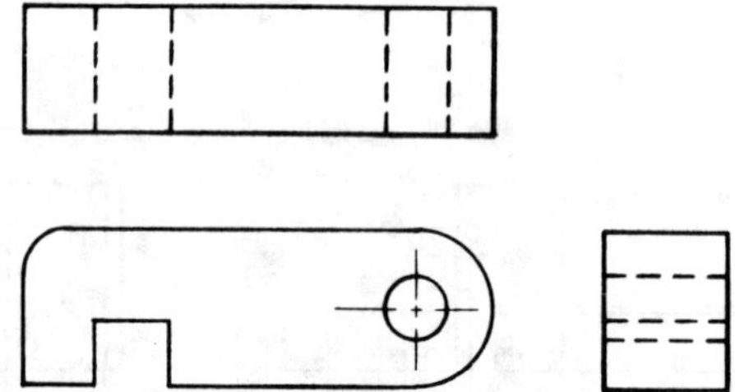

Assignment: Draw an isometric from the three view drawing.

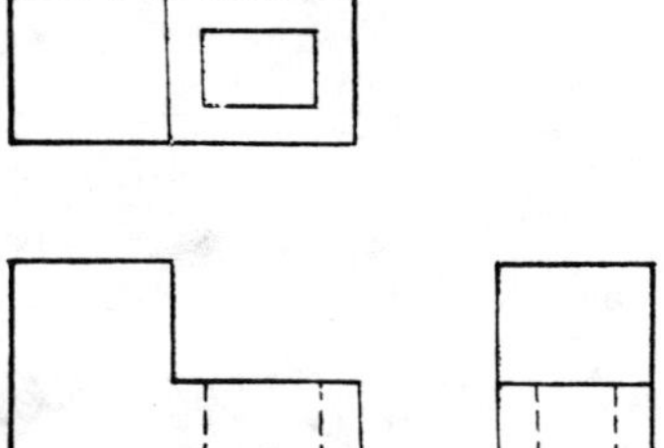

Assignment: Draw an isometric from the three view drawing.

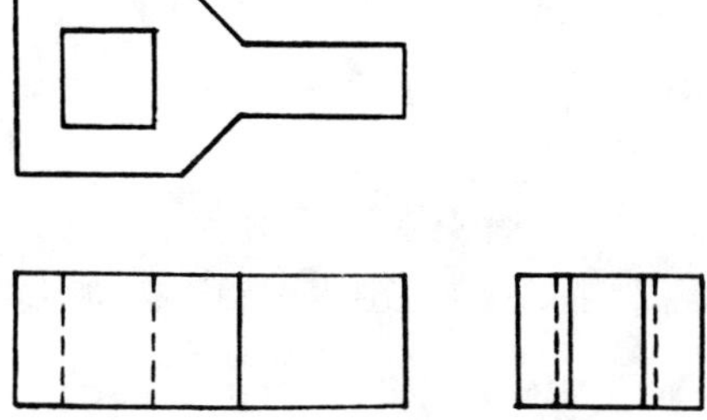

UNIT END TEST

Fill in the blanks with the correct word.

1. A right angle has an angle of ____________ degrees.
2. Triangles are classified as ____________, ____________, or ____________ triangles.
3. If a hexagon is drawn inside a circle, a ____________ degree triangle is used.
4. A polygon is a plane figure that has ____________ angles and ____________ sides.
5. There are ____________ basic views of an object that are used in working drawings.
6. The three principal dimensions are ____________, ____________, and ____________.
7. Surfaces that cannot be seen are represented by ____________ lines.
8. Sections are used to show ____________.
9. The two most common types of pictorial drawings used in technical drawing are ____________ and ____________.
10. Isometric drawing is based on the theory of ____________.

Add the missing line or lines.

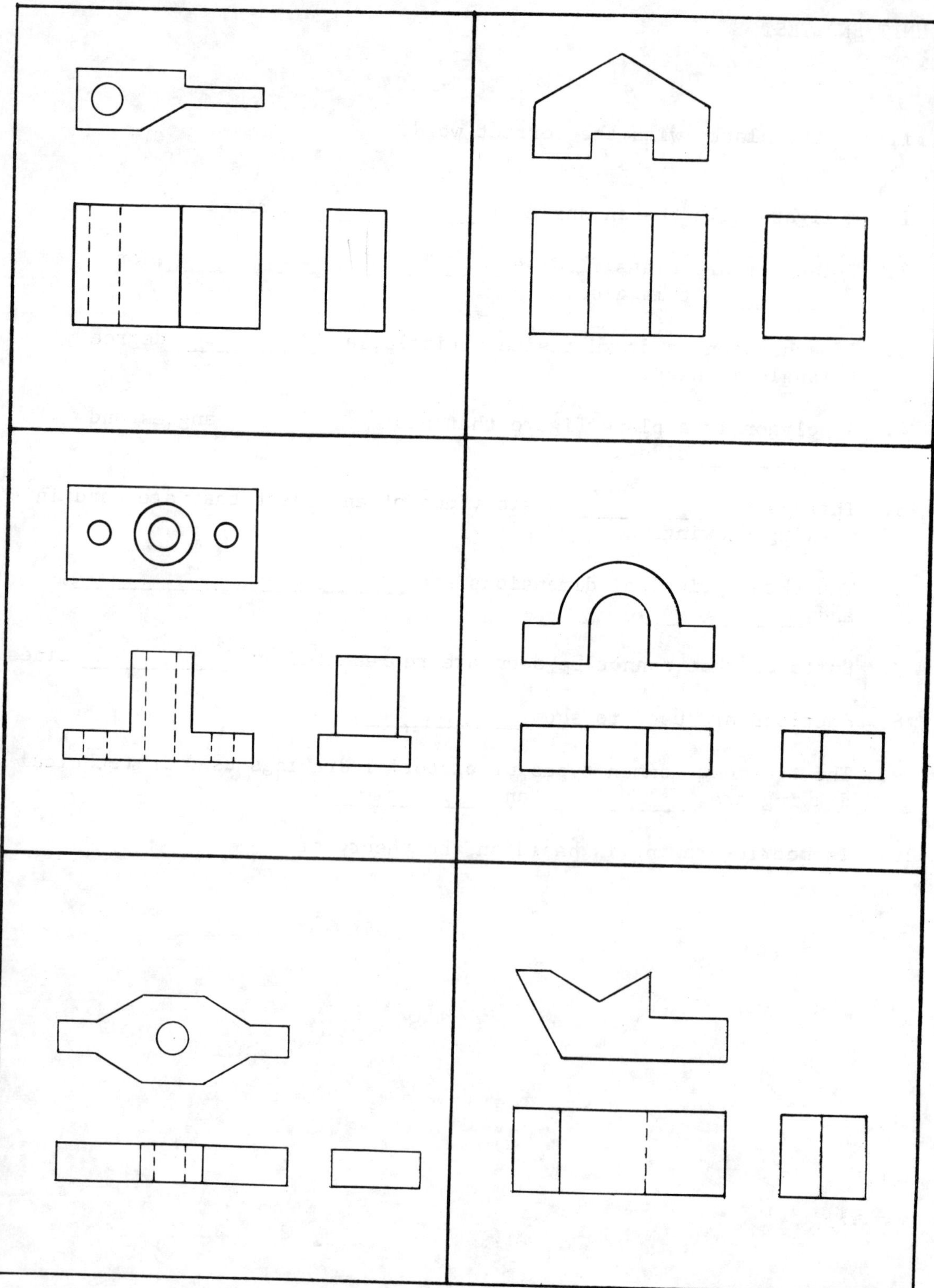

Chapter 4
DIMENSIONING

If a drawing is to be complete and if the object or structure is intended to be built, a drawing must have dimensions and notes. For without the proper dimensions and notes, mechanics would have difficulty in obtaining the correct size of an object. The dimensions give particular sizes and notes give related information. The correct dimensions are just as important, or more important, than the views that describe the object.

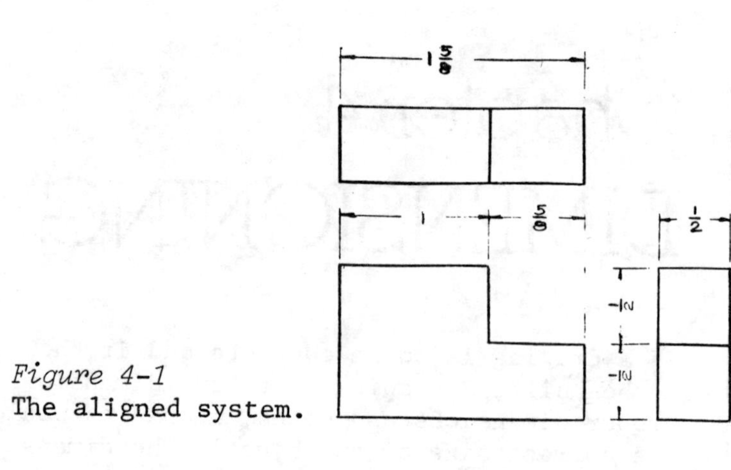

Figure 4-1
The aligned system.

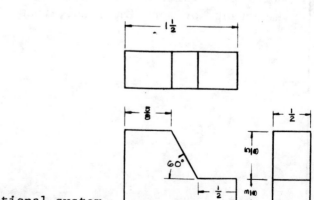

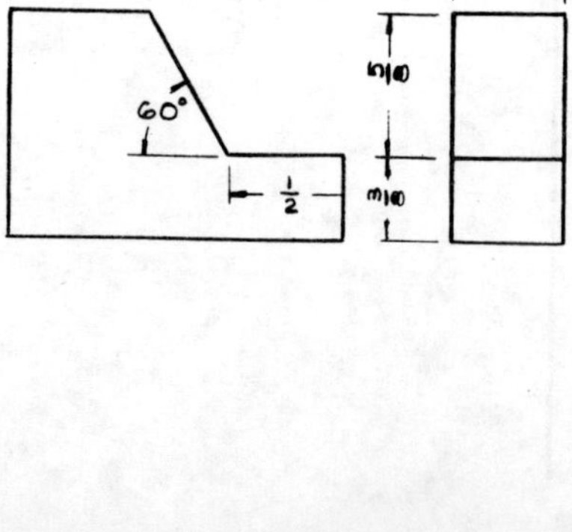

Figure 4-2
The unidirectional system.

DIMENSIONING

The two ways to correctly dimension a drawing are the aligned system and the unidirectional system. The aligned system of dimensioning has all the dimensions placed in line with the dimension line (Figure 4-1). The unidirectional system of dimensioning places the dimensions to read from the bottom of the drawing (Figure 4-2).

There are certain types of lines that are used in the dimensioning of an object. Four of the most common types of lines are extension lines, dimension lines, center lines, and leaders (Figure 4-3). An extension line is started 1/16 inch beyond the object and is terminated 1/8 inch past the last dimension line. Dimension lines extend from extension line to extension line and are terminated by an arrowhead. In engineering drawing, a gap is left in the middle of the dimension line. The first dimension line should be placed 3/8 inch to 1/2 inch from the object, and the remaining dimension lines should be spaced 1/4 inch to 3/8 inch apart. The arrowheads that terminate the dimension line should be approximately 1/8 inch long and one-third the length in width. A center line is composed of a series of long and short dashes. The long dash is approximately 1/2 inch in length while the short dash is approximately 1/8 inch long. The long and short dash is seperated by a 1/16-inch gap. A leader is an inclined line with a horizontal shoulder. It is terminated by an arrowhead that touches a specific detail. Parallel to the shoulder line a note is used to describe the detail.

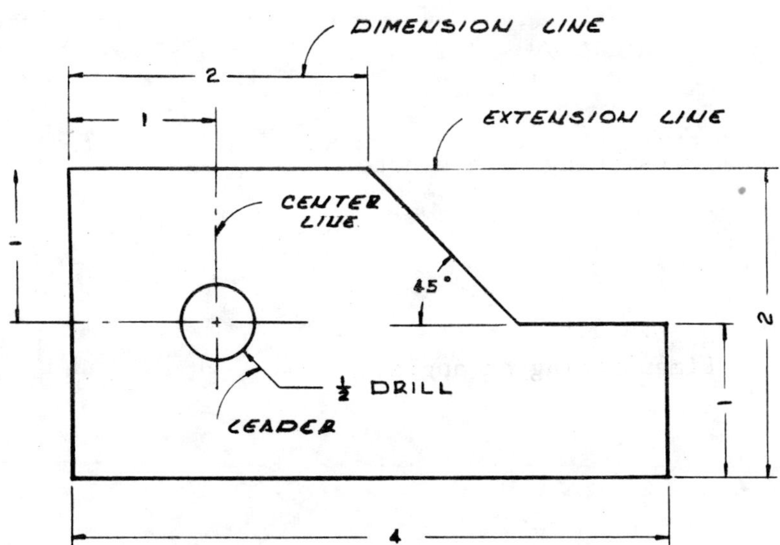

Figure 4-3
Lines for dimensioning.

DIMENSIONING: CIRCLES, ARCS, ROUNDS, FILLETS, AND ANGLES

A circle is dimensioned by giving its diameter. The diameter can be given outside the circle or inside the circle, or a leader can be used (Figure 4-4). The letter D or DIA is used after the dimension.

An arc is dimensioned by giving its radius. The radius should be placed on the inside of the arc, but if the arc is small the radius may be placed on the outside (Figure 4-5).

Rounds and fillets are dimensioned in the same manner as an arc, but if the rounds and fillets are uniform, only one or two dimensions are necessary. In some cases a note is used to denote the size of the rounds and fillets (Figure 4-6).

The dimension line for an angle is drawn as an arc. The dimension for the angle should be dimensioned so that the dimension may be read from the bottom of the sheet (Figure 4-7).

ALL FILLETS AND ROUNDS $\frac{1}{4}$ R

Figure 4-4
Dimensioning a circle.

Figure 4-5
Dimensioning an arc.

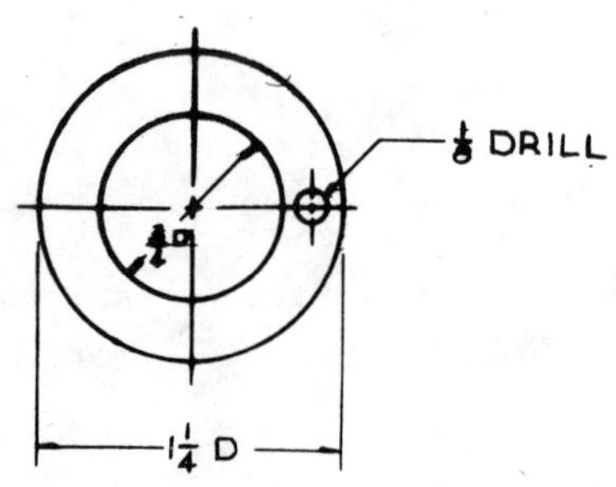

Figure 4-6
Dimensioning with a note.

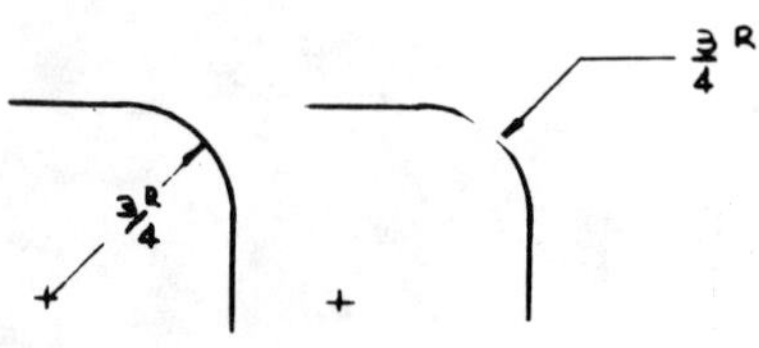

Figure 4-7
Dimensioning an angle.

Assignment: Dimension the angle block.

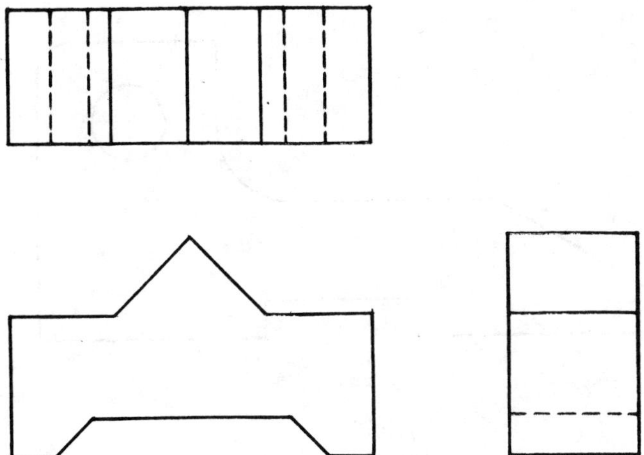

Assignment: Dimension the cap plate.

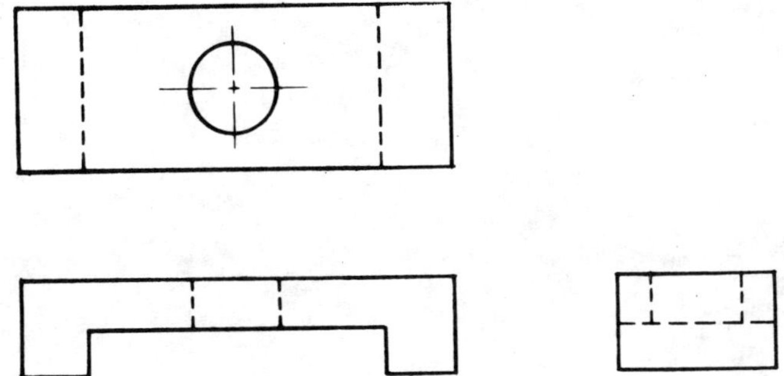

Assignment: Dimension the front view of the saddle bracket.

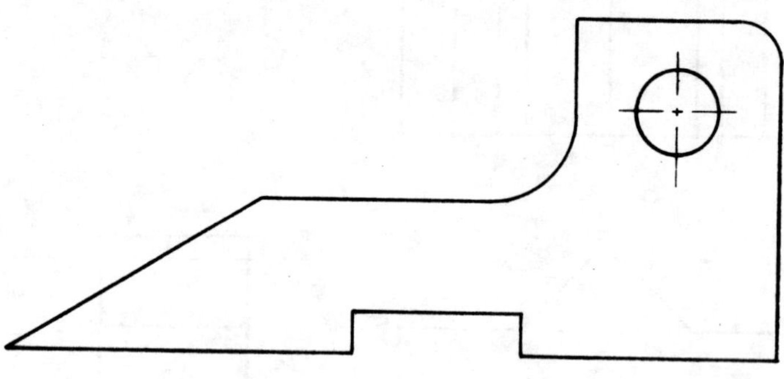

UNIT END TEST

1. Four of the most common lines used in dimensioning are: ____________, ____________, ____________, and ____________.

2. An extension line is started ____________ inch beyond the object.

3. Dimension lines are terminated ____________ inch past the last dimension line.

4. The first dimension line should be placed ____________ inch from the outline of the object.

5. A ____________ is composed of a series of long and short dashes.

6. A circle is dimensioned by giving its ____________.

7. An arc is dimensioned by giving its ____________.

8. The dimension line for an angle is drawn as an ____________.

9. Leaders are usually drawn at a ____________ degree angle.

10. Arrowheads are usually ____________ inch long.

Chapter 5
ARCHITECTURAL SYMBOLS

In architectural drawing, symbols are used to characterize certain features. To reduce confusion over the meaning of different symbols, the American Standards Association (ASA) and the United States Department of Defense have standardized certain symbols.

PLUMBING SYMBOLS

1. Compressed air
2. Vent
3. Cold water
4. Hot water
5. Check valve
6. Hot water return
7. Gas
8. Sprinkler line
9. Hose bib
10. Water closet
11. Shower stall
12. Lavatory
13. Water heater
14. Sump pit
15. Bathtub
16. Shower
17. Urinal
18. Thermostat
19. Floor drain
20. Soil stack plan
21. Gate valve
22. 90-degree elbow
23. 45-degree elbow
24. Elbow turned up
25. Elbow turned down
26. Tee
27. Clean out
28. Trap

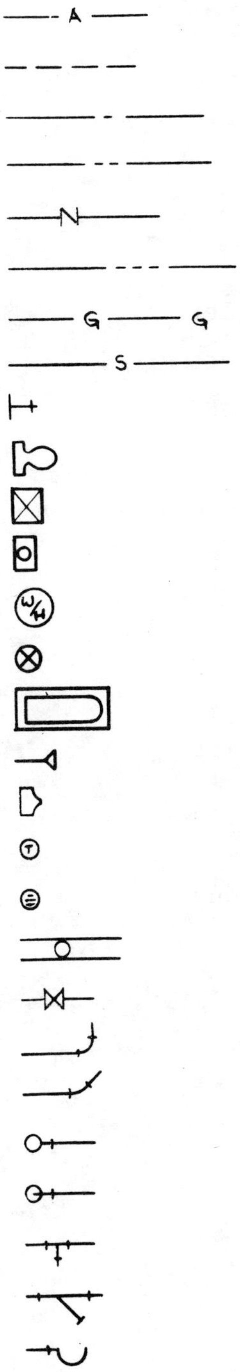

ELECTRICAL SYMBOLS

1. Ceiling fixture outlet
2. Wall fixture outlet
3. Pull switch light
4. Drop cord
5. Recessed outlet fixture
6. Fluorescent fixture
7. Duplex convenience outlet
8. Single recepticle outlet
9. Weather proof convenience outlet
10. 222 volt outlet
11. Split wired convenience outlet
12. Floor outlet
13. Lighting panel
14. Power panel
15. Buzzer
16. Television antenna outlet
17. Bell
18. Outside telephone
19. Interconnecting telephone
20. Single-pole switch
21. Double-pole switch
22. Dimmer switch
23. Floodlite

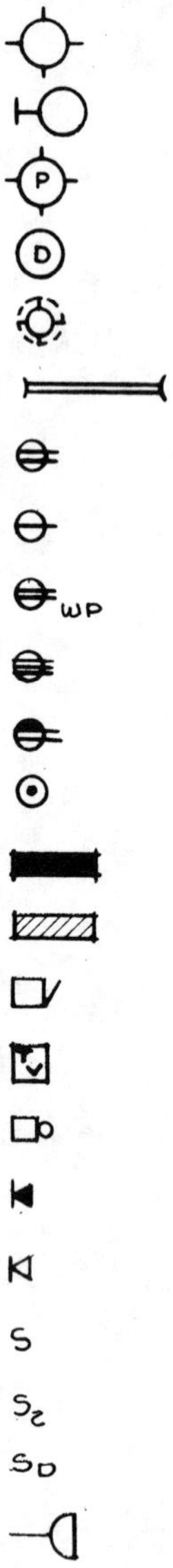

MATERIAL SYMBOLS

Material	Plan	Elevation	Section
1. Brick			
2. Firebrick			
3. Ashlar			
4. Rubble			
5. Concrete			
6. Concrete block			
7. Wood			
8. Batt insulation			
9. Gravel			
10. Terrazzo			
11. Rigid insulation			
12. Plywood			
13. Glass			
14. Marble			
15. Sand			
16. Earth			
17. Rock			
18. Steel			
19. Tile			
20. Flashing			
21. Water			
22. Cast iron			

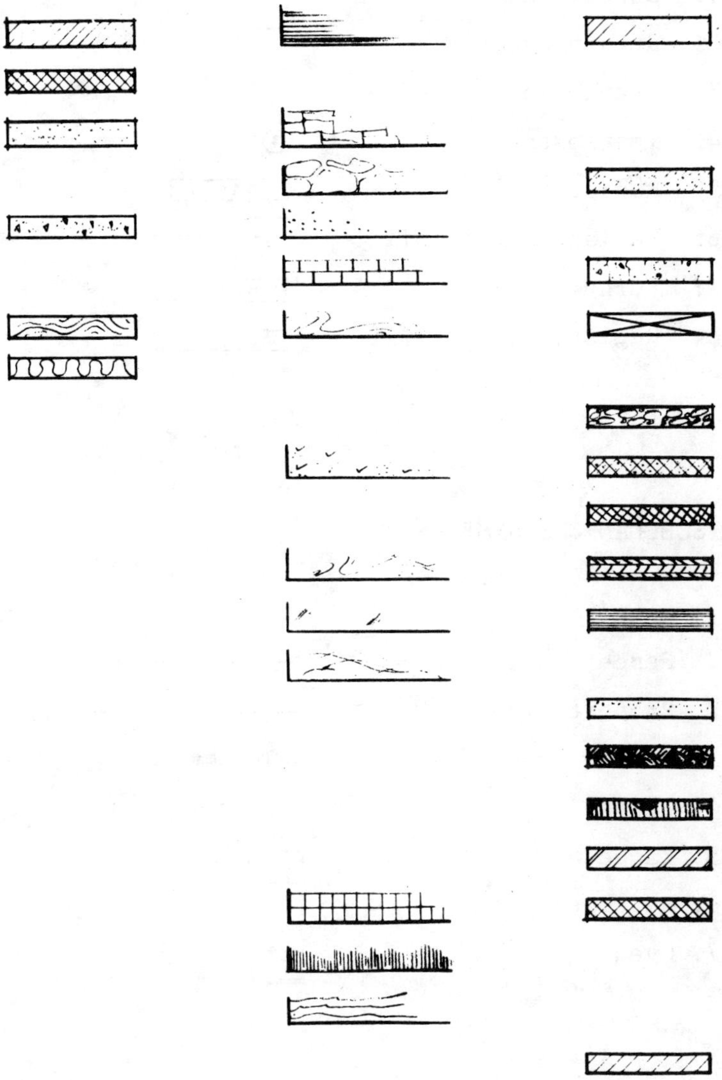

HEATING SYMBOLS

1. Supply duct
2. Return duct
3. Change in duct size
4. Thermostat
5. Radiator
6. Radiant Panel coil
7. Furnace
8. Register

MISCELLANEOUS SYMBOLS

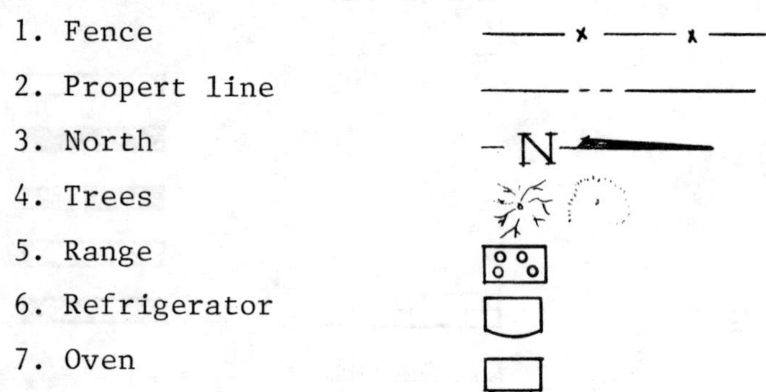

1. Fence
2. Propert line
3. North
4. Trees
5. Range
6. Refrigerator
7. Oven

Assignment: Draw the symbols for:

1. cold water line
2. gas line
3. water heater
4. shower
5. thermostat
6. floor drain
7. gate valve
8. 90-degree elbow
9. ceiling fixture outlet
10. pull switch light
11. buzzer
12. television antenna outlet
13. bell
14. single pole switch
15. double pole switch
16. supply duct
17. fence

18. tree

19. batt insulation

20. gravel

21. flashing

22. earth

23. plywood

24. brick

25. concrete

Assignment: Identify the symbols.

1.

2.

3.

4.

5.

6.

7.

8. Ⓣ

9.

10.

11.

12. Ⓟ

13.

14.

15. S

16. S_D

17.

18.

19.

20.

21. ——— x ———

22. ——— - ———

23.

24.

25. $\ominus_{W.R}$

Chapter 6
SKETCHING

Sketching is an important means of communication, an effective way to get an idea across, and is a necessity in any type of drafting. Sketches are used for many reasons, but in most cases they are used to record ideas and formulate new ones.

MATERIALS

The only materials needed for sketching are pencil, paper, and eraser. Most sketches are made with an H or F pencil. The pencil should have a long tapered point that is slightly rounded (Figure 6-1). The paper can be either plain tracing paper, or it can be cross-sectioned. The cross-sectional paper has light lines printed on one side and is very beneficial to beginning students.

One of the most important aspects of sketching is to hold the pencil properly. The pencil should be held naturally about 1-1/2 inches from the point. Comfortable strokes should be taken, avoiding sloppy lines. The lines should be drawn in a single stroke; however, if it is necessary small gaps can be left (Figure 6-2). A right-handed person draws from left to right and top to bottom.

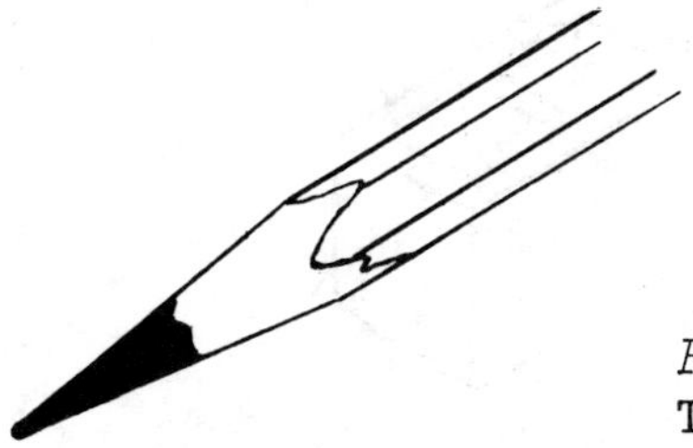

Figure 6-1
The pencil should have a rounded point.

Figure 6-2
Lines should be drawn in a single stroke.

PICTORIAL SKETCHES

A pictorial sketch is a simple means of expressing an idea. There are several types of pictorials but the one that is most often used is the isometric (Figure 6-3). An isometric sketch is built around axes of three lines. Height is represented by a vertical line, and the dimensions of width and depth are represented by lines drawn at a 30-degree angle with the horizontal.

The first step in the construction of an isometric sketch is to lay out the axes (Figure 6-4). The dimensions of height, width, and depth are then placed on the three axes. The isometric shape is then lightly blocked in. The corners do not have to terminate percisely but may cross. Once the outline of the figure is blocked in, details are added and the lines are darkened in (Figure 6-5).

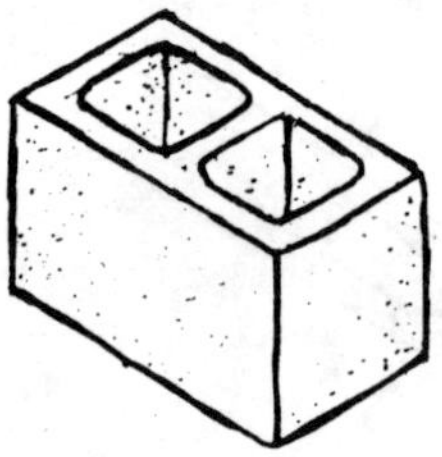

Figure 6-3
Isometric sketch.

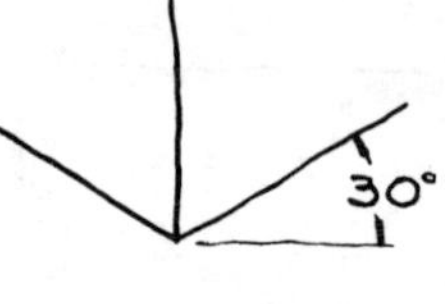

Figure 6-4
Isometric axis.

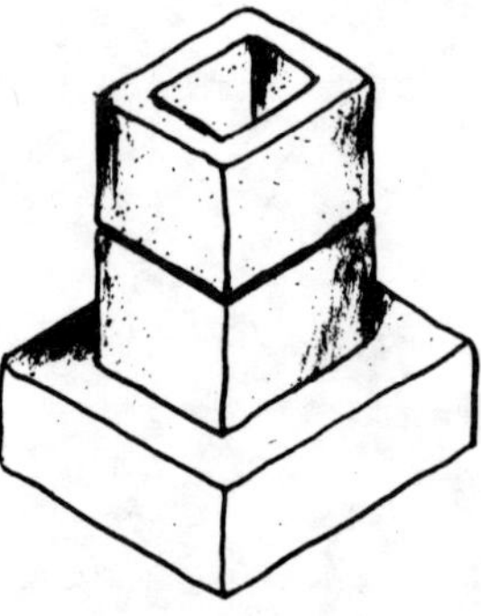

Figure 6-5
Sketched lines should be dark.

FLOOR PLANS

In developing a set of architectural floor plans, one of the first steps is to sketch tentative ideas on grid paper (Figure 6-6). The grid paper allows an expression of ideas to formulate in their proper scale. Since the grids are to scale, it is not necessary to dimension the sketch. However, for later convenience, it is sometimes wise to dimension the sketch. Some of the detail work, such as convenience outlets, lights, and ceiling joists direction, are omitted from the sketch and later added to the floor plan. The exterior walls are dark, wide, and usually drawn with an H or F pencil. The interior walls are drawn with a 2H pencil and are relatively light lines. The closets are accented by making a series of parallel lines perpendicular to the long dimension.

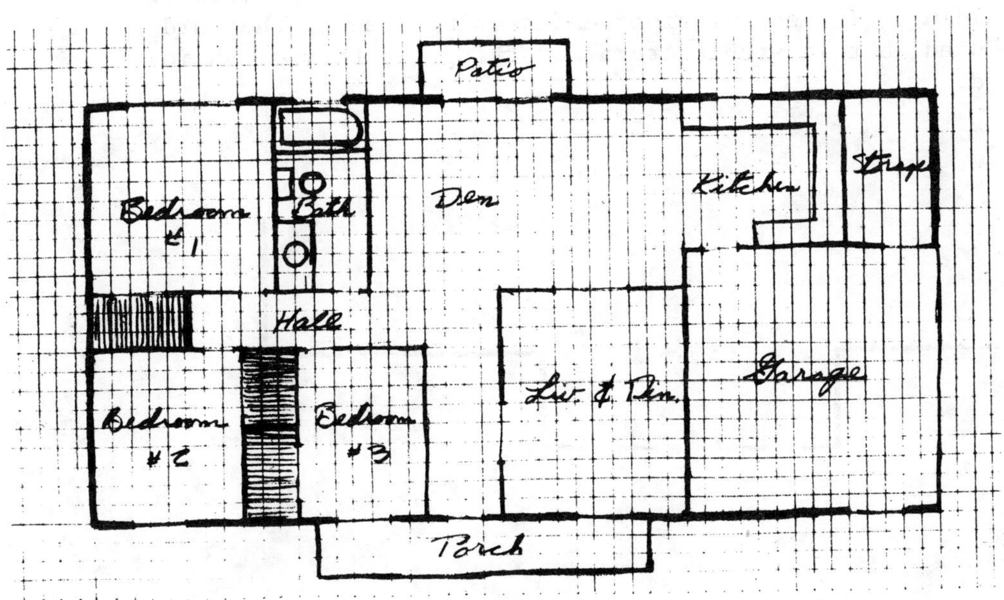

Figure 6-6
Grid sketch.

ELEVATIONS

Most elevations are sketched by first placing a clean sheet of tracing paper over the developed floor plan sketch. The features are then transferred from the floor plan to the elevation (Figure 6-7). The features are projected by using light construction lines drawn perpendicular to the floor plan. The dimension of width is projected, but the dimension of height is not. The height of a door is 6'-8", but windows vary in height, the size determined by a particular architectural style. The outline of the elevation is lightly sketched in, details are added later. One of the most important things to remember is to keep the right proportion.

Note: The term elevation is used to denote a particular view of a building. In mechanical or engineering drawing the word "view" is used, but in architectural drafting the term elevation is used.

FRONT ELEVATION

Figure 6-7
Elevation sketch.

Assignment: Draw a series of parallel horizontal lines.

Assignment: Draw a series of parallel vertical lines.

Assignment: Make an isometric sketch of a brick.

Assignment: Make an isometric sketch of a bathroom vanity.

Assignment: Sketch the floor plan of a house that has three bedrooms, one bath, kitchen, living room, den, and garage. *Note:* This sketch will be used for an assignment in Chapters 7-18.

Assignment: Design an elevation for the sketch of the floor plan.

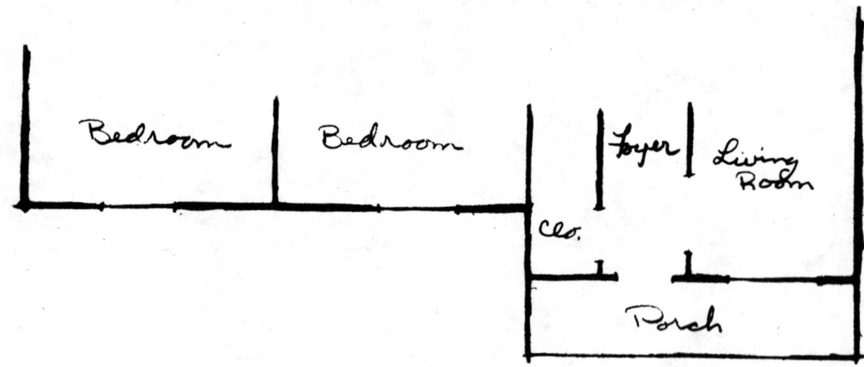

UNIT END TEST

Make a sketch of a switch plate cover.

Make a sketch of a kitchen floor plan.

Chapter 7
FLOOR PLAN

The floor plan is merely an extension of the grid sketch with dimensions and details added. The floor plan is made up of individual components, each playing a significant part in the development of the floor plan. Doors are added to gain entrance to rooms; windows are used as a source of ventilation and light; individual rooms are planned to include the kitchen, the bathroom, bedrooms, dining room, living room, and utility room; and electrical outlets and electrical fixtures are symbolized.

WALLS

The first step in the actual drafting of the floor plan is to draw a single line outside of the house. After the general outline has been drawn, exterior and interior walls are developed. Most residential homes are built with exterior walls of either brick veneer or wood siding. The plan view of a brick veneer wall is drawn by depicting 4-inch brick, 1-1/2 inch air space, and a 3-1/2 inch stud wall (Figure 7-1). An exterior frame wall with wood siding and single interior wall are draw as parallel lines 3-1/2 inches apart (Figure 7-2).

Note: **Crosshatching lines are the symbol for brick, and a grain pattern is the symbol for stud walls.**

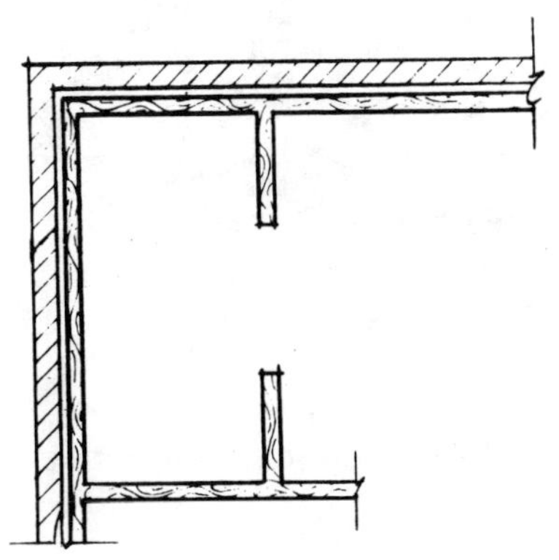

Figure 7-1
Brick veneer.

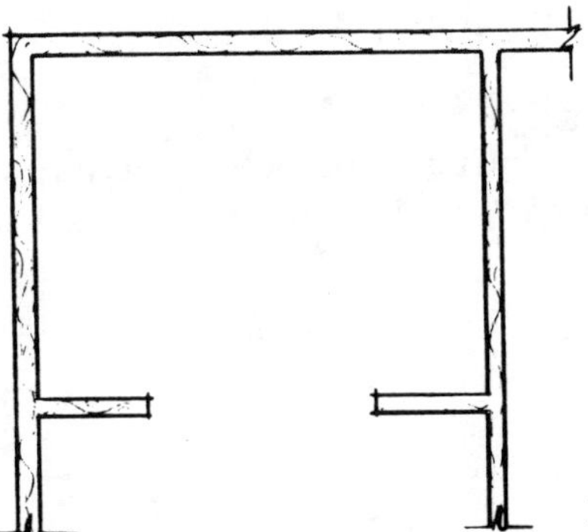

Figure 7-2
Exterior frame wall.

DOORS

Doors are used to gain entrance to a room and provide a certain amount of privacy. There are three basic types of doors that are used in homes: (1) sliding doors (Figure 7-3); (2) swinging doors (Figure 7-4); (3) folding doors (Figure 7-5). The sliding door operates on an overhead track and is used primarily in closets. Swinging doors operate on two or more hinges and in most cases provide an entrance to a room. Folding doors also operate on overhead tracks and are popular closet doors and sometimes serve as room dividers.

Figure 7-3
Sliding doors.

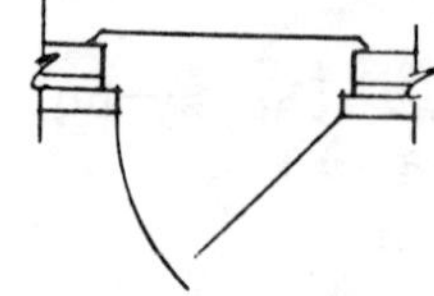

Figure 7-4
Swinging doors.

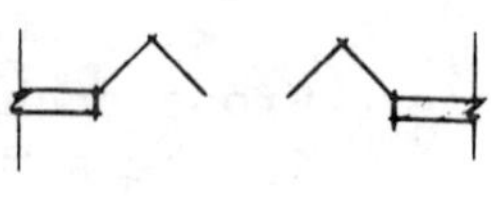

Figure 7-5
Folding doors.

Three other types of doors that are sometimes used are accordian (Figure 7-6), double acting (Figure 7-7), and pocket doors (Figure 7-8).

The accordian door has many narrow leaves of wood or plastic. This type of door operates on a track in the head jamb and can be used as a movable wall.

A double-acting door swings in either direction and can be panelled, flush, or louvered. A double-acting door is often used between the kitchen and dining room, or it is used in an area that has a great deal of traffic.

A pocket door is usually a flush door and requires no space along a wall when the door is open. The door units are purchased preassembled and are not suitable as an exterior door.

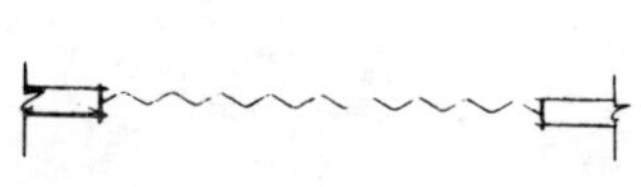

Figure 7-6
Accordian door.

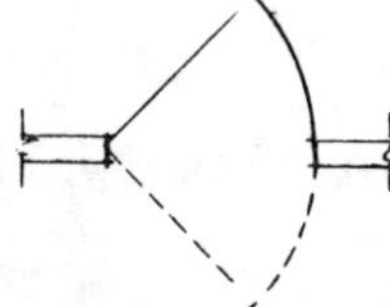

Figure 7-7
Double-acting door.

Figure 7-8
Pocket door.

WINDOWS

Window units are a source of light and, in some cases, provide ventilation. There are many different types of window units. Some of the more popular are double-hung, casement, horizontal sliding, awning, hopper, and fixed units. Double-hung windows (Figure 7-9) are equipped with two operating sashes. Each sash moves vertically and provides 50% ventilation. Horizontal sliding windows (Figure 7-10) have a minimum of two sashes and operate horizontally. Casement windows (Figure 7-11) are hinged on one side and swing in or out. The windows are usually operated by either a crank or lever.

Three other types of windows that are sometimes used are hopper, awning, and fixed windows.

Hopper windows (Figure 7-12) have the sash hinged at the bottom and are a variation of the awning window. The hopper window provides draft-free ventilation, for the incoming air is deflected upward. This particular type of window is sometimes used in basements.

The awning window (Figure 7-13) is hinged at the top and swings out horizontally. Most awning windows have one or more sashes and are operated by a crank.

A fixed window (Figure 7-14) is sometimes called a picture window and provides no ventilation. The window is usually large and is made of 1/4-inch plate glass or insulating glass.

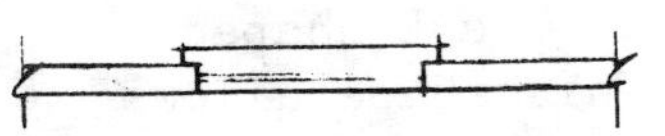

Figure 7-9
Double-hung window.

Figure 7-10
Horizontal slide window.

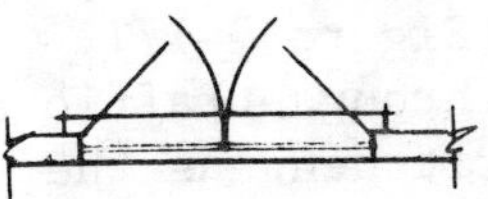

Figure 7-11
Casement window.

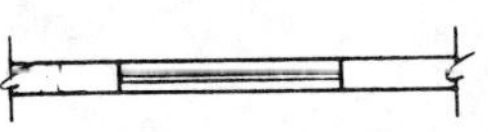

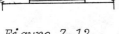

Figure 7-12
Hopper window.

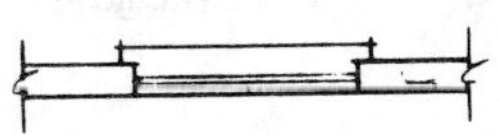

Figure 7-13
Awining window.

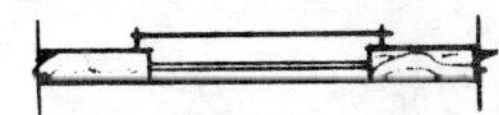

Figure 7-14
Picture window.

THE KITCHEN

A kitchen is divided into three main areas of activity--cooking, refrigeration and sanitation. To maintain an efficient work area each activity area should possess certain characteristics. The cooking area should have a working surface on both sides of the range plus working space near the double oven. This area should also have some storage space and should be located near the serving area. The area on both sides of the range should have heat-resistant countertops, and the cooking area should be well ventilated.

The sanitation area includes a dishwasher, sink, and garbage disposer. The sink should have a work area of 24 inches on either side. Storage space should be provided for fruits, vegetables, and cooking utensils. The refrigeration area should be located near a service entrance. This area should have at least 15 inches of counter space adjacent to the refrigerator.

The three major work areas form a "work-triangle." The work triangle is an important factor in determining how well a kitchen is planned. To establish the work triangle, measure from the center of the range to the center of the refrigerator to the center of the sink. The total length of the triangle should be less than 22 feet but more than 13 feet. The recommended distances between the work areas are: sink to refrigerator, 4 to 7 feet; sink to range, 4 to 6 feet; and range to refrigerator, 4 to 9 feet.

There are three basic types of kitchen plans: the U-shaped (Figure 7-15); the L-shaped (Figure 7-16); and the corridor kitchen (Figure 7-17). The U-shaped kitchen has the advantage of eliminating through-traffic and can have a compact work triangle. The L-shaped kitchen has the cabinets along two adjacent walls. This shape allows for a breakfast area without sacrificing space from the work area. The corridor kitchen has the cabinets placed on two parallel walls. This type of arrangement can serve as a passageway between other parts of the house. If this type of arrangement is used, the floor space between the two cabinets should be a minimum of 4 feet.

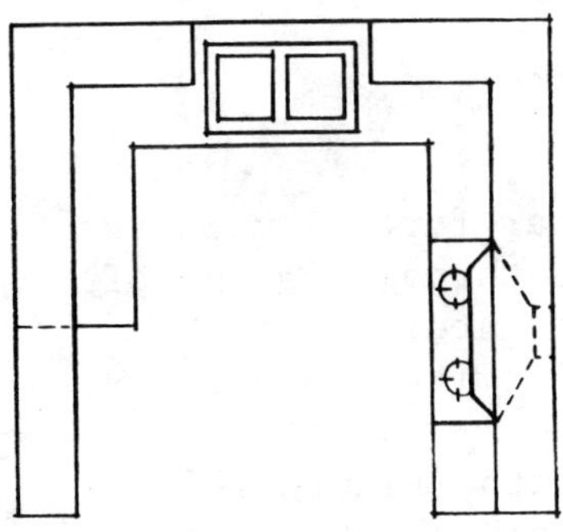

Figure 7-15
U-shaped kitchen.

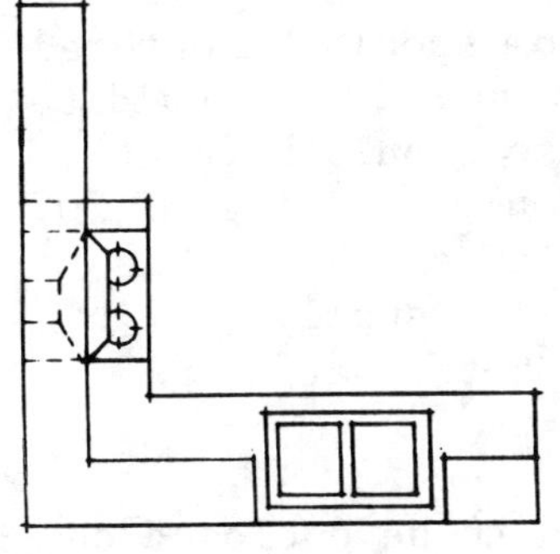

Figure 7-16
L-shaped kitchen.

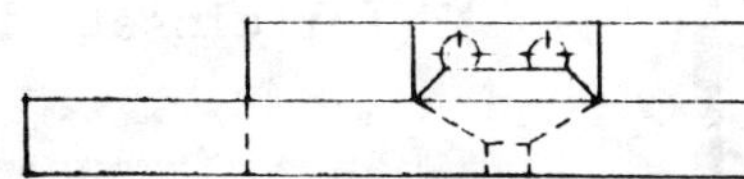

Figure 7-17
Corridor kitchen.

THE BATHROOM

The bathroom is a private retreat and grooming center for all members of a family. The arrangement of the plumbing and bathrooms is one of the mechanical and design pivot points of a house. Intelligent preplanning is a vital factor in accomplishing uniformity and economy.

Every house is required to have at least one bath (Figure 7-18), but most have at least a bath and a half. A full bathroom has a tub, lavatory, and water closet (commode). A half-bath has only a water closet and lavatory (Figure 7-19). The bath should be at least 5 feet by 8 feet and located near the bedrooms. The bathroom should be entered from the hall, and when it is located in a two-story house, it should be placed near the head of the stairs. A two-story house should have at least 1-1/2 baths, The water closet requires a minimum wall area of 30 inches and should not be visible from other rooms (Figure 7-20). The lavatory can be wall hung, but the built-in lavatory is usually preferred (Figure 7-21). In the master bath or in a bath that is shared, twin lavatory installation is often desired.

Most bathtubs are 5'-0" x 2'-6" and are required to be enclosed on three sides (Figure 7-22). The minimum size for a shower is 30" x 30" (Figure 7-23).

The bathroom door should swing into the bath and afford maximum privacy. The width of the door should be 2'-4" or 2'-6". The bathroom should be well lighted, ventilated, and heated. For proper ventilation, an exhaust fan or a window may be used.

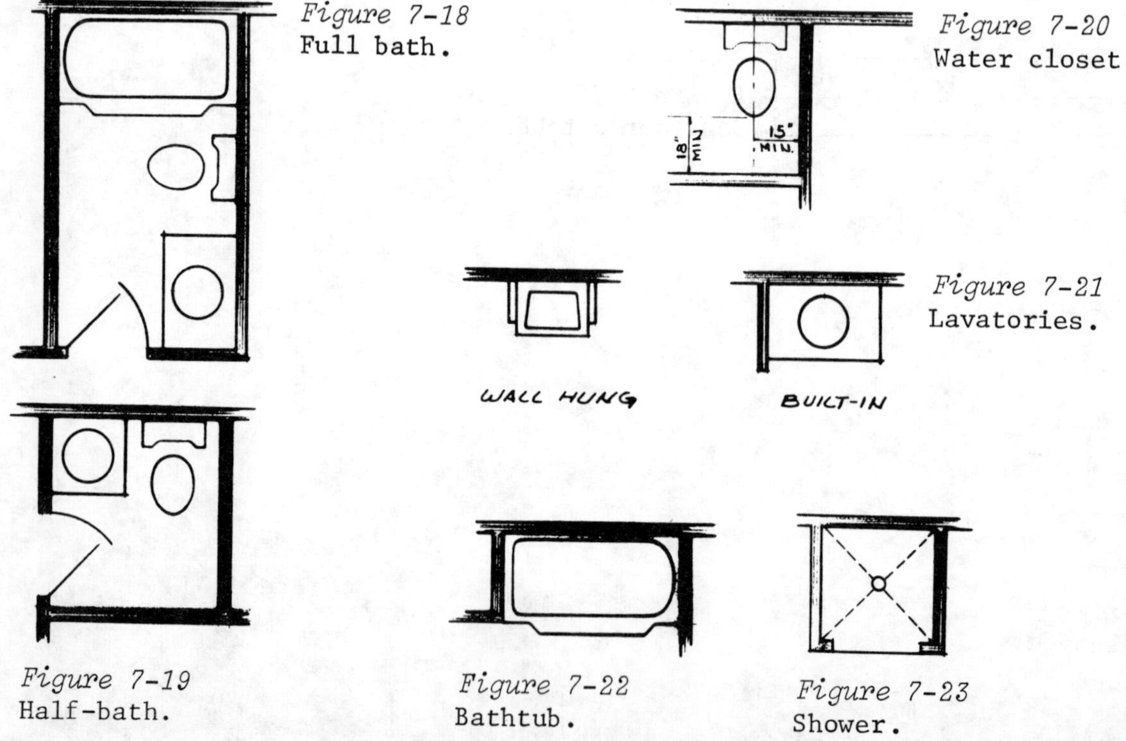

Figure 7-18
Full bath.

Figure 7-20
Water closet.

Figure 7-21
Lavatories.

Figure 7-19
Half-bath.

Figure 7-22
Bathtub.

Figure 7-23
Shower.

STAIRS

There are five basic plans that can be used for stairs. They are: (1) the straight-run (Figure 7-24); (2) the L-shaped (Figure 7-25); (3) the narrow U (Figure 7-26); (4) the winder (Figure 7-27); and (5) the double L or U (Figure 7-28).

The straight-run stair leads from one level to another without a turn and is the most popular of the five stair designs. The L-shaped stair has one landing and makes a 90-degree turn at the landing. The narrow U stair has two flights of stairs in reversed directions, the two flights run parallel to each other, and they make a 180 degree turn at the landing. The winder is the most difficult stair to construct and is the most dangerous. The winder is dangerous because it does not provide adequate footage. If winders are used they should not come to a point. The double L or U has two landings and makes two 90-degree turns. This particular type of stair is not often used.

The width of a main stair is 2'-8" clear of the hand rail. A basement stair requires 2'-6" clear of the hand rail. There are several parts of a stair, each designed for a specific purpose. The tread is the horizontal member of the stair and is the part of the stair that is stepped on. Most treads are 10 to 11 inches in width. The riser is the vertical face of the stair and is placed directly below the tread. The total run is the horizontal length of the stairs, and the stairwell is the opening in which a set of stairs is placed. The total rise is the vertical distance from one floor to another. To find the number of treads required for the floor plan, divide the total rise by 7 and subtract 1. The seven is the average height of a riser, and there is always one less tread than the total number of risers.

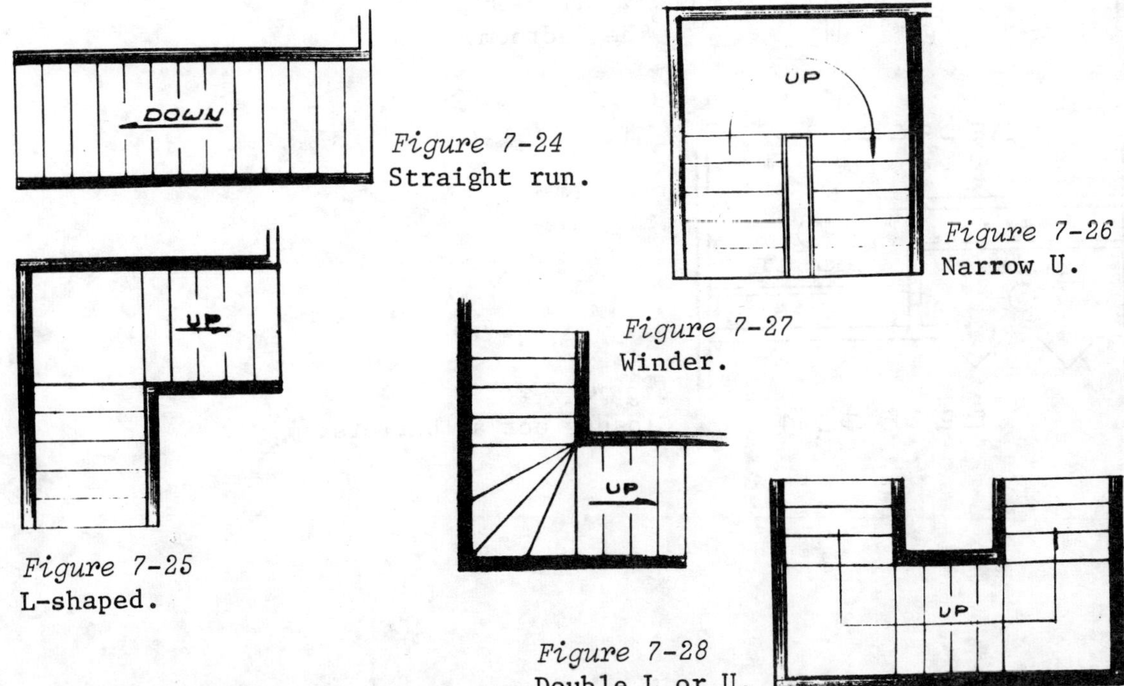

Figure 7-24
Straight run.

Figure 7-26
Narrow U.

Figure 7-27
Winder.

Figure 7-25
L-shaped.

Figure 7-28
Double L or U.

THE BEDROOM

A bedroom should contain a minimum of 100 square feet and should only be accessible by a hall. In most cases the bedroom should be located in a separate wing and on the quiet side of the lot. The children's bedrooms should be adjacent to or near the master bedroom (Figure 7-29). To act as a buffer between the bedrooms, the closets and baths should be strategically located (Figure 7-30). If possible, there should be windows on two walls of each bedroom. The windows allow for cross-ventilation. The window area should be at least 15% of the floor area. However, there should be at least one uninterrupted wall area of ten feet. The door to the bedroom should be at least 2'-6" in width and should swing into the bedroom.

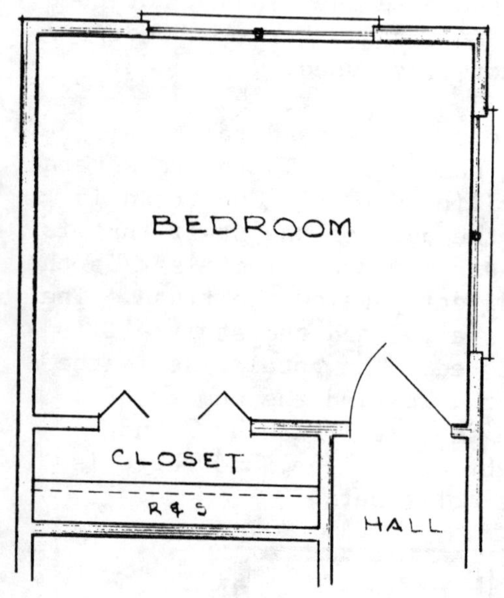

Figure 7-29
The bedroom.

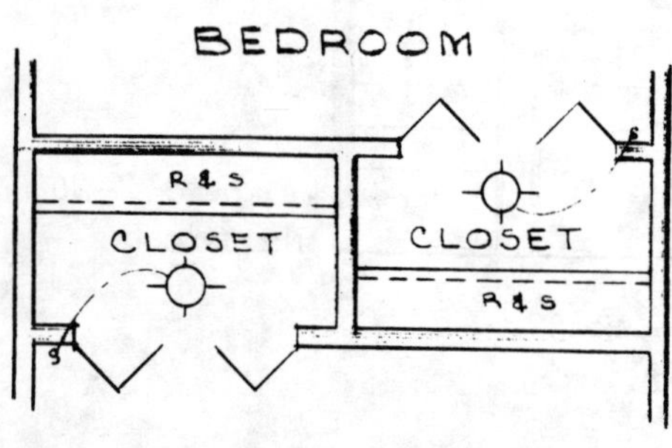

Figure 7-30
Closets act as buffers.

THE DINING AND LIVING ROOM

The dining room should be located between the kitchen and the living room area. There are two basic plans that can be used for a living room. The plan that is most widely accepted is the living room-dining room combination. In this type of arrangement there are no walls to separate the two rooms (Figure 7-31). The other arrangement is to have the dining room and living room separate (Figure 7-32). If the two rooms are separate, they should be adjacent to each other and have a large opening between them. The living room should have direct access from the entry and should not provide passage to other parts of the house. The dining room and living room should have about 300 square feet and should be isolated from the bedrooms.

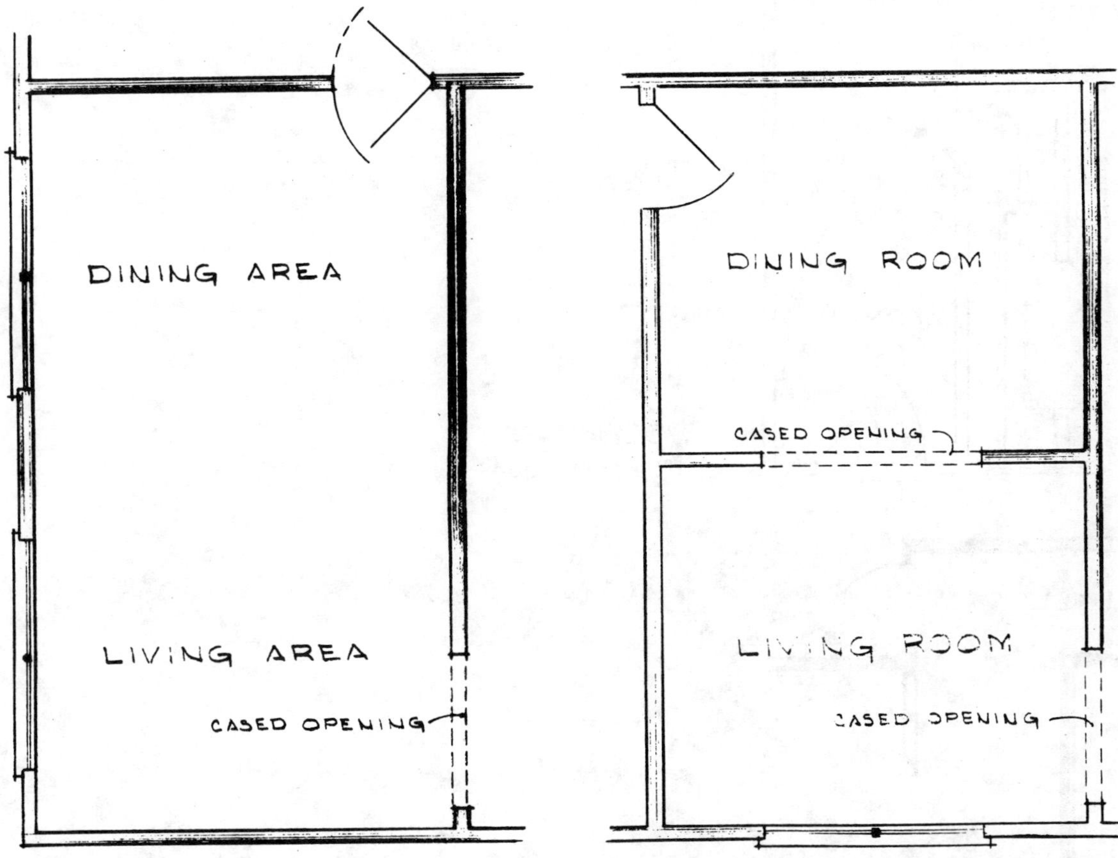

Figure 7-31
Living and dining area.

Figure 7-32
Separate living and dining rooms.

THE ENTRANCE AND THE HALL

The entrance way should lead to the central area of the house and open into a hall (Figure 7-33). There is no standard size for an entry, but most are about 5' x 6'. The entry door should be covered by a porch or overhang. The entry can be walled off, or it can be an extension of the living room. In some cases, a divider can be used to separate the two areas (Figure 7-34).

The recommended width of a hall is 3'-6". The minimum width is 3 feet and the maximum width is 4 feet. The total area of the hall should be kept as small as possible.

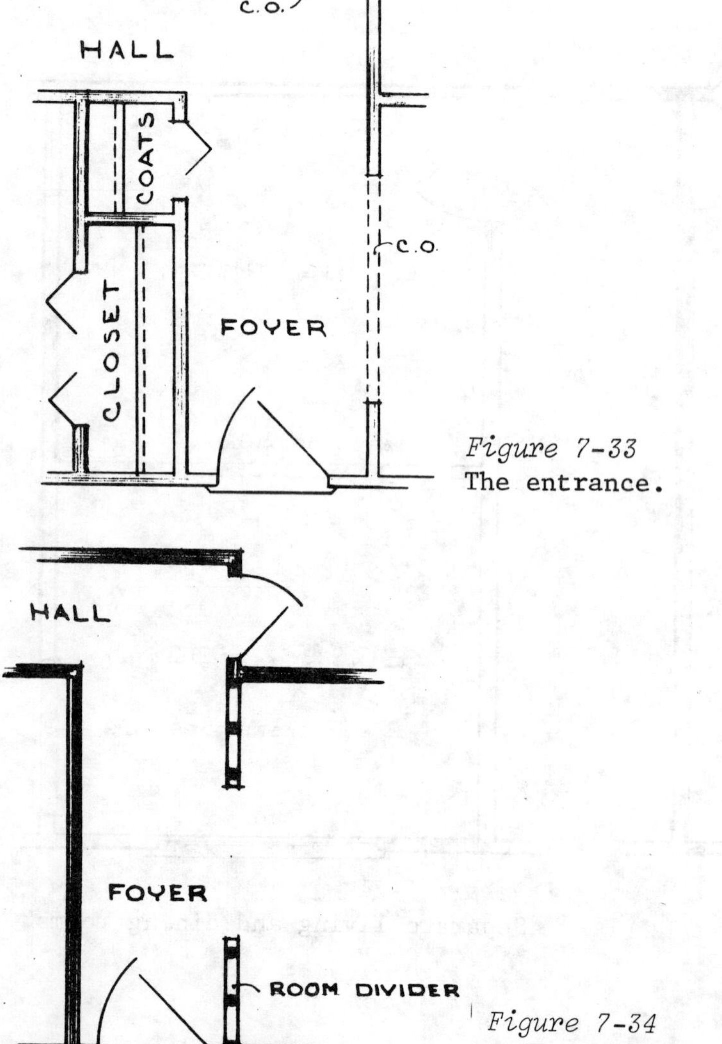

Figure 7-33
The entrance.

Figure 7-34
Use of the room divider.

CLOSETS

Closets are used to store different items that are not in use. The three types of closets are: bedroom, coat, and linen, each filling a specific need.

A bedroom closet should have a minimum of four linear feet of closet rod space, and it should have a depth of two feet. There are many types of doors that can be used, but a bi-fold door provides the most accessibility (Figure 7-35). The closet should also be properly lighted. To act as a buffer for noise, the closets should be placed on interior walls. The minimum size of a coat closet is 2' by 2', but a more efficient size would be 2' x 3'. The coat closet should be located near the front door. If the house has a foyer, the coat closet should be adjacent to it (Figure 7-36).

At least one linen closet should be built in each house. The average size of a linen closet is 1'-6" deep and 3 feet in width (Figure 7-37). There should be ten square feet of linen space for a two bedroom home and fifteen square feet for a three-bedroom home.

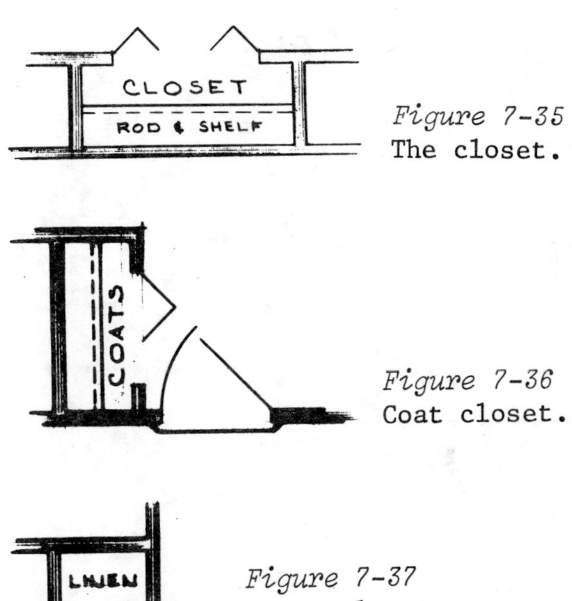

Figure 7-35
The closet.

Figure 7-36
Coat closet.

Figure 7-37
Linen closet.

THE UTILITY ROOM

The utility room houses the washer and dryer and should be located near the kitchen and back door (Figure 7-38). The washer and dryer should be located side by side, and if possible a counter top and sink should be included in the utility room. The sink is used for hand washable items, and the counter top is used for folding clothes. If possible the dryer should be located on an outside wall for venting. The minimum floor area for a utility room is 60 square feet.

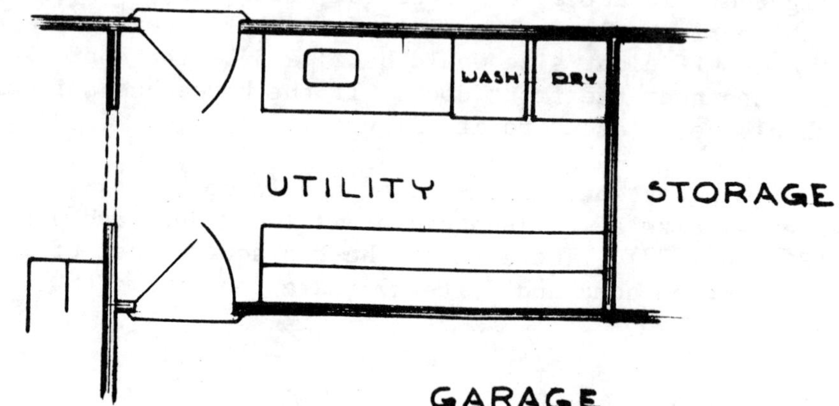

Figure 7-38
The utility room.

GARAGE OR CARPORT

A garage is enclosed on three sides and can be completely enclosed with a door (Figure 7-39). The carport is popular in the South and has one or more open sides (Figure 7-40). The garage or carport is usually attached to the house and has an entrance near the kitchen. The minimum size of a garage or carport is: one car 10' x 18' and two cars 18' x 18'. The floor should be concrete, 4 inches above grade, and sloped toward the entrance.

A garage can have one door or two small doors. An eight-foot door is the minimum size for a garage door. The garage door should be kept simple in design. The wall between the garage and house should be fire resistant, usually 5/8-inch gypsum or plaster is used.

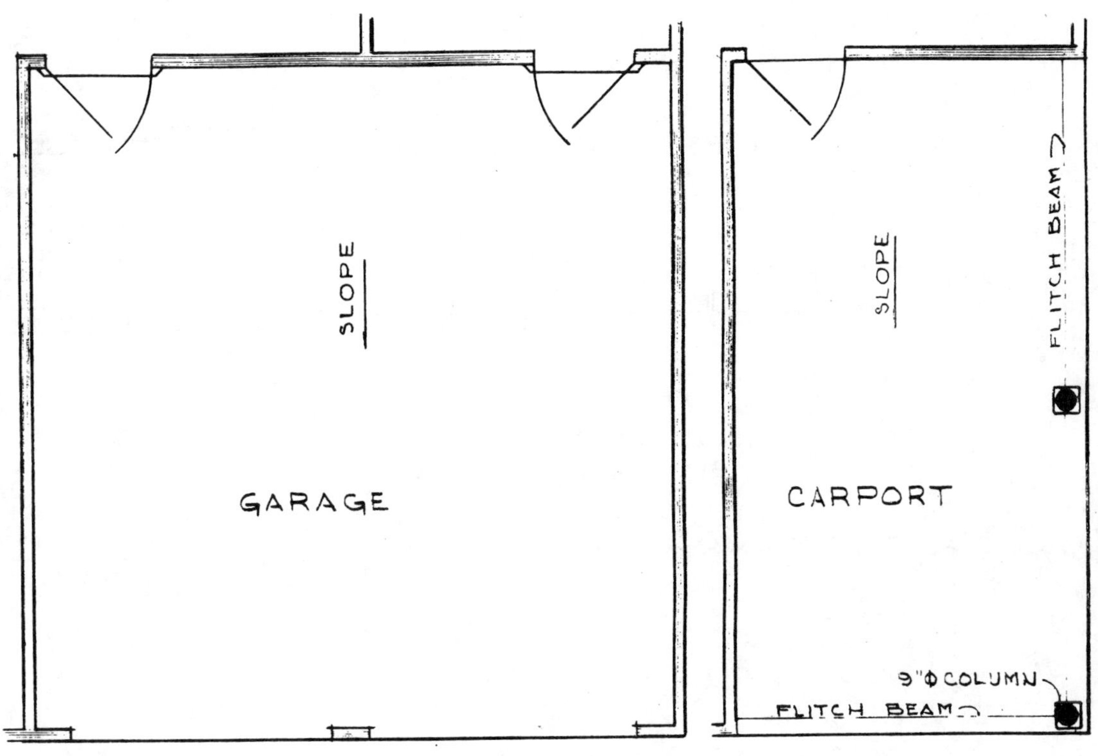

Figure 7-39
Two-car garage.

Figure 7-40
One-car carport.

ELECTRICAL OUTLETS

In the living areas of a home, electrical outlets should be spaced 8 feet apart (Figure 7-41). Other areas, such as halls, carports, foyers, and storage rooms, should be provided with at least one electrical outlet. A circle 3/16 of an inch in diameter with two short lines perpendicular to the stud wall is the symbol used for convenience outlets. If a 220-volt outlet is needed, a third line is added to the circle. For outdoor use, outlets are sometimes placed on patios, porches, and in carports. These outlets usually have a cover over them and are designated on the floor plan by placing a WP by the outlet symbol.

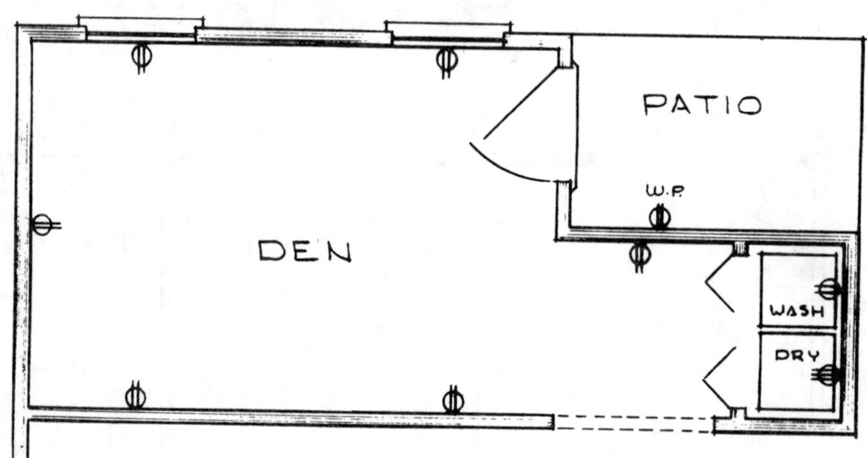

Figure 7-41
Electrical outlets.

ELECTRICAL FIXTURES

Each room or area of a house should be properly lighted. Each living area of the house requires a minimum of one fixture, and if the area is larger than 150 square feet, there should be two fixtures. The kitchen usually has two fixtures, one overhead and one over the sink (Figure 7-42). A hall should have ceiling fixtures 15 feet apart, and the stairway should have adequate lighting controlled at the head and foot of the stairs. Each closet should have a light fixture that can be operated by a pull cord or switch (Figure 7-43). Each entrance should have one or more light fixtures, and each garage should have a ceiling fixture for every two cars (Figure 7-44).

Most of the fixtures are controlled by a wall switch. The symbol for the wall switch is the letter S. The symbol for the ceiling fixture is a circle with four short lines protruding from it. To connect the switch and fixture, a curved center line is used. The switch should be located on the doorknob side of the door. If a room has two entrances, a three-way switch should be used (Figure 7-45). A three-way switch is used to turn on a fixture at one location and turn it off at another.

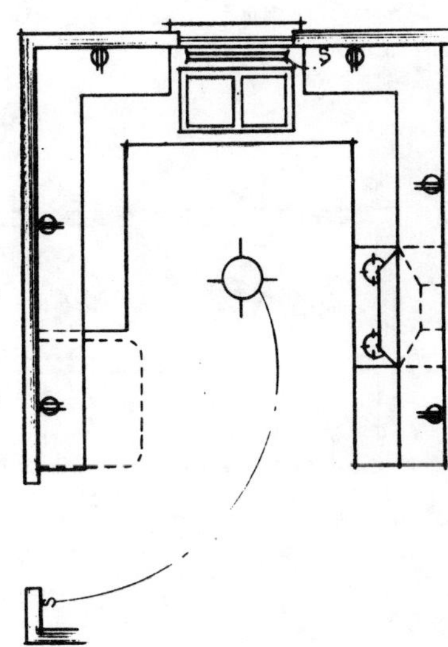

Figure 7-42
Kitchen light fixture.

Figure 7-43
Closet light fixture.

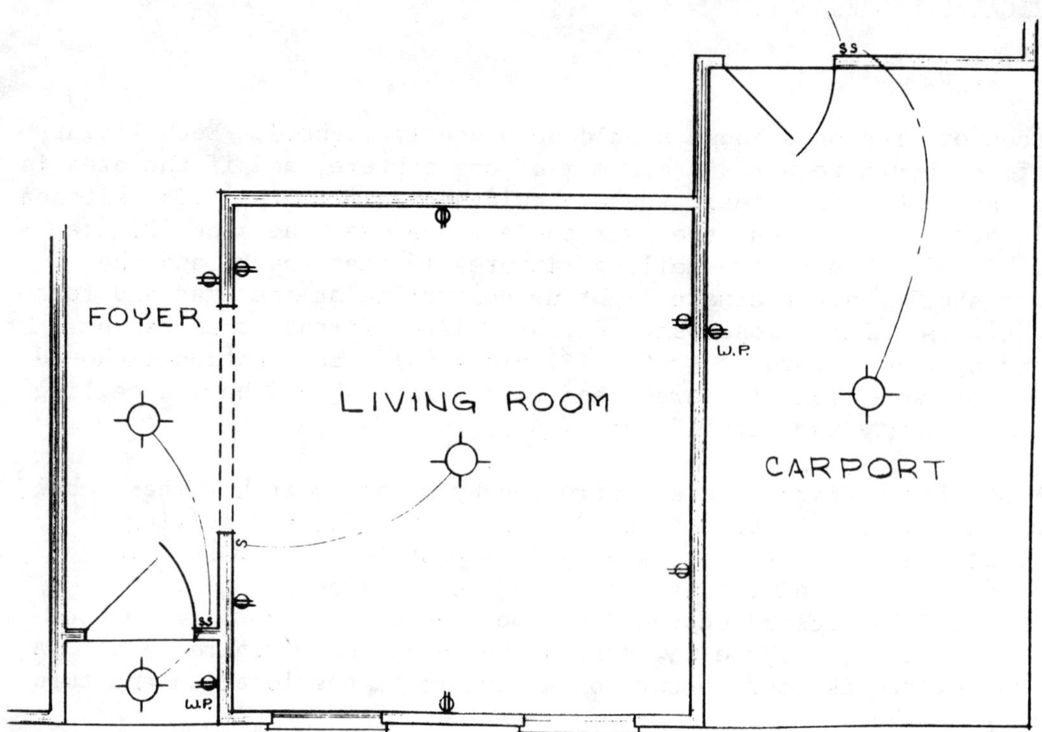

Figure 7-44
Entrance fixture.

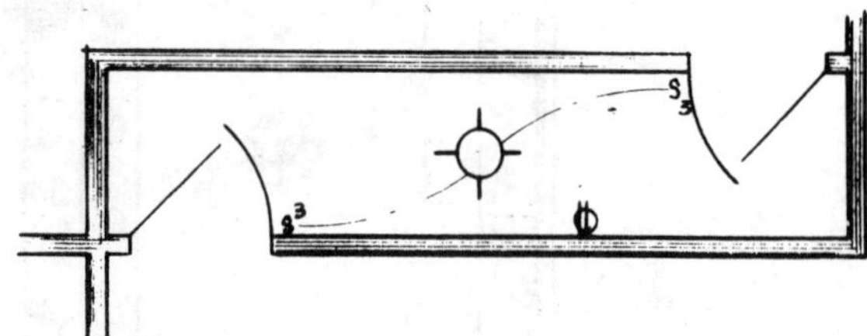

Figure 7-45
Three-way switch.

DIMENSIONING

There are several methods of dimensioning a wood frame house. One method that is used extensively is to place three sets of dimension lines on the outside of the building (Figure 7-46). The first dimension line measures from the outside surface of the stud wall to the center line of windows, doors, and partitions. The second dimension line measures from the outside stud wall to the center of partitions. The third dimension line is an overall dimension line, measuring from outside stud wall to outside stud wall. In some cases it may be necessary to place dimension lines on the inside of the building. If dimension lines are placed on the inside, they should be carefully placed so they will not interfere with other lines.

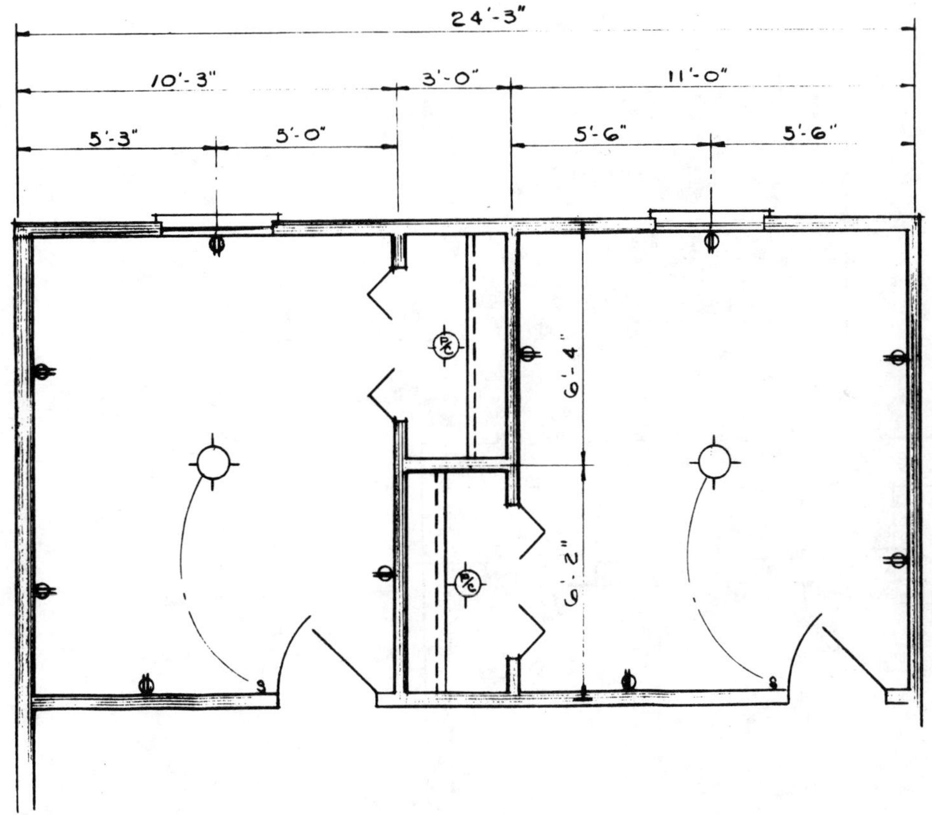

Figure 7-46
Dimensioning.

In architectural drafting, the dimension lines are continous and can be terminated by a dot, slash, circle, or arrowhead (Figure 7-47). The dimensions should not be crowded. All dimensions are given in feet and inches and should be 3/32 to 1/8 inch high.

If the plan is a basement plan or the building is constructed of solid masonry, the size of the door opening is given (Figure 7-48). The size of the walls is also indicated on the floor plans.

Each floor plan should have dimensions on all sides, and an overall dimension should be placed on all sides.

Note: 1. Avoid duplication of dimensions.

2. Use notes to clarify certain features.

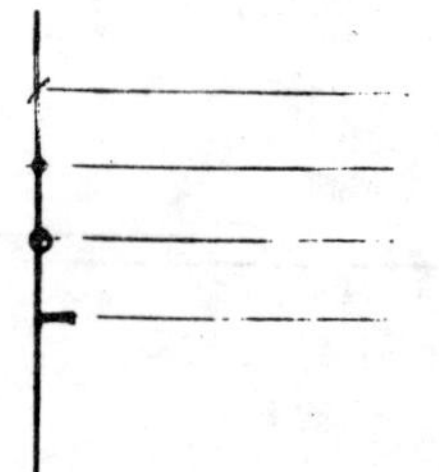

Figure 7-47
Dimension line termination.

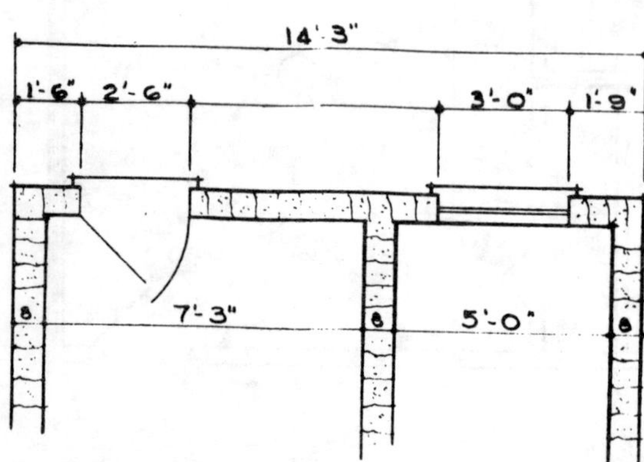

Figure 7-48
Dimensioning.

Assignment: Complete the corner section of a home with siding.

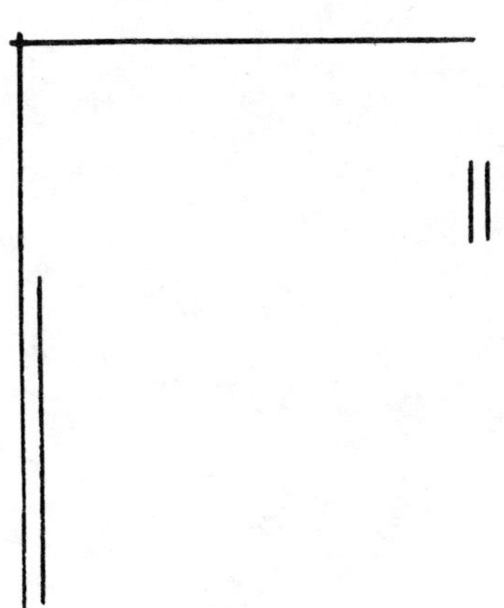

Assignment: Complete the corner section of a brick veneer home.

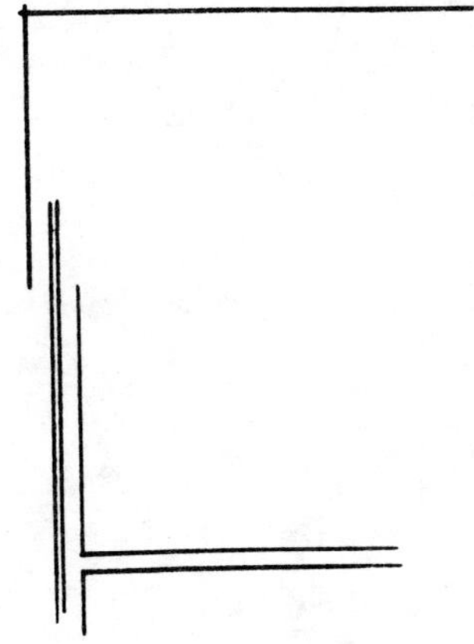

Assignment: Add the doors to the floor plan as indicated.

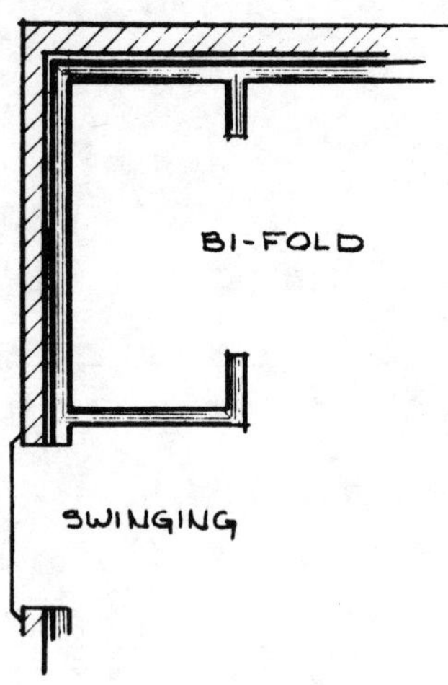

Assignment: Add the doors to the floor plan as indicated.

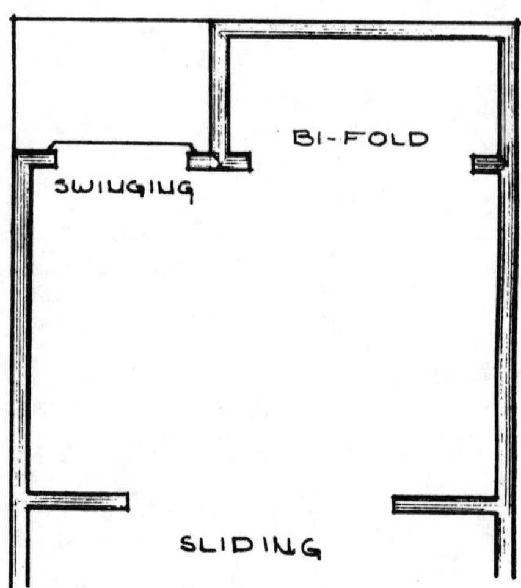

Assignment: Add the doors to the floor plan as indicated.

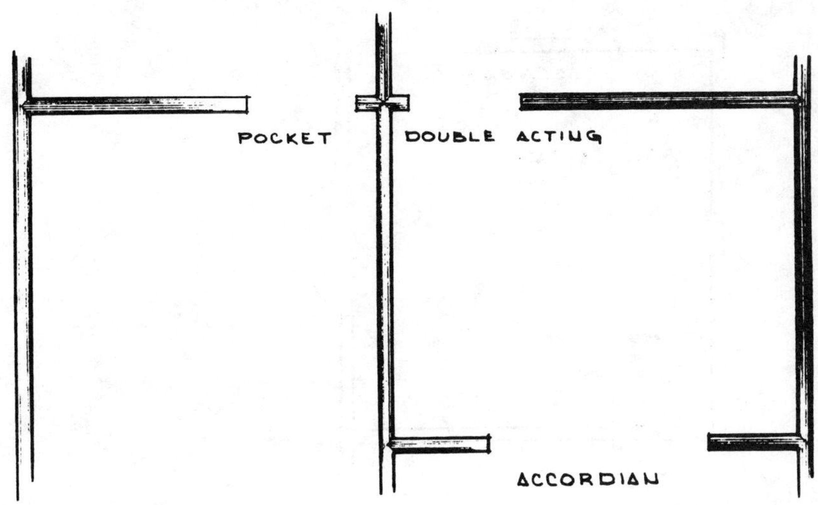

Assignment: Add the windows to the floor plan as indicated.

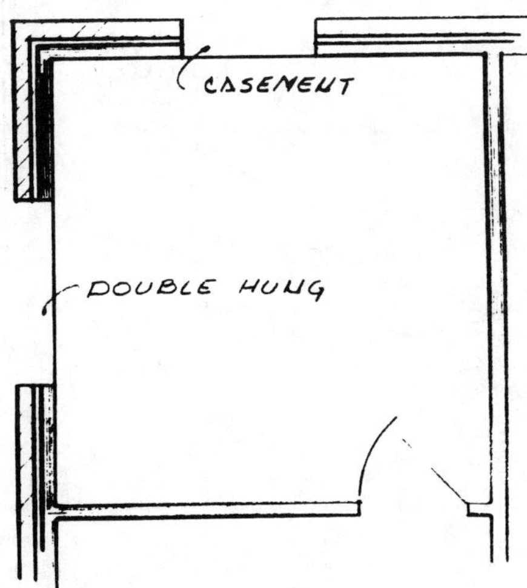

Assignment: Add the windows to the floor plan as indicated.

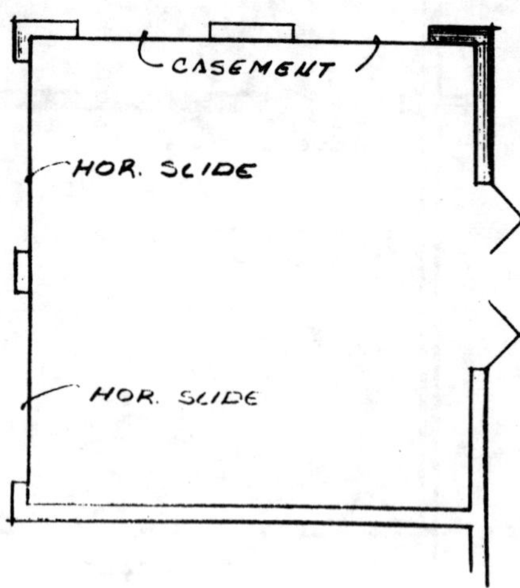

Assignment: Add the windows to the floor plan as indicated.

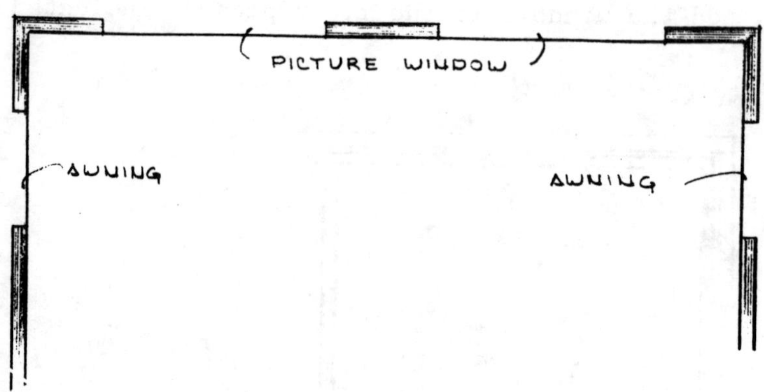

Assignment: **Design a U-shaped kitchen.**

Assignment: **Design an L-shaped kitchen.**

Assignment: **Design a corridor kitchen.**

Assignment: Design a full bath with two lavatories.

Assignment: Design a half-bath.

Assignment: Design a bath with a shower, water closet, and lavatory.

Assignment: Draw the plan view of a straight-run stair that has 13 risers to the basement of a house. The total rise is 8'-6".

Assignment: Draw the plan view of an L-shaped stair that has 15 risers to the second floor of a house. The total rise is 8'-9".

Assignment: Design a master bedroom that has 150 square feet.

Assignment: Design a living room and dining room.

Assignment: Design an entrance that has 36 square feet and has an adjacent coat closet.

Assignment: Design an entrance way and living room that is separated by a room divider.

Assignment: Design a bedroom closet that has twenty square feet.

Assignment: Design a coat closet that has eight square feet of floor area.

Assignment: Design a utility room.

Assignment: Design a two-car garage.

Assignment: Place electrical outlets in the proper location.

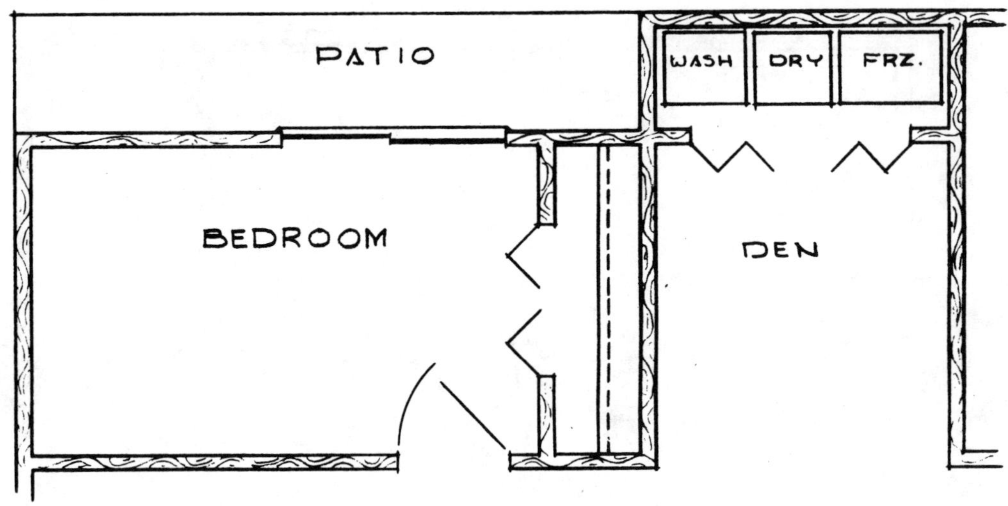

Assignment: Place the switches and fixtures in their proper location.

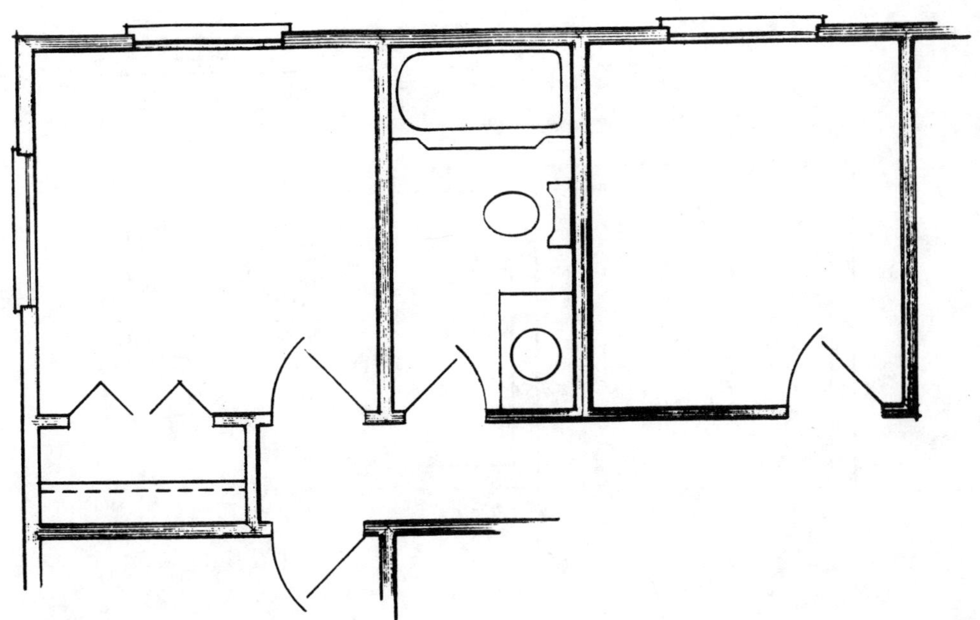

Assignment: Place the necessary dimensions on the wood frame house.

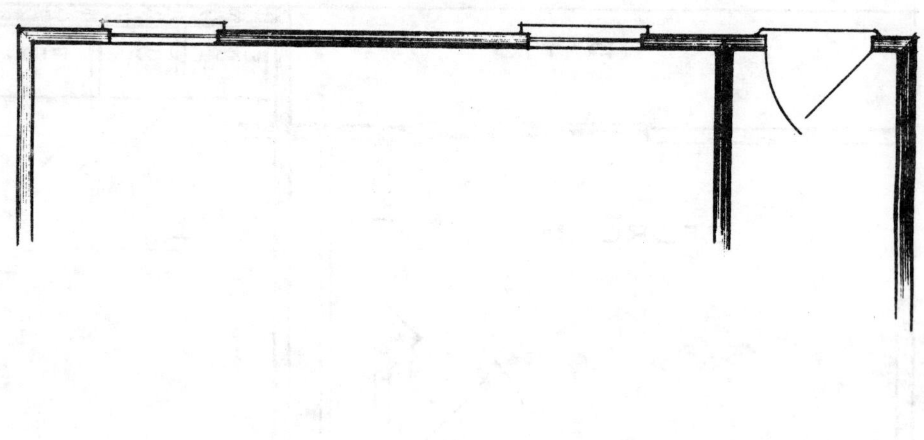

Assignment: Place the necessary dimensions on the floor plan.

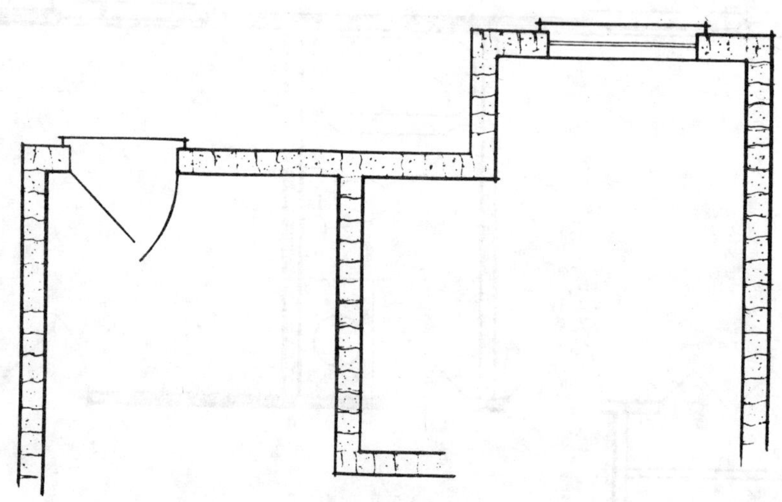

UNIT END TEST

1. The three basic types of doors used in homes are ___________, ___________, and ___________.

2. Double-hung windows are equipped with ___________ operating sashes.

3. Hopper windows have the sash hinged at the ___________.

4. The total length of the work triangle should be less than ___________.

5. The minimum size for a shower is ___________ X ___________.

6. The ___________ is the horizontal member of the stair and is the part of the stair that is stepped on.

7. The door to a bedroom should be at least ___________ in width.

8. The recommended width of a hall is ___________.

9. The minimum size of a coat closet is ___________.

10. The minimum size of a two-car garage is ___________.

Unit End Assignment:

Draw a floor plan, using the developed sketch from chapter 6. Use a sheet of tracing paper 18 x 24 inches. Be sure to include a border line and a title block.

Chapter 8
THE FOUNDATION PLAN

The foundation plan is a plan view drawing used in the construction of the foundation. It usually includes: (1) the size and shape of the foundation, (2) size and location of footings, (3) beams and pilasters, (4) dimensions and notes, and (5) the scale to which the foundation plan was drawn.

There are three basic types of foundations used in light construction: (1) slab-on-grade, (2) crawl space, and (3) basement.

SLAB-ON-GRADE

In areas that have warm climates a slab-on-grade is a popular type of foundation (Figure 8-1). In most cases, the foundation plan for a slab-on-grade is drawn by placing a sheet of tracing paper over the floor plan and tracing the general outline of the floor plan. Hidden lines are then placed parallel to the outside wall. The hidden line indicates the inside of the footings. In most cases the width of the footings is 12 inches. If the building is to be brick veneer, another parallel line is drawn 5-1/2 inches from the outside of the foundation. The 5-1/2 inches represents the brick shelf and will be a continuous line unless there is a door opening. Cutting plane lines are then drawn in areas of the slab that will need detailing.

Note: 1. The details of the footings are usually drawn on the same sheet of paper as the foundation plan but to a larger scale.

2. Any time the slab elevation changes, a line will indicate that change. For example, the floor slab is 4 inches higher than the carport slab; therefore, a line is used to show the elevation change.

3. A brick shelf will not run across the door but will be placed beneath the windows.

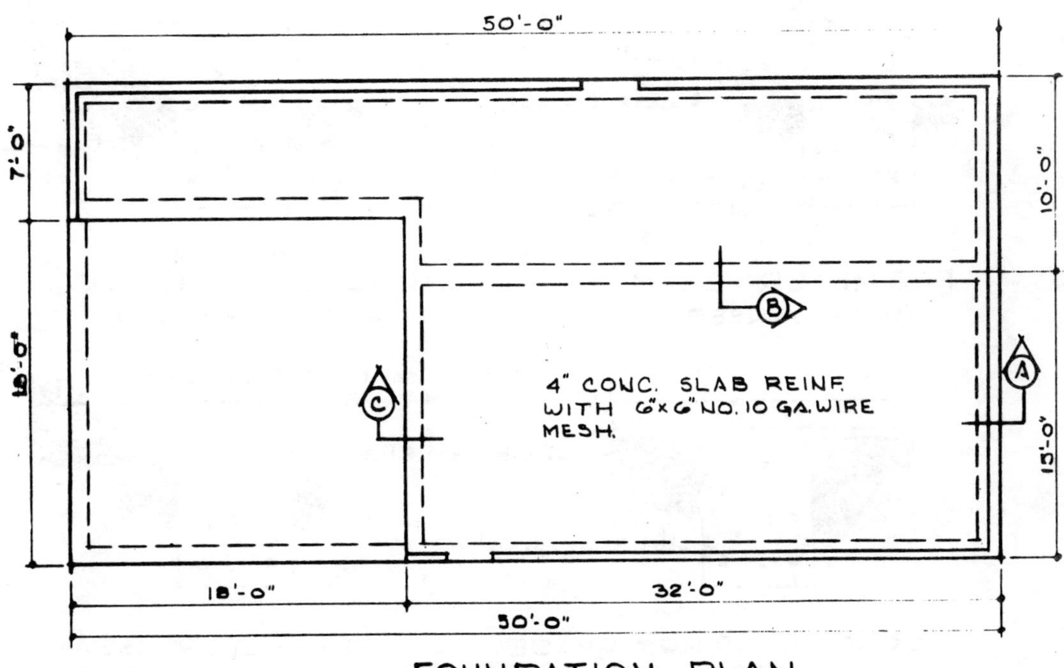

Figure 8-1
Foundation plan.

4. The cutting plane line indicates the direction in which the observer is looking at the object.

5. A cutting plane line is placed in every location that has a different type of footing.

6. In most cases brick is not placed under the carport, so a brick ledge is not shown.

FOOTINGS FOR A SLAB-ON-GRADE

The footings (Figure 8-2) for a slab-on-grade are usually 12 inches wide and extend 6 inches into undisturbed soil; according to most building codes the slab elevation is 8 inches above grade. The footings are usually reinforced with No. 4 or No. 5 reinforcement bars. The slab is reinforced with 6 x 6 No. 10 gauge welded wire mesh. Directly beneath the slab, a polyethylene vapor barrier is placed. The polyethylene is used as a vapor stop and controls moisture that might penetrate the slab. Another means of controlling moisture is to place a 4-inch base course of wash gravel or crushed stone beneath the floor slab. The base course acts as a capillary stop against moisture that might rise through the underlying soil. The base course usually rests on fill dirt. The fill should be well tamped and free of debris and organic matter.

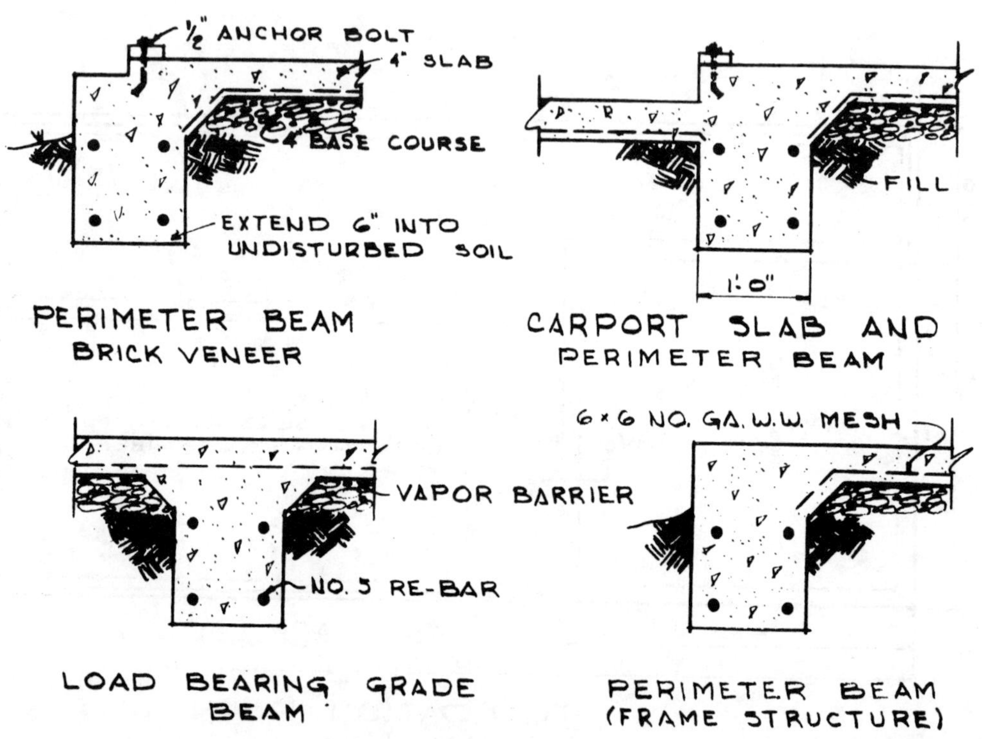

Figure 8-2
Footings.

Note: 1. A 1/2-inch anchor bolt is used to secure the bottom plate to the slab. An anchor bolt is not placed in the load-bearing grade beams.

2. A load-bearing grade beam, in most cases, is placed under a load-bearing wall. If roof trusses are used, a load-bearing grade beam is not required.

BASEMENTS

In several geographic locations a foundation system that forms a basement is a popular type of foundation (Figure 8-3). The foundation is comprised of load-transmitting elements such as: foundation walls, pilasters, and columns. The transmitting elements receive the load of the superstructure and transmit the load to the footings.

The foundation plan is usually drawn by placing a sheet of tracing paper oever the floor plan and lightly tracing the general outline of the floor plan. The outline of the floor plan and the floor plan itself should be removed from the drawing board; the outline of the floor plan is then placed back on the board. A line 8 inches from the outline is drawn around the perimeter of the plan. The line 8 inches from the general outline represents the width of the concrete block, the most common material used for foundation walls. Parallel lines are then drawn on either side of the concrete block wall. The lines are hidden lines and represent the width of the concrete footings. A rule of thumb for the footing size is: the footing width equals twice the width of the foundation wall.

Isolated footings are usually included in the foundation plan. The isolated footings support columns that are placed beneath girders and beams. The footings are 24 inches square and 12 inches deep and are represented by hidden lines on the foundation plan.

Note: 1. Placed concrete can be used for foundation walls, but because of the expensive form work, it is not the most popular.

2. Pilasters may be added to the foundation wall. The pilasters add strength to the wall and may be used to support a beam.

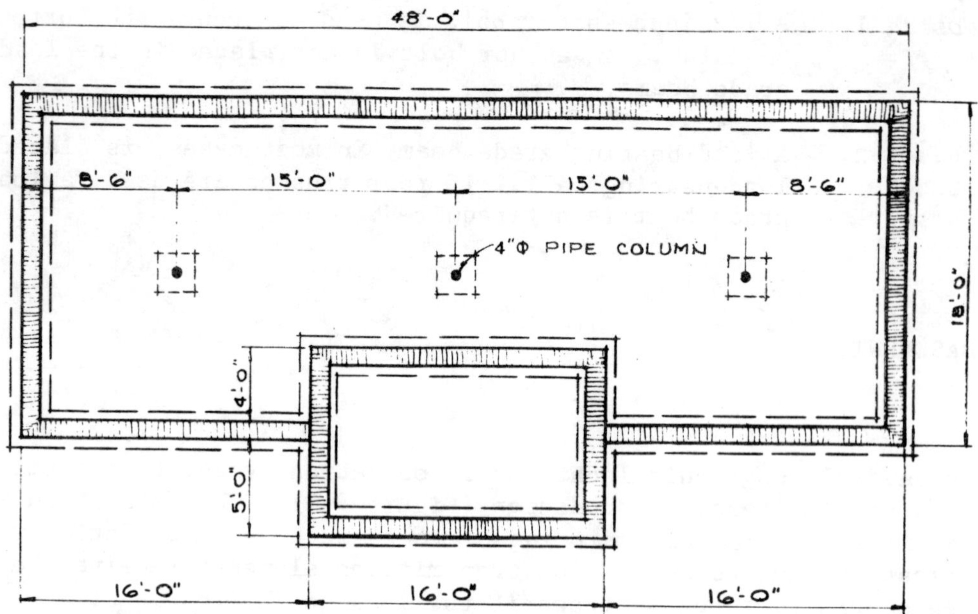

Figure 8-3
The foundation plan.

FOOTINGS

A footing is usually a concrete pad, although other materials may be used (Figure 8-4). There are several methods employed in the construction of footings, but most of the footings are stepped at the base of the foundation wall. The projection of the footing equals one-half the width of the footing. The thickness of a footing should equal the thickness of the foundation wall or be at least 12 inches thick. The footing should extend into the undisturbed soil 6 inches and be placed 3 inches below the frost line.

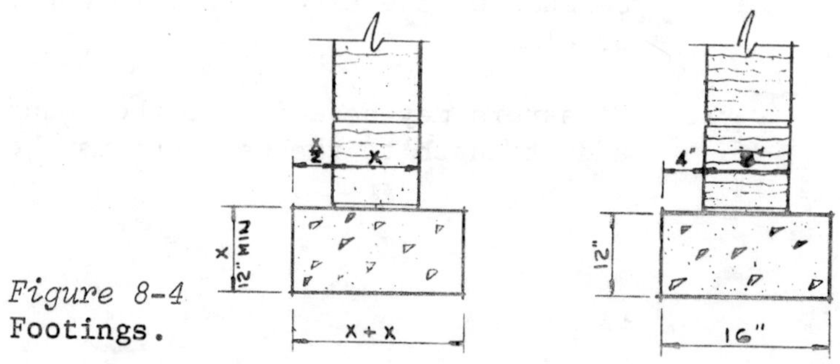

Figure 8-4
Footings.

BASEMENT WALLS

Basement walls (Figure 8-5) are usually constructed of 8-inch concrete blocks, although 12-inch blocks or placed concrete can be used. The bottom of the foundation wall is placed on a concrete footing, and the top of the wall should project past the finish grade 8 inches. One of the major problems in a foundation of this type is the possibility of water penetration through the foundation wall. To prevent water penetration, several precautionary methods are taken: (1) the foundation wall may be parged with cement mortar, (2) hot tar may be mopped over the wall, and (3) a sheet of .006 polyethylene can be placed over the foundation wall.

At the base of the foundation wall, a 4-inch drain tile is placed. The drain tile is used to carry ground water to a storm sewer or a dry stream bed. To aid in the percolation of the ground water, the drain tile is surrounded by wash gravel or crushed stone.

Note: 1. A 1/2-inch expansion joint is usually placed at the intersection of the foundation wall and basement floor.

2. The drain tile is usually placed at the intersection of the foundation wall and footing.

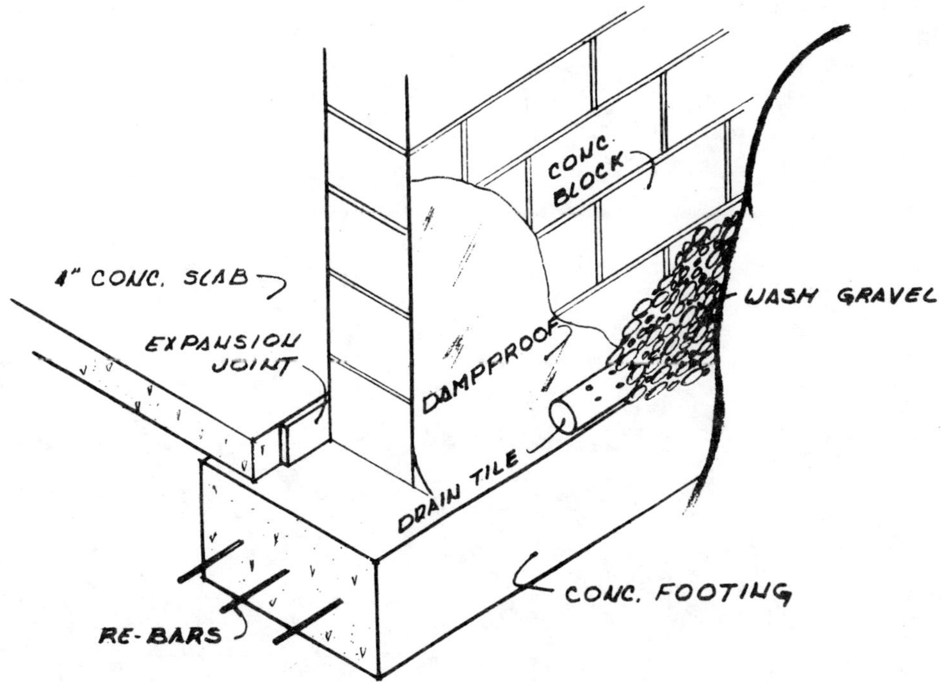

Figure 8-5
Basement wall.

STEPPED FOOTINGS

In areas that have a sloping terrain, it is often more economical to use a stepped footing (Figure 8-6). A stepped footing is composed of horizontal and vertical steps. As a rule of thumb, the vertical step should not exceed 3/4 of the distance of the horizontal step. The horizontal step should not be less than 2 feet. The formula for the width of the stepped footing is: the width of the footing should equal twice the thickness of the foundation wall.

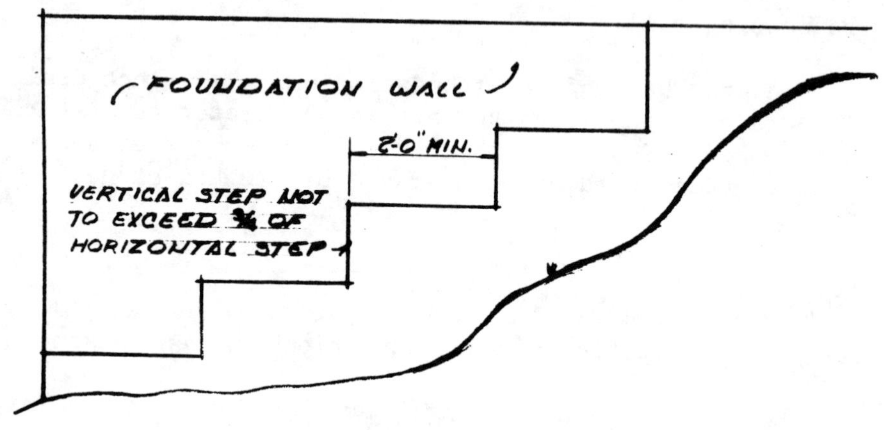

Figure 8-6
Stepped footing.

PIER FOUNDATION

In relatively warm climates, free-standing masonry piers are sometimes used as a foundation system (Figure 8-7). The foundation plan is simple, showing only the locations of the masonry piers, beams, and joist. The masonry units are usually 8 inch x 8 inch x 16 inch concrete blocks. The blocks rest on a reinforced concrete pad. The spacing of the piers depends upon the size of the framing members, but in most cases the piers are spaced 8 feet on center.

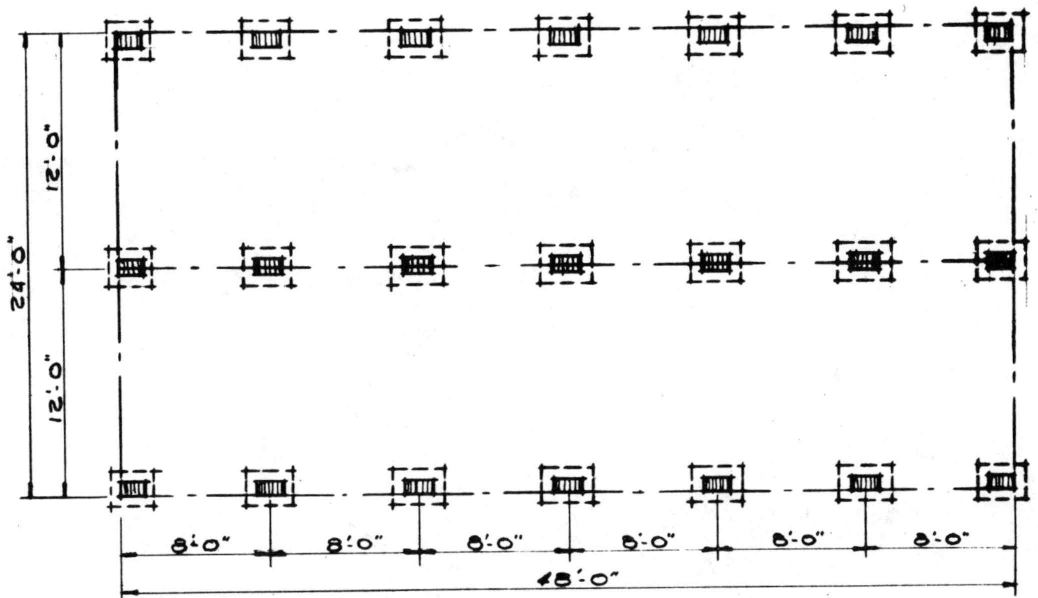

Figure 8-7
Pier foundation.

PIERS

Masonry piers (Figure 8-8) are usually constructed from 8-inch x 8-inch x 16-inch concrete blocks. To distribute the load of the superstructure, the piers are placed on reinforced concrete pads. The top of the pier should be a minimum of 18 inches above grade and topped with a metal termite shield.

Note: The footing should rest on undisturbed or well-tamped soil.

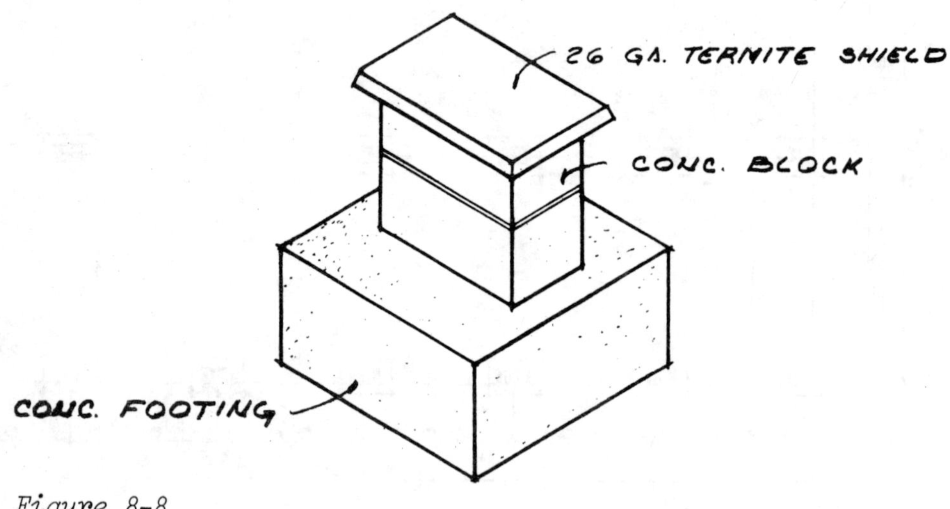

Figure 8-8
Pier.

CRAWL SPACE

In many areas of the country, foundation systems consist of a foundation wall, footing, and interior piers (Figure 8-9). The foundation wall and piers are usually made of concrete blocks placed on concrete footings.

The foundation plan is drawn by first placing a clean sheet of tracing paper over the developed floor plan. The general outline of the floor plan is then lightly traced. The floor plan is removed from the board, and the outline of the floor plan is taped to the board.

A line parallel to the outline of the floor plan is drawn. The line is drawn on the inside and represents the width of the foundation wall. In most cases the width is 8 inches, although 12-inch blocks can be used. The footings are then drawn. The footings are represented by dashed lines parallel to the foundation wall. The width of the footing is usually twice the width of the foundation wall.

Interior piers are placed within the foundation wall and are placed on isolated footings. They should be spaced 8 feet on center and should be placed under load-bearing partitions.

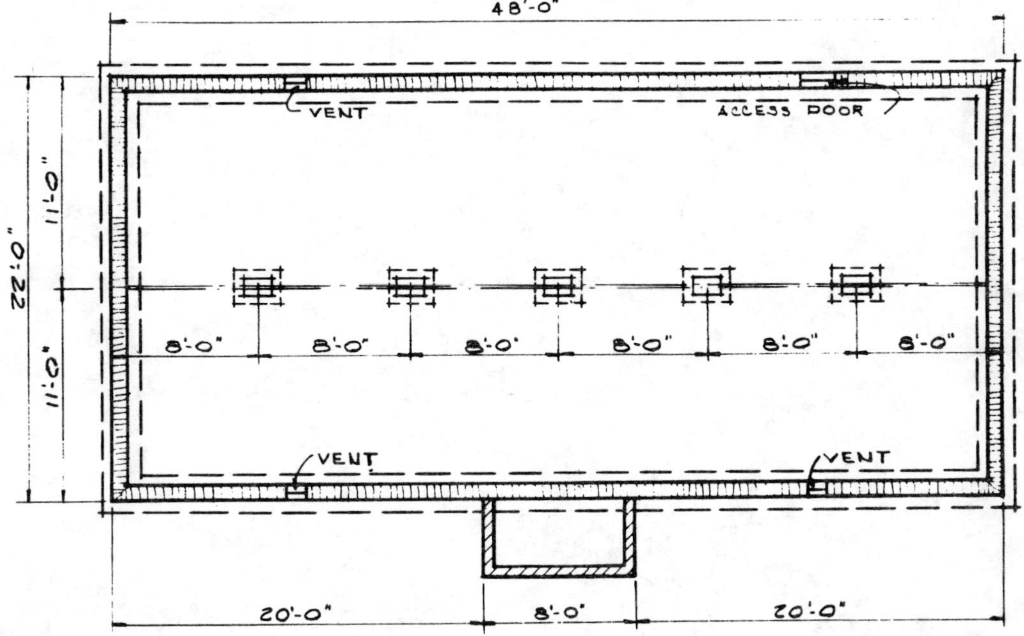

Figure 8-9
Foundation plan.

Assignment: Complete the foundation plan for a slab-on-grade. Include dimensions, notes, and the cutting plane lines.

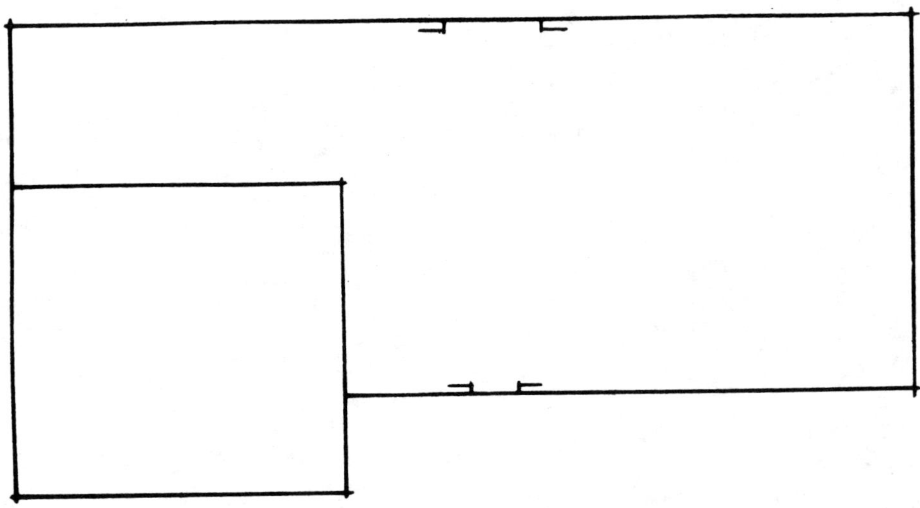

Assignment: Complete the footing detail, dimensioning the necessary parts.

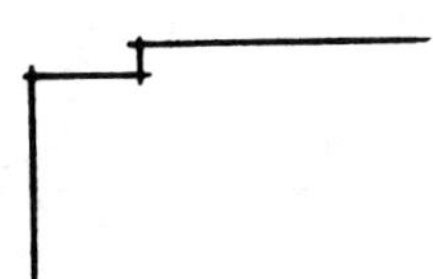

Assignment: Draw a detail for a load-bearing grade beam.

Assignment: Complete the footing detail, dimensioning the necessary parts.

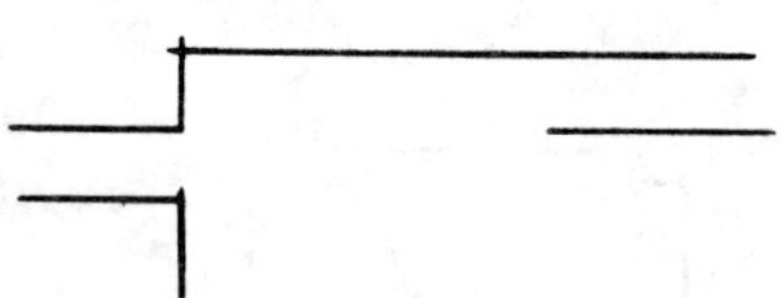

Assignment: Draw a grade beam detail for a structure that has plywood siding.

Assignment: Complete the foundation plan (basement).

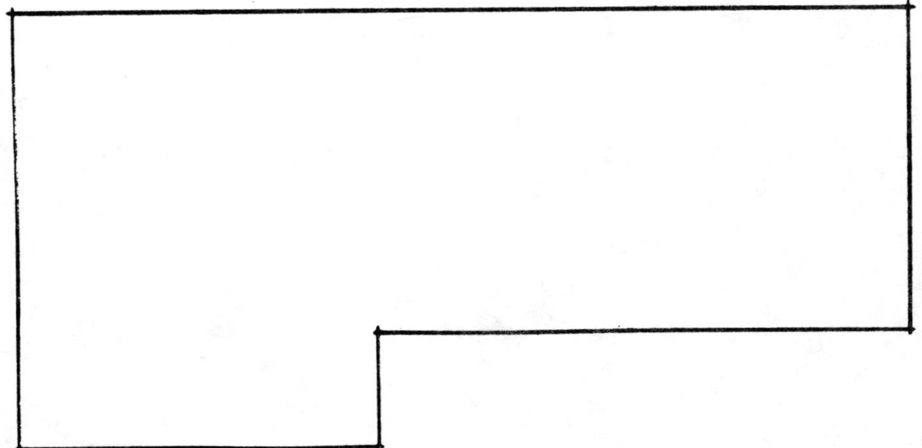

Assignment: Complete the footing detail below, dimensioning the necessary parts.

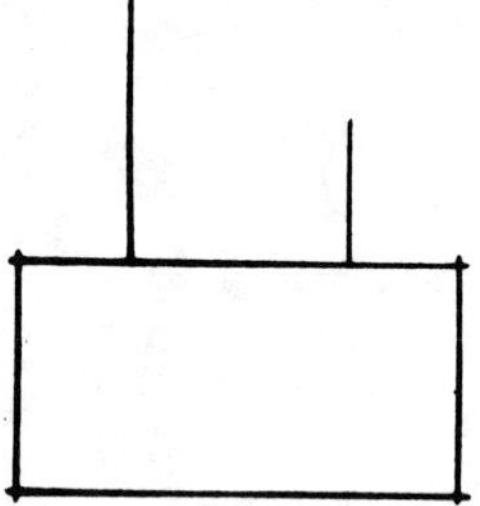

Assignment: Draw a 12-inch concrete foundation wall with a reinforced footing of appropriate size.

Assignment: Draw a detail of a basement wall. Include dimensions and notes.

Assignment: Draw an isometric of a stepped footing.

Assignment: Complete the masonry pier foundation plan.

Assignment: Draw a detail of a free-standing masonry pier.

Assignment: Complete the foundation plan (crawl space).

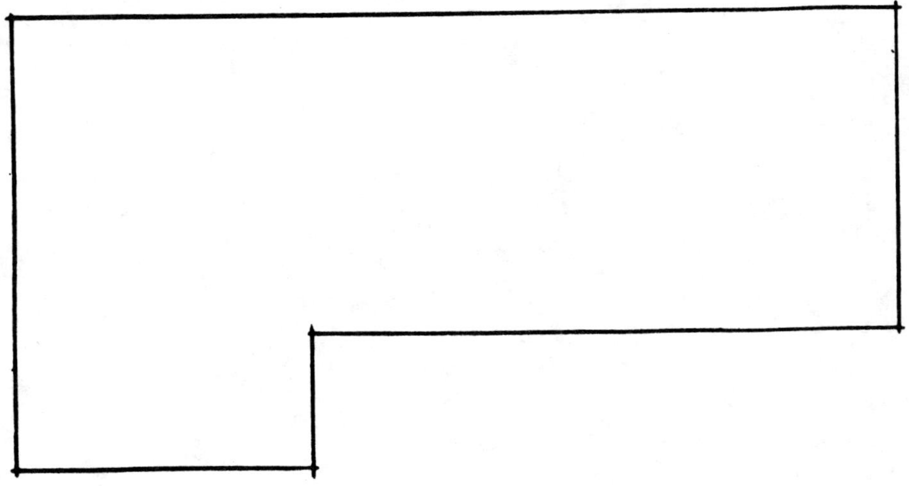

UNIT END TEST

Sketch the footing details for the foundation plan.

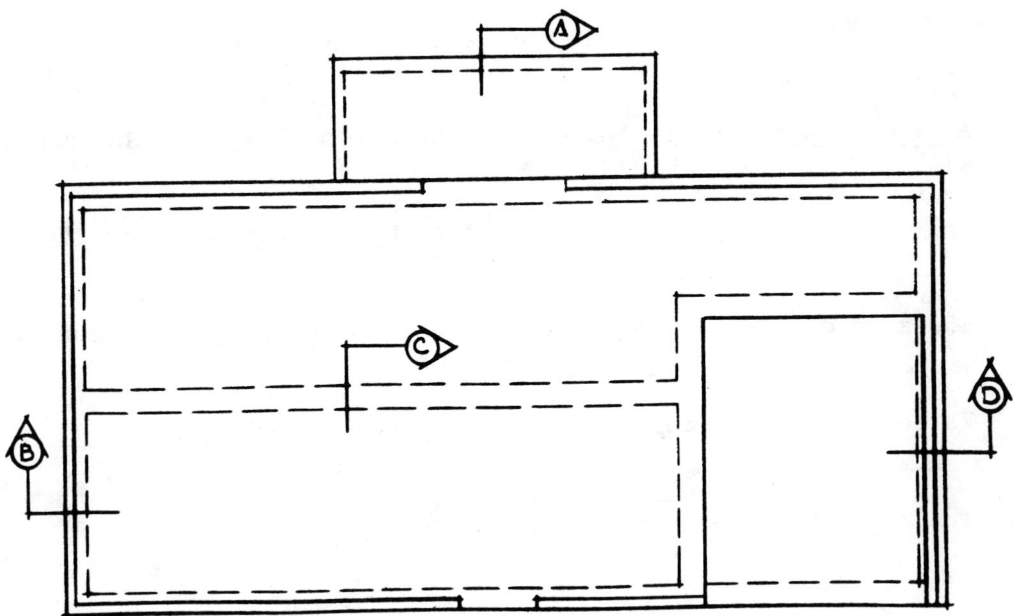

Fill in the blank:

1. The size of a brick ledge for a slab-on-grade is ___________.

2. The three types of spread foundations are ___________, ___________, and ___________.

3. Footings for a slab-on-grade are usually ___________ wide.

4. A slab is usually reinforced with ___________.

5. Two types of material used for base course are ___________, and ___________.

6. A ___________ is used to secure the bottom plate to the concrete slab.

7. The size of the concrete block used in basement walls is ___________ x ___________.

8. The size of the isolated footing used under columns is usually ___________ x ___________.

9. Three methods of damp proofing a foundation wall are ___________, ___________, and ___________.

10. The minimum size of a crawl space is ___________.

Sketch the symbols used for:

concrete　　gravel　　earth　　concrete block

undisturbed earth　　wire mesh　　re-bars　　anchor bolt

Unit End Assignment:

Draw a foundation plan for the floor plan developed in Chapter 7.

Chapter 9
DETAILS

A "detail" is a section of a particular feature of a building which is used to describe that feature. For an adequate description, the detail should be drawn to a scale larger than 1/4" = 1'-0"; be fully dimensioned; have sufficient notes; and contain the correct symbols. Some of the features that are usually detailed are windows, doors, cornices, fireplaces, stairs, and kitchen cabinets.

CORNICE DETAIL

The cornice detail is used to show the construction details at the intersection of the wall, wall frame, and the roof. There are several methods employed in the construction of a cornice, but one of the most widely used cornice details has a horizontal soffit.

In the drafting of the cornice, the wall frame, the ceiling joist, and rafter are first laid out (Figure 9-1). The rafter is laid out from the inside top corner of the wall frame. The slope of the rafter is usually found by using an architectural template that has a roof pitch indicator, or the slope can be determined by measuring from the inside of the wall frame to a point 12 feet along the joist. A vertical measurement is then made that corresponds with the rise of the roof; this point and the inside of the wall frame are then connected by a straight line, indicating the bottom side of a rafter. This creates a notch in the rafter called the "birds-mouth." The rafter is usually projected past the wall frame two feet, although it can be projected any distance. The rigid insulation, ledger, and the lookout are then added to the detail (Figure 9-2). The lookout and ledger are two-by-fours and should be located 1/2 inch below the bottom of the rafter tail. A 2 x 4 piece of deadwood and a 3/8-inch plywood soffit are added to the bottom of the lookout (Figure 9-3). The outside face of the deadwood should be placed 5 inches from the rigid insulation. The addition of the frieze, fascia, and shingle strip completes the construction of the cornice. To finish the detail, the interior wall finish is placed; insulation added to the exterior wall and attic; roof sheathing and shingles added; and the bricks are placed behind the frieze (Figure 9-4).

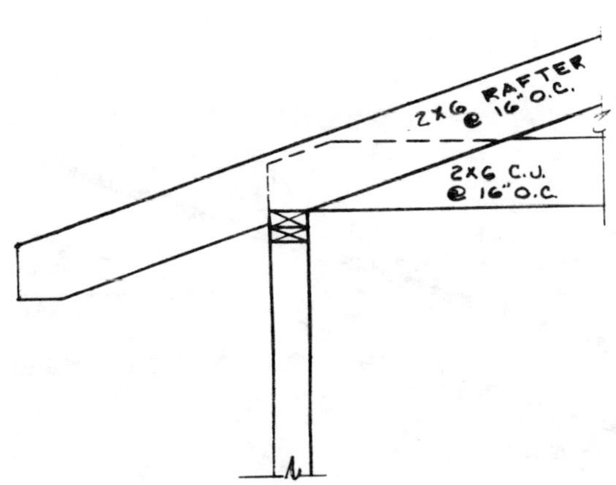

Figure 9-1
Cornice detail, step 1.

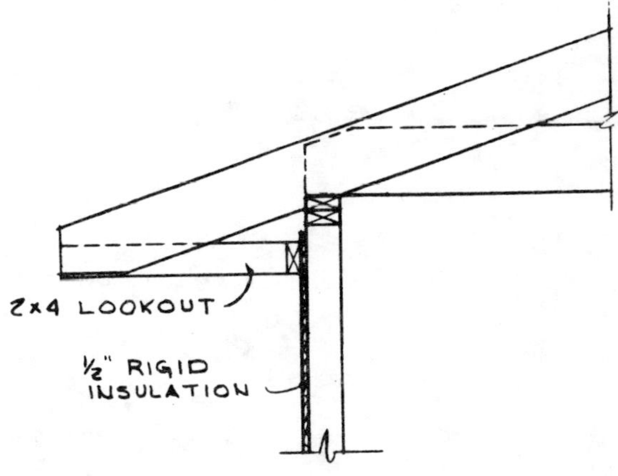

Figure 9-2
Cornice detail, step 2.

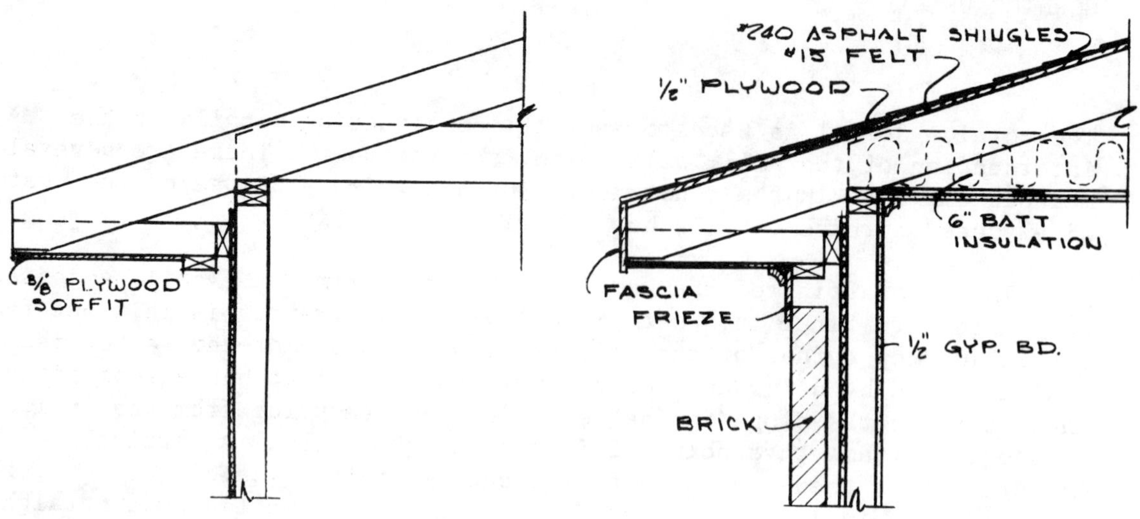

Figure 9-3
Cornice detail, step 3.

Figure 9-4
Cornice detail, step 4.

A cornice for a wood frame building with lap siding is built similar to brick veneer cornice, but the dead wood and frieze are omitted. To change the style of cornice, the soffit can be nailed directly to the bottom side of the rafter tails (Figure 9-5). This technique is quite simple and requires only a fascia, soffit, and a piece of trim to cover the joint at the intersection of the soffit and siding.

Note: To ventilate the attic, small vents are sometimes placed in the soffit.

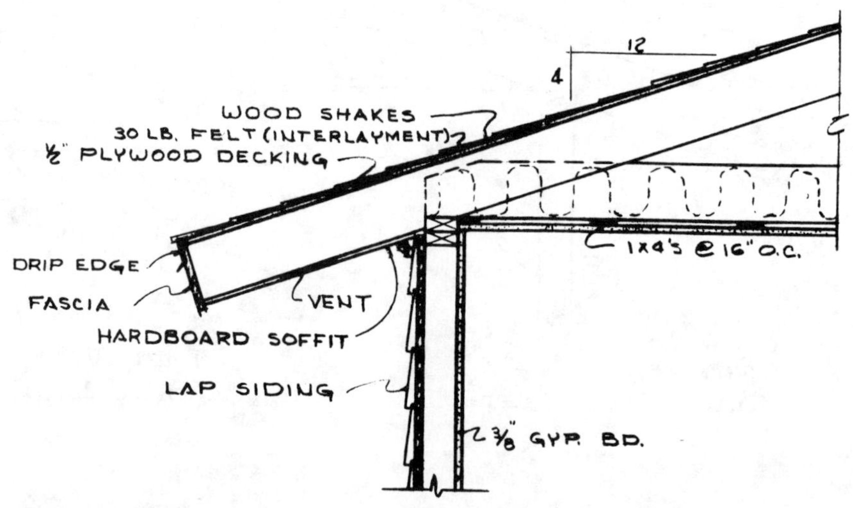

Figure 9-5
Cornice detail.

SILL DETAIL

The sill detail is usually included in the vertical wall section. It is used to show the construction details of the joist, sill plate, header, and wall frame.

The section is started by drawing the foundation wall, termite shield, and sill plate (Figure 9-6). The sill plate should be anchored to the foundation wall with anchor bolts spaced 8 feet on center. The joist and header are then drawn in, placing the header flush with the outside of the foundation wall (Figure 9-7). The subfloor is drawn next, and the exterior wall and finish floor are placed (Figure 9-8). To complete the detail, the sheathing and exterior siding are drawn in.

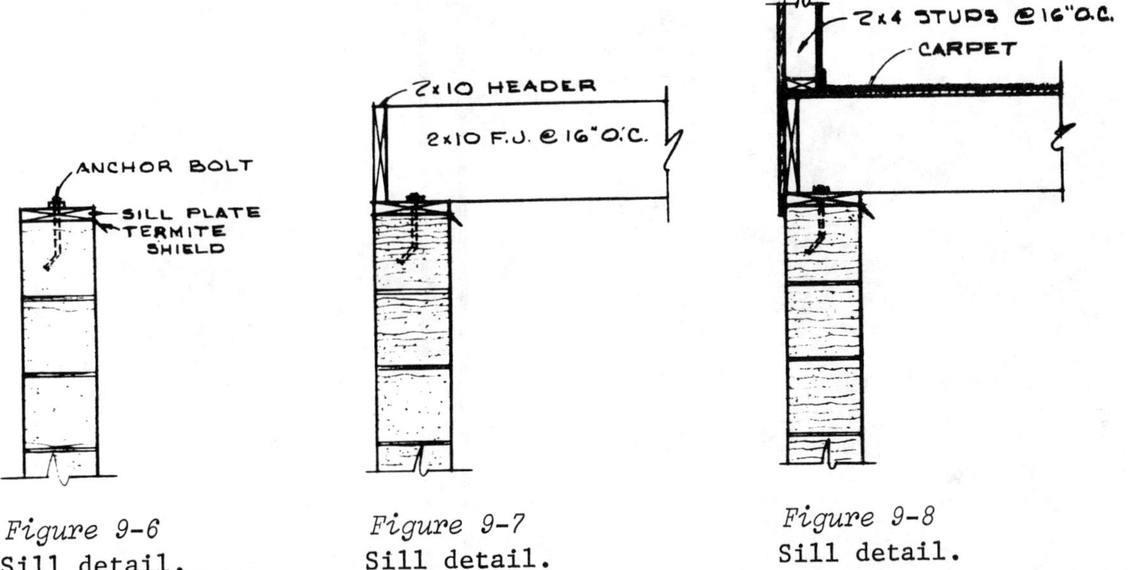

Figure 9-6
Sill detail.

Figure 9-7
Sill detail.

Figure 9-8
Sill detail.

TYPICAL WALL DETAIL

In most cases a vertical wall section is drawn. It includes the cornice detail, footing detail, sill detail, and in some cases a window detail is added (Figure 9-9). If all the exterior walls are the same, only one wall section is needed; if there are construction variations, there should be more than one wall section.

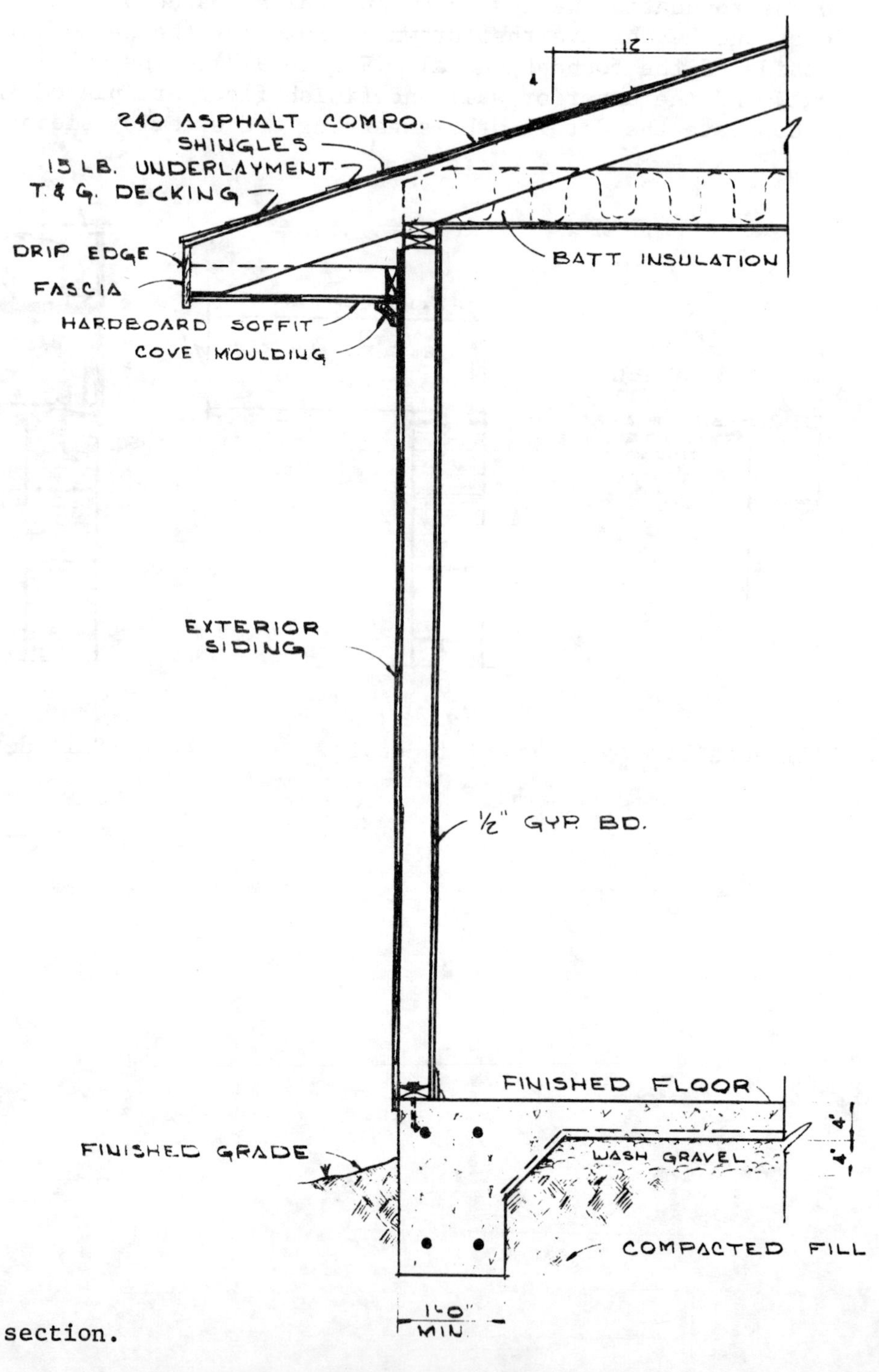

Figure 9-9
Typical wall section.

EXTERIOR DOOR DETAIL

Exterior door details are drawn in three parts: the head detail; the jamb detail; and the sill detail (Figure 9-10). The details should line up vertically, with the head drawn at the top, the sill at the bottom, and the jamb placed between the head and sill.

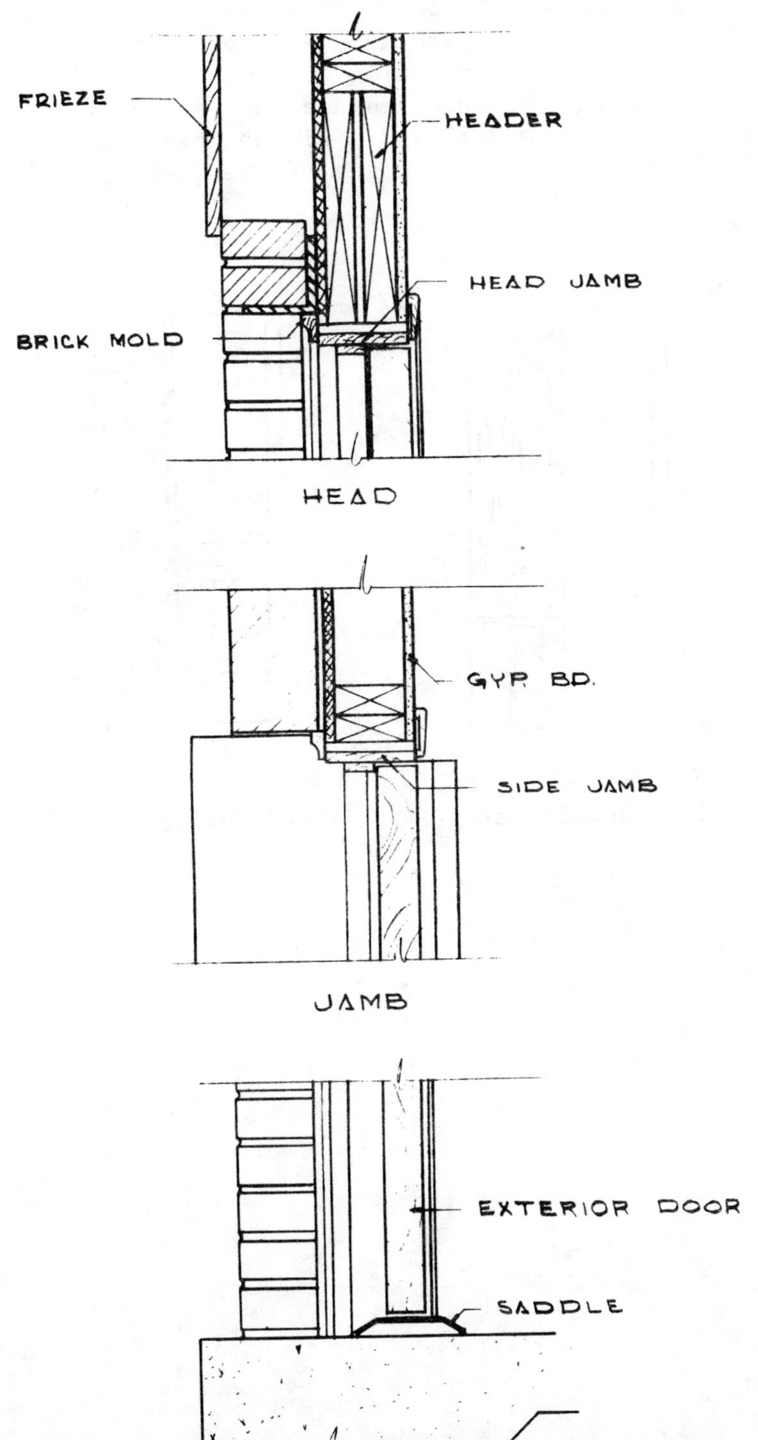

Figure 9-10
Exterior door detail.

EXTERIOR DOOR DETAIL (Head)

The head is a full section that shows the location of the header, head jamb, door stop, interior wall finish, exterior wall finish, moulding, and door. The construction of the head detail is centered around two 2-inch x 2-inch headers. Each header is 1-1/2 inches in width and has a 1/2-inch space between the two headers. A door jamb is slipped into the rough door opening; the width of the door jamb is equal to the rough opening plus the thickness of the rigid insulation and interior wall finish (Figure 9-11). The jambs are preassembled and have a 1-inch x 2-inch door stop nailed to them (Figure 9-12). To finish the detail, exterior and interior trim is placed over the edges of the jamb (Figure 9-13).

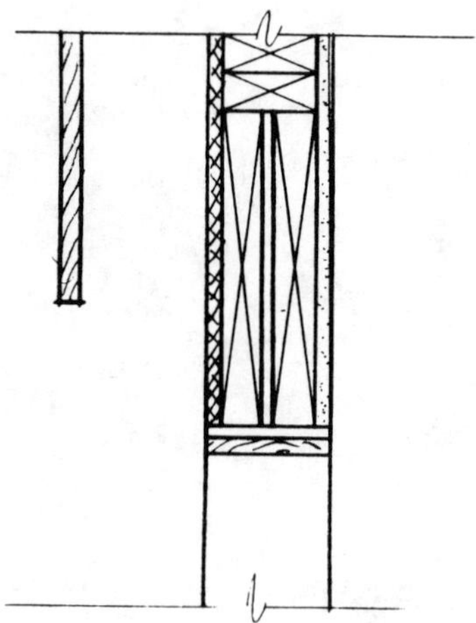

Figure 9-11
Head detail, step 1.

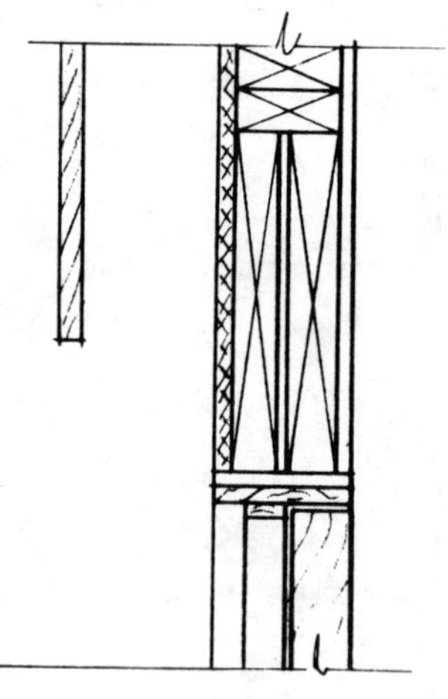

Figure 9-12
Head detail, step 2.

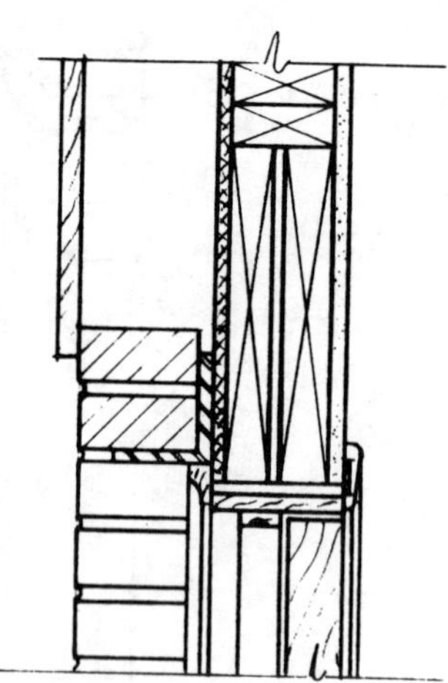

Figure 9-13
Head detail, step 3.

EXTERIOR DOOR DETAIL (Jamb)

A jamb detail is a revolved section in the door detail. It shows what the door section would look like if you were looking directly down on it. The jamb detail is drawn by first showing a stud, cripple, rigid insulation, and interior wall finish (Figure 9-14). The jamb, door stop, door, and trim are then added to the rough opening (Figure 9-15). To complete the detail a sill and threshold are added (Figure 9-16).

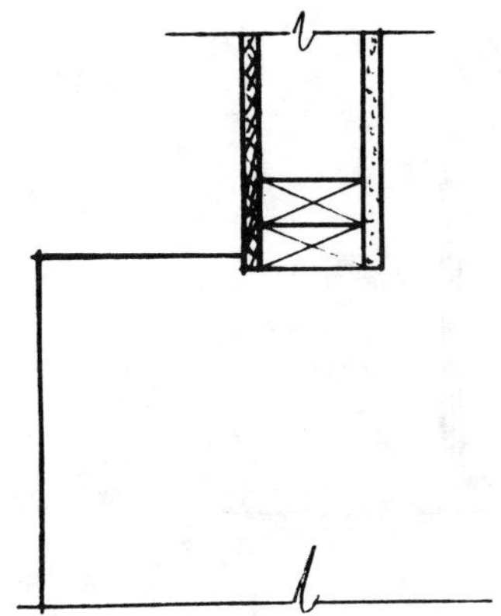

Figure 9-14
Jamb detail, step 1.

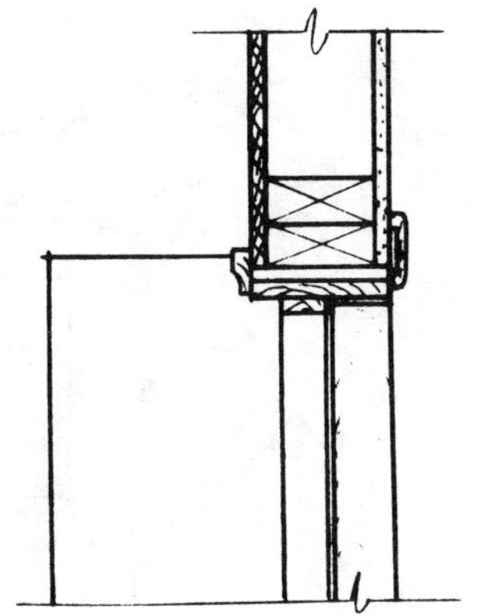

Figure 9-15
Jamb detail, step 2.

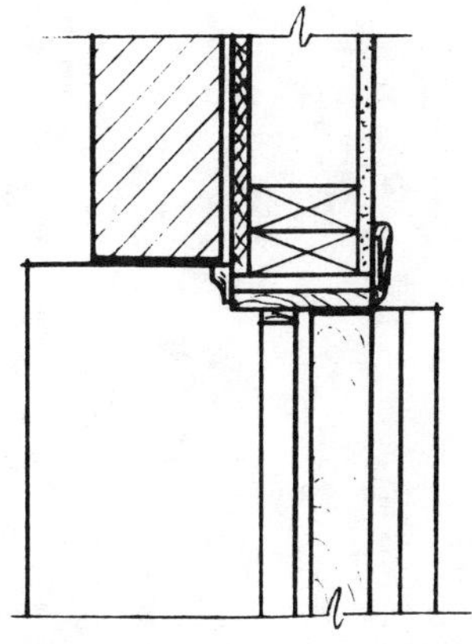

Figure 9-16
Jamb detail, step 3.

EXTERIOR DOOR DETAIL (Sill)

The sill detail is the lowest part of the door detail. It shows a section of the threshold and the bottom of the door. The threshold can be made of several materials, but an aluminum threshold is often used. The detail is started by drawing the floor frame, or the concrete slab. The section of the threshold and door is then drawn in (Figure 9-17). To complete the detail, vertical lines are added to indicate the placement of the jamb and trim.

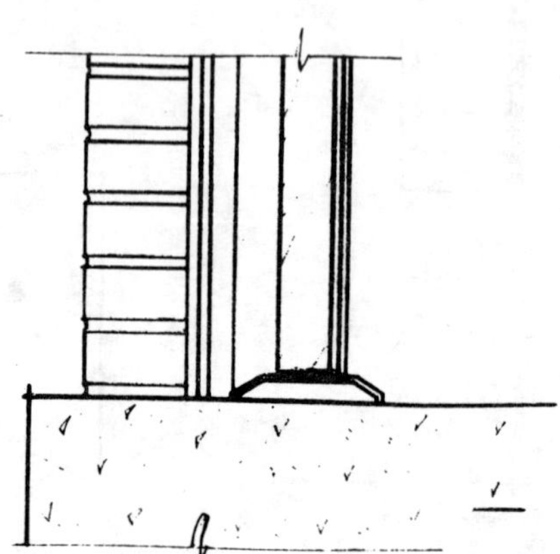

Figure 9-17
Sill detail.

WINDOW DETAILS

Window details are drawn in three parts: the head, jamb, and sill (Figure 9-18). The details should line up vertically, with the head drawn at the top, the sill at the bottom, and the jamb placed between the head and sill.

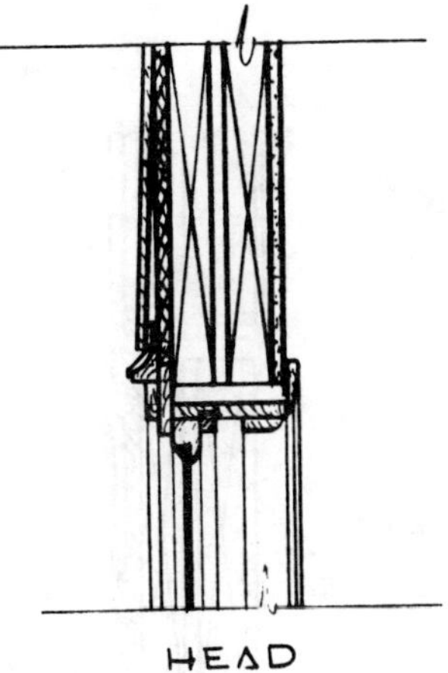

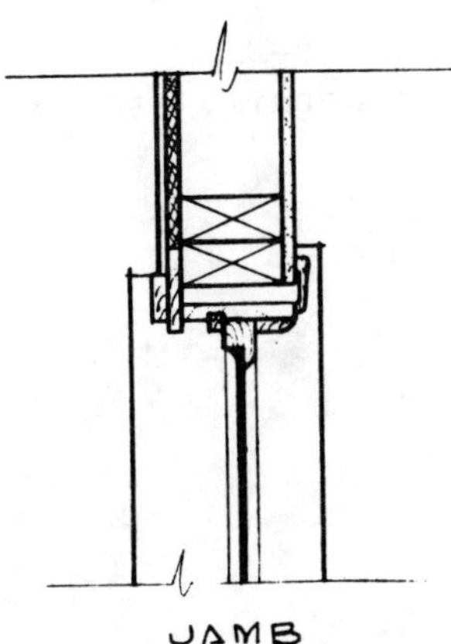

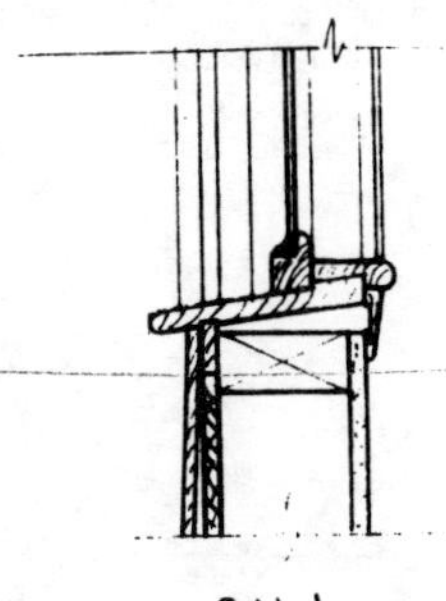

Figure 9-18
Window detail.

WINDOW DETAIL (Head)

The head is a section taken through the top of the window. It shows the location of the header, jamb, trim, stops, and sash. The detail is started by drawing the headers, rigid insulation, and the interior wall finish (Figure 9-19). The window jamb, casement, sill, and trim are then added to the detail (Figure 9-20). To complete the detail, the glass and sash are added (Figure 9-21).

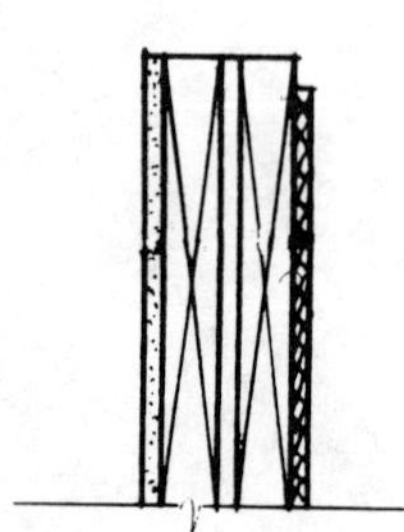

Figure 9-19
Head detail, step 1.

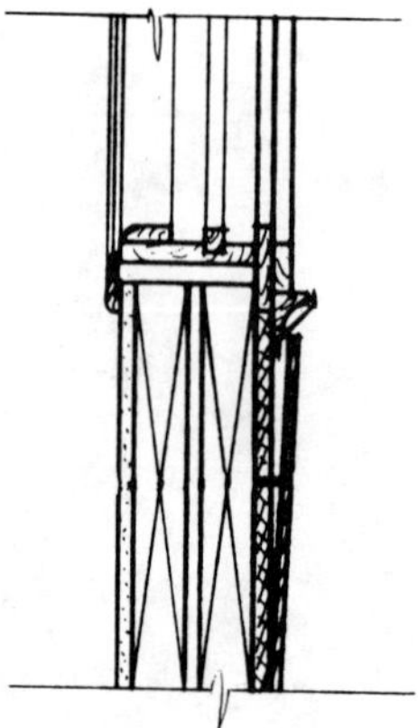

Figure 9-20
Head detail, step 2.

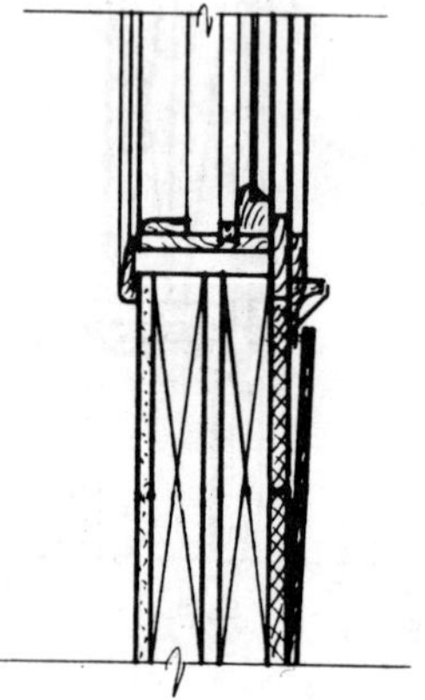

Figure 9-21
Head detail, step 3.

WINDOW DETAIL (Jamb)

A window jamb detail is used to show the top view of the window in section. The detail is drawn by first showing the rough opening, jamb, and trim. The top view of the sill and apron are then drawn in (Figure 9-22). To complete the detail, the window sash is added (Figure 9-23).

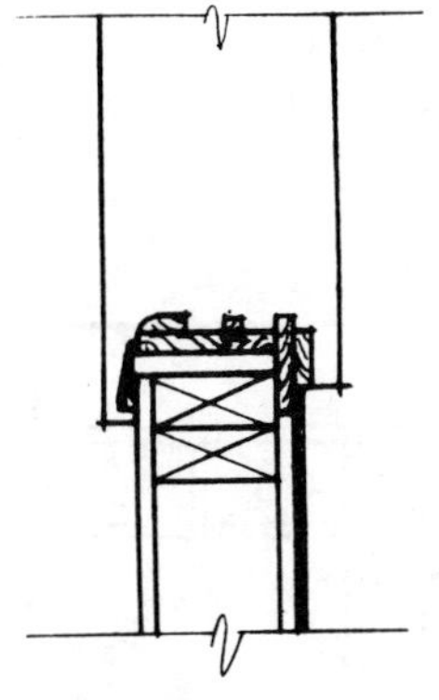

Figure 9-22
Jamb detail, step 1.

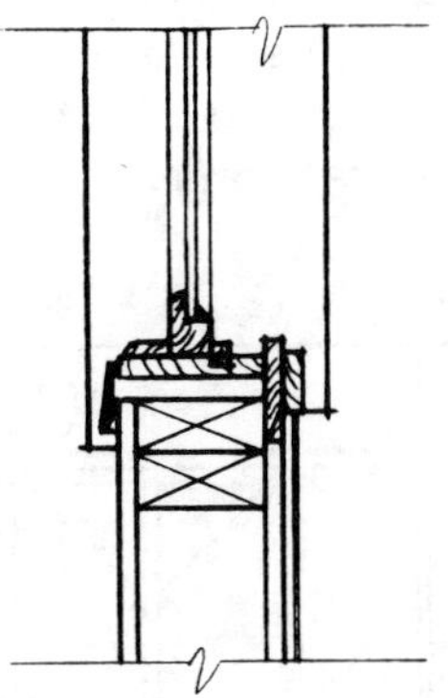

Figure 9-23
Jamb detail, step 2.

WINDOW DETAIL (Sill)

The sill detail is the lowest part of the window detail and is used to show the relationship of the sill, stool, sash, and apron. The detail is started by drawing the rough opening and the wall finish materials (Figure 9-24). The sill, stool, and apron are then drawn in the rough opening (Figure 9-25). The sash is added, and vertical lines representing trim and stops are drawn in to complete the detail (Figure 9-26).

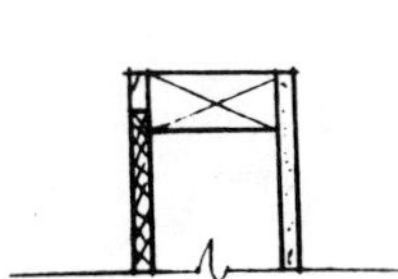

Figure 9-24
Sill detail, step 1.

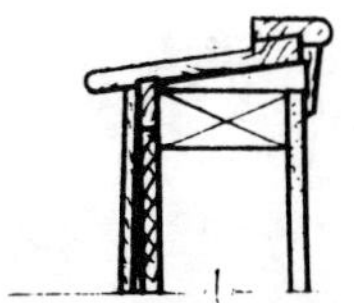

Figure 9-25
Sill detail, step 2.

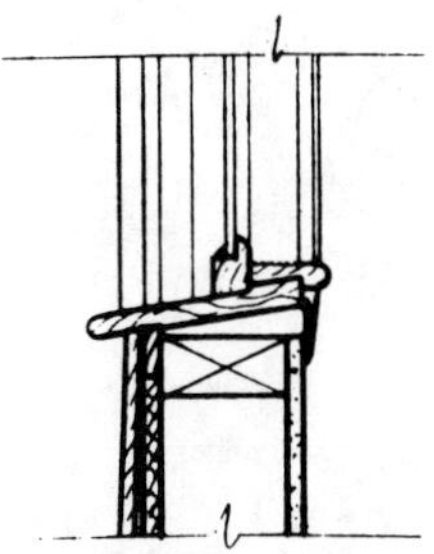

Figure 9-26
Sill detail, step 3.

KITCHEN CABINET DETAILS

The kitchen cabinet details usually include a section of the cabinets and an elevation of the cabinets (Figure 9-27). A section is drawn if there is a cabinet perpendicular to the cabinet that is in elevation. The section usually gives only the basic outline of the cabinet and the vertical dimenions. Some of the basic dimensions are: base cabinet width 2'-0"; wall-hung cabinet width 1' 0"; base cabinet height 3'-0"; wall-hung cabinet height 2' 6"; and furr down 12". The elevations are used to show location of appliances, direction of door swing, number and location of drawers and doors, and in some cases a manufacturer's number may be indicated on the elevations.

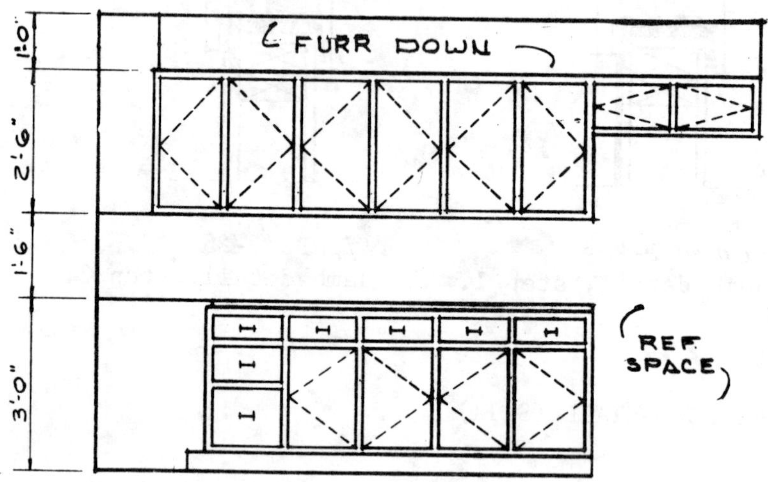

Figure 9-27
Kitchen cabinet detail.

STAIR DETAIL

The stair detail layout is started by drawing the joist and finish floor for the second story and the finish floor line for the first floor (Figure 9-28). The distance from finish floor to finish floor is the total rise. The riser and treads are then laid out using a grid system (Figure 9-29). The number of risers is found by dividing the total rise by seven.

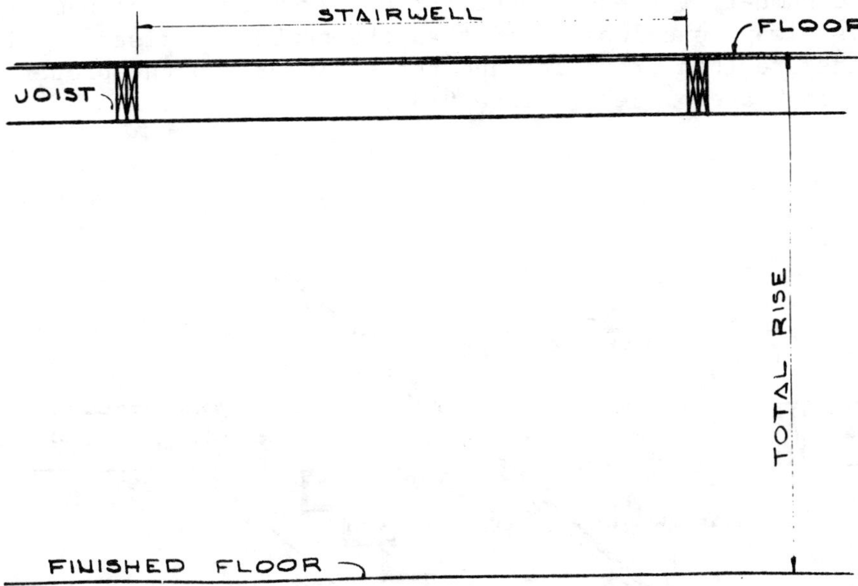

Figure 9-28
Stair detail, step 1.

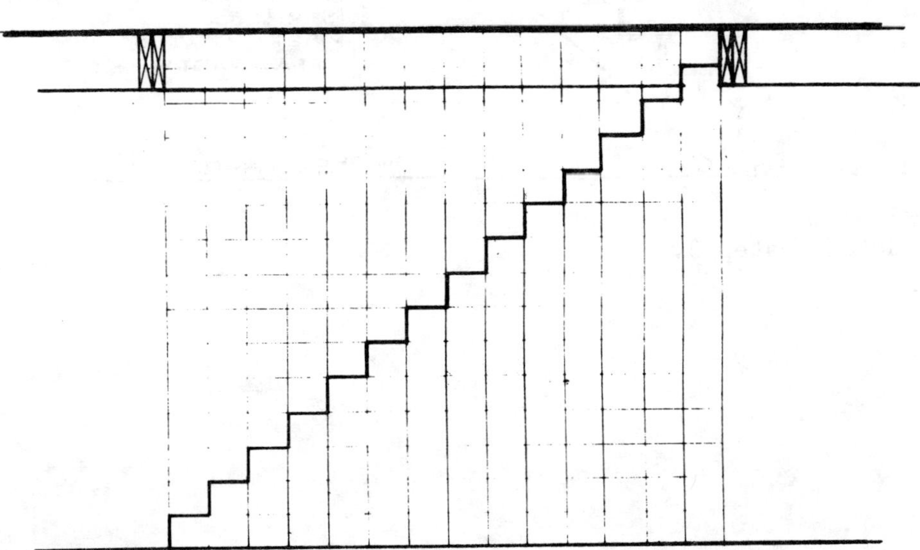

Figure 9-29
Stair detail, step 2.

EXAMPLE: Total Rise = 106 inches

$$\frac{106}{7} = 15.14$$

Total No. of risers = 15

To find the number of treads, subtract one from the total number of risers (there is always one less tread than the number of risers). The risers and treads are then drawn in, and the stringer and the proper notes and dimensions are placed (Figure 9-30).

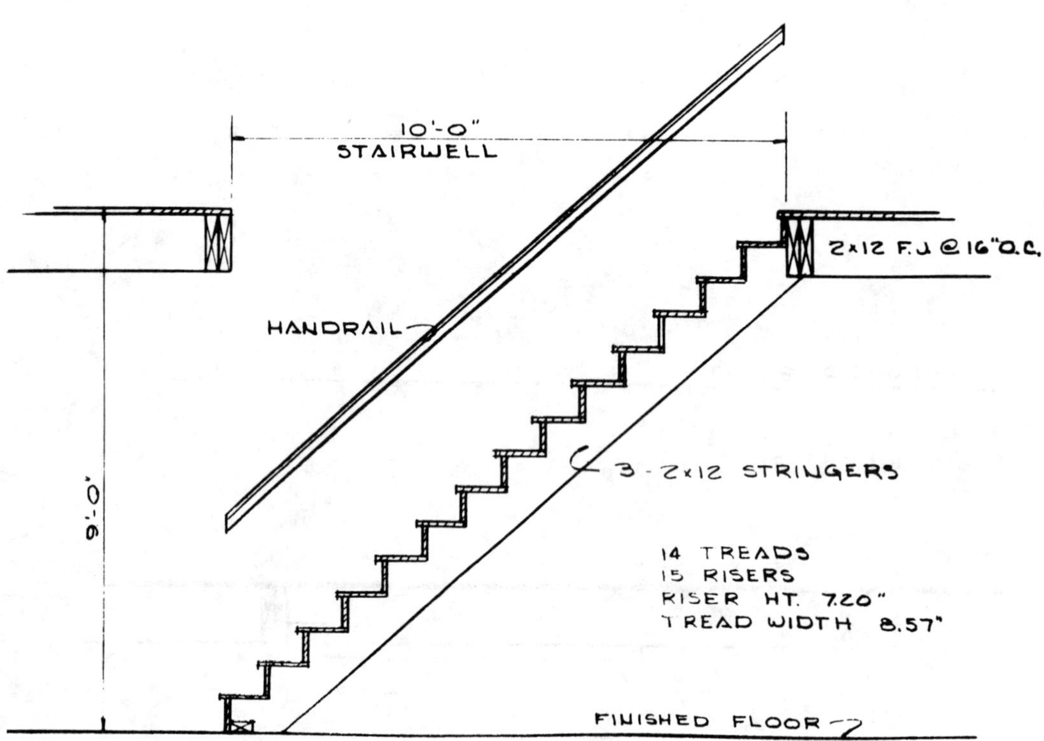

Figure 9-30
Stair detail, step 3.

Assignment: Draw a cornice detail for a brick veneer building that has a roof with a 1/8 pitch (3-12).

Assignment: Complete the cornice detail for a brick veneer building that has a roof with a ¼ pitch (6-12).

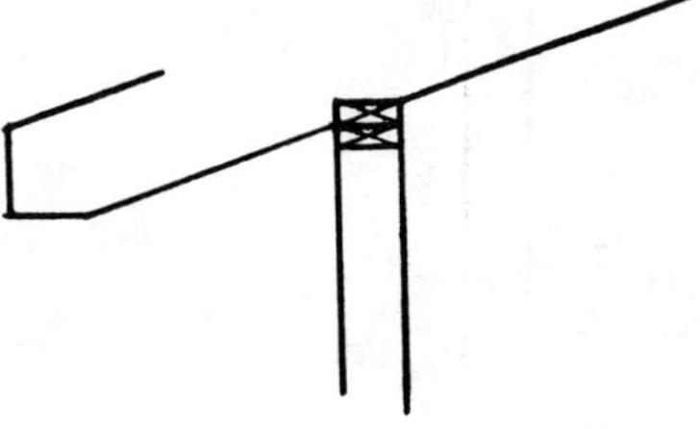

Assignment: Complete the cornice detail, using a sloping soffit.

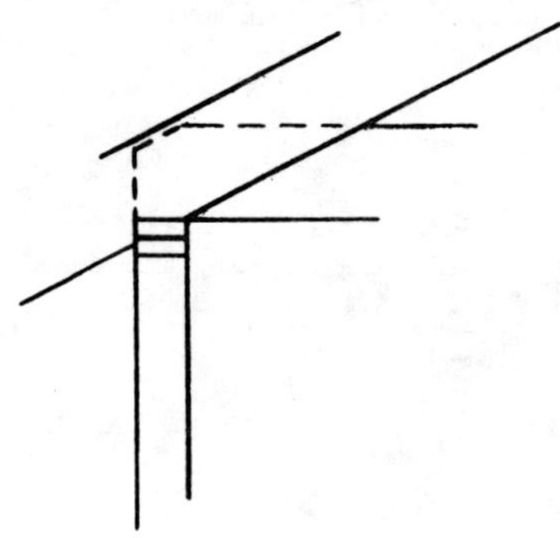

Assignment: Complete the cornice, using a horizontal soffit.

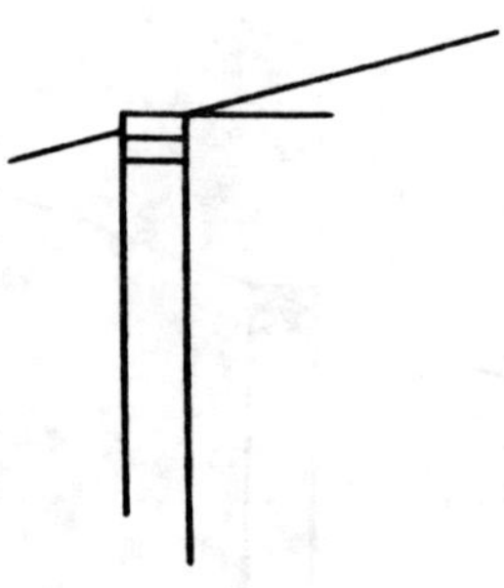

Assignment: Draw a sill detail for a house that has a crawl space.

Assignment: Draw a sill detail for a house that has a basement.

Assignment: Draw a typical wall section for a house that has: (1) a 1/8 roof pitch; (2) horizontal soffit; (3) a crawl space; and (4) is a brick veneer.

Assignment: Draw a head detail for an exterior door used in brick veneer construction.

Assignment: Draw a head detail for an exterior door used in frame construction.

Assignment: Draw a jamb detail for an exterior door used in brick veneer construction.

Assignment: Draw a jamb detail for an exterior door used in frame construction.

Assignment: Draw a sill detail for an exterior door used in brick veneer construction.

Assignment: Draw a sill detail for an exterior door used in frame construction.

Assignment: Draw an exterior door detail (head, jamb, sill).

Assignment: Draw a head detail for a double-hung window in a wood frame building.

Assignment: Draw a head detail for a double-hung window in a brick veneer building.

Assignment: Draw a jamb detail for a double-hung window in a brick veneer building.

Assignment: Draw a jamb detail for a double-hung window in a wood frame building.

Assignment: Draw a sill detail for a double-hung window in a brick veneer building.

Assignment: Draw a sill detail for a double-hung window in a wood frame building.

Assignment: Draw a window detail (head, jamb, sill).

Assignment: Draw the details for the kitchen cabinets.

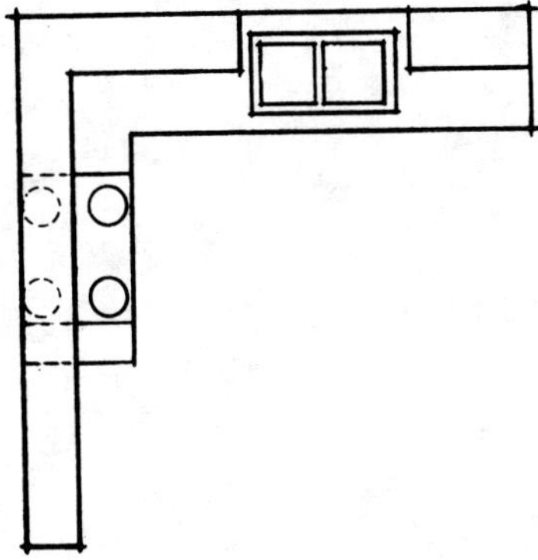

Assignment: **Complete the stair detail.**

FINISHED FLOOR

STAIR DETAIL

SCALE: ½" = 1'-0"

UNIT END TEST

Fill in the blanks:

1. The rafter is usually projected past the wall frame ____________ feet.
2. The lookout is nailed to the ____________.
3. Lookouts are usually spaced ____________ inches on center.
4. The sill plate is anchored to the foundation wall with ____________ spaced ____________ on center.
5. A typical wall detail includes the ____________, ____________, and ____________ detail.
6. Exterior door details are drawn in three parts: the ____________, ____________, and ____________.
7. A header is ____________ inches in width.
8. A jamb detail is a ____________ section.
9. The ____________ detail is the lowest part of the door detail.
10. There is always ____________ less tread than the total number of risers.

Unit End Assignment:

Draw the details for the developed floor plan from Chapter 7. Use a sheet of tracing paper 18 x 24 inches. Be sure to include a border line and a title block.

Chapter 10
ELEVATIONS

An elevation is a modified orthographic drawing that shows one side of an object. Most buildings require four elevations, one on each side. Interior elevations can be shown, but in most cases an interior elevation is considered as a detail.

All surface materials on the elevations are indicated by symbol or notes. Grade lines, floor and ceiling level, and some important dimensions should also be included.

Some of the most prominent features of an elevation are: windows, doors, roofs, and surface materials.

DOUBLE-HUNG WINDOWS

The location of windows can be projected from the floor plan, or they can be measured. The windows should be sufficiently detailed, and if hinged they should show the direction of swing.

The first step in the drawing of a window elevation is to draw the casings (Figure 10-1). The width of the casing may vary, but in most cases it is 1-1/2 inches wide. The height and width of the window depend on the size of the window. The rail and stile sashes are then drawn in very lightly (Figure 10-2). These sizes also vary depending on the manufacturer, but in most cases they are 1 to 1-1/2 inches in width. The upper sash check rail (Figure 10-3) and the muntins (Figure 10-4) are added to complete the elevation.

Note: 1. A brick or wooden sill may be added under the window, and a drip cap may be placed over the window.

2. The number of muntins depends on the size and type of window.

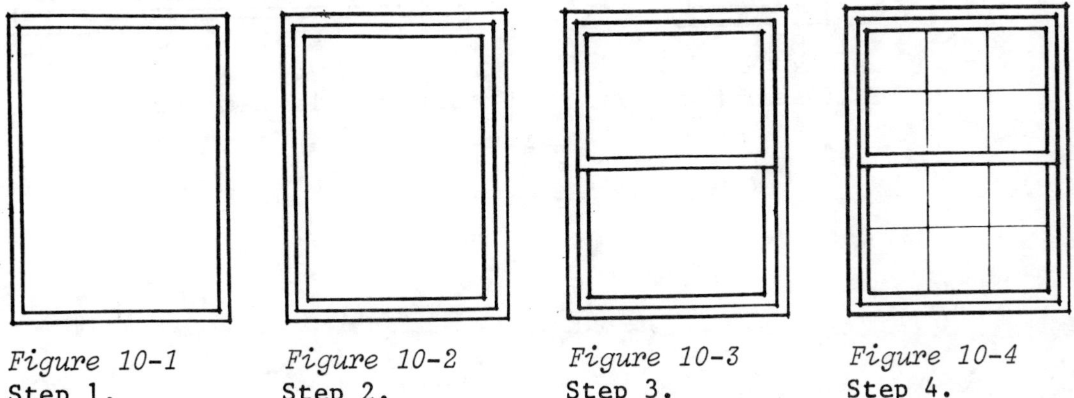

Figure 10-1 Step 1.

Figure 10-2 Step 2.

Figure 10-3 Step 3.

Figure 10-4 Step 4.

CASEMENT AND SLIDING WINDOWS

A casement window is drawn similar to a double-hung window. The exception is that the upper sash rail is omitted and a dashed line is added (Figure 10-5). The dashed line indicates the direction the window will open. The window is hinged on the side where the two dashed lines intersect.

Sliding windows are drawn in the same manner as a double-hung window, but they are placed horizontally rather than vertically (Figure 10-6). In most cases the muntins are omitted from sliding windows.

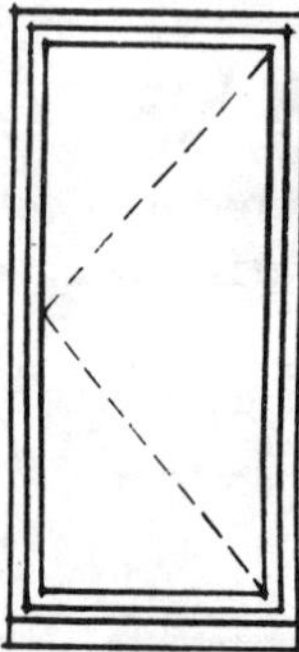

Figure 10-5
Casement window.

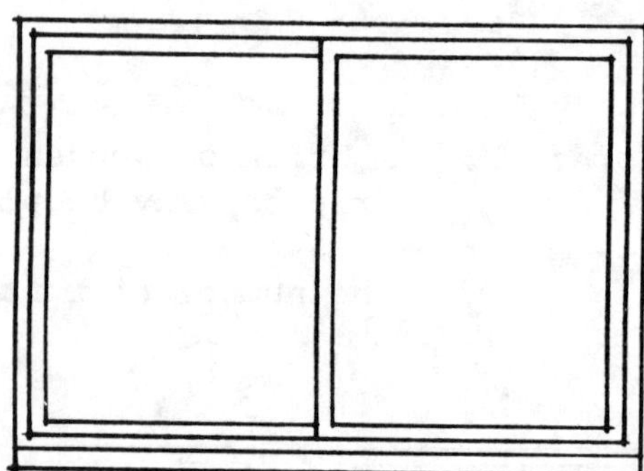

Figure 10-6
Sliding glass window.

DOORS

Doors in elevation are first drawn by drawing the general outline of the door (Figure 10-7). The width of most exterior doors is 2'-8" or 3'-0"; the height is almost always 6'-8". The door casings are then drawn around the door (Figure 10-8). The casings are usually one-by-fours. If the door is set in brick veneer, a 1 x 2 strip of brick molding should be placed over the casing. At the bottom of the door a threshold is added (Figure 10-9). If the door has panels or windows, these should also be added (Figure 10-10).

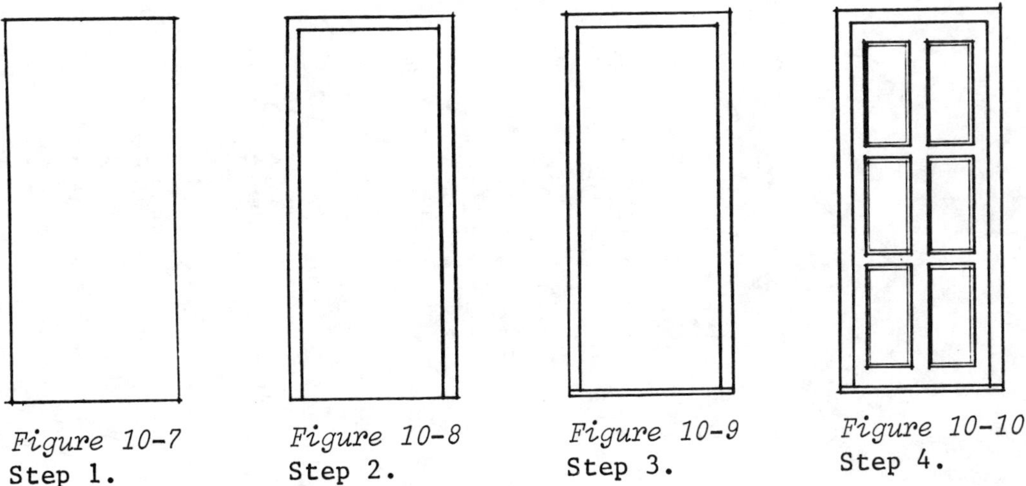

Figure 10-7 Step 1.

Figure 10-8 Step 2.

Figure 10-9 Step 3.

Figure 10-10 Step 4.

GABLE ROOFS

Once the general shape of the house is blocked in, the roof is added. If the gable end is drawn first, the height of the frame wall should first be located. From the top of the inside frame wall, the roof slope is drawn (Figure 10-11). The slope can be achieved by using an architectural template that has a roof pitch indicator, or the slope can be laid out with an architect's scale. Measuring perpendicular to the bottom side of the rafter, the top side of the rafter is located (Figure 10-12). The other side of the gable is drawn in, and the cornice is blocked in. The return of the rake cornice is usually blocked in to form a "bird-box" (Figure 10-13). Once the roof and cornice are complete, other features of the elevation are added (Figure 10-14).

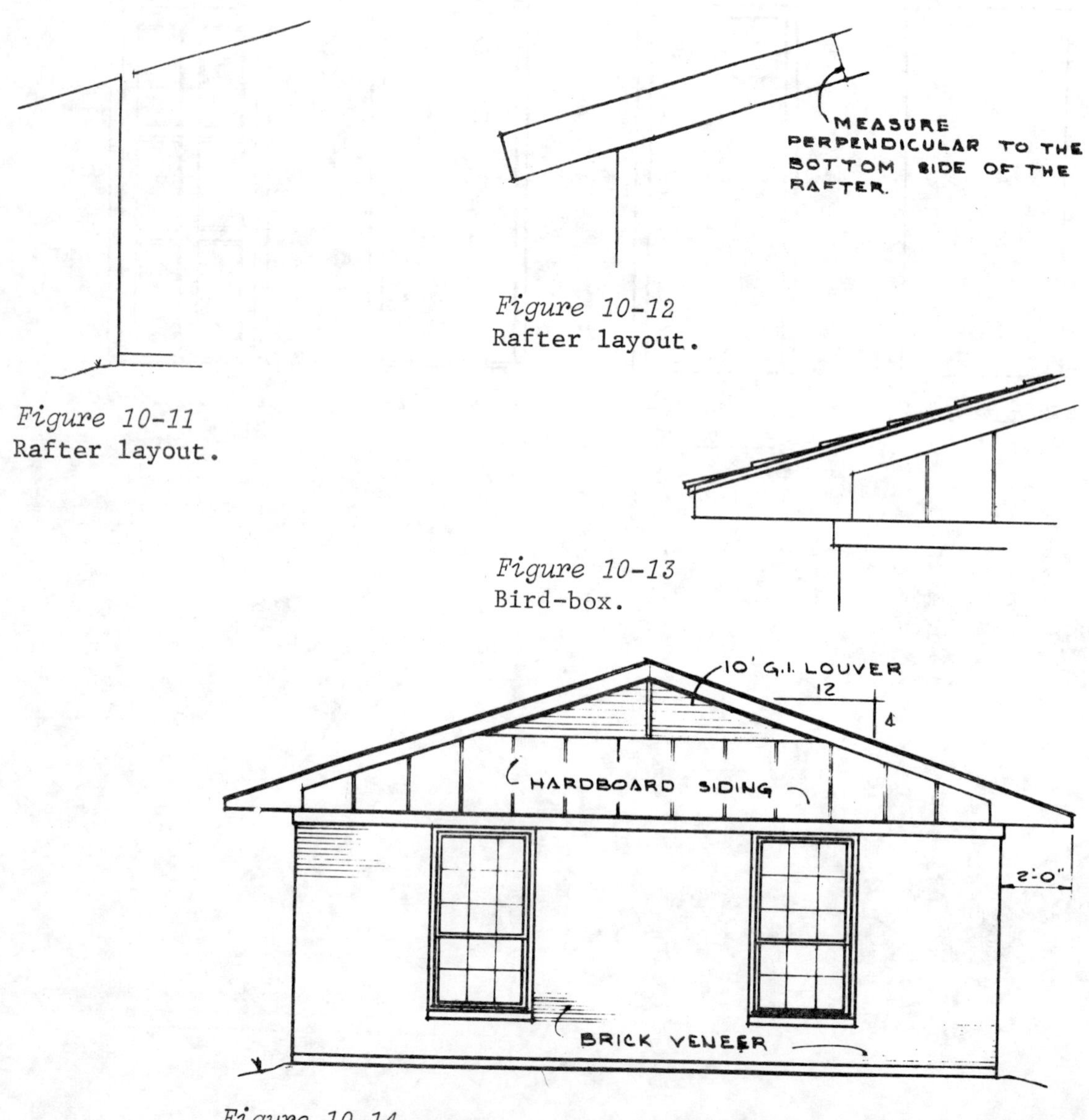

Figure 10-11
Rafter layout.

Figure 10-12
Rafter layout.

Figure 10-13
Bird-box.

Figure 10-14
Left side elevation.

HIP ROOFS

A hip roof can be drawn by blocking the building in and projecting the fascia past the building to the desired overhang (Figure 10-15). From the end of the fascia, the slope is laid out (Figure 10-16). Measuring from the end of fascia, the total span is marked. Using the same slope, a line is drawn from the end of the span until it intersects the other sloping line (Figure 10-17). The intersection of the two lines is the height of the ridge. The other end of the roof is drawn in, and the hip line and ridge line are darkened in (Figure 10-18).

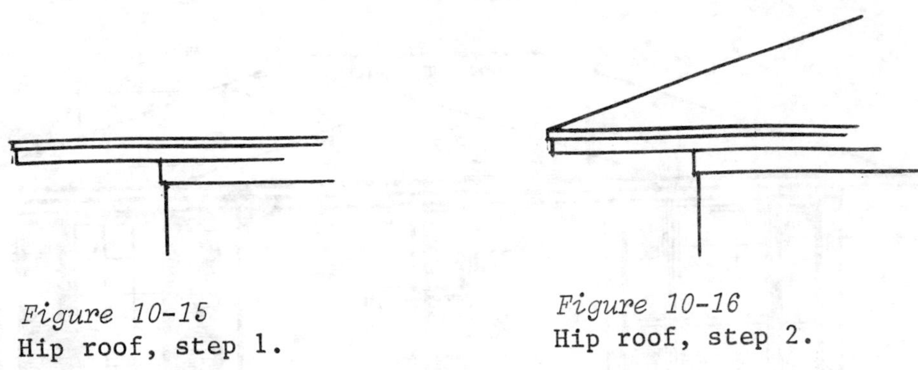

Figure 10-15
Hip roof, step 1.

Figure 10-16
Hip roof, step 2.

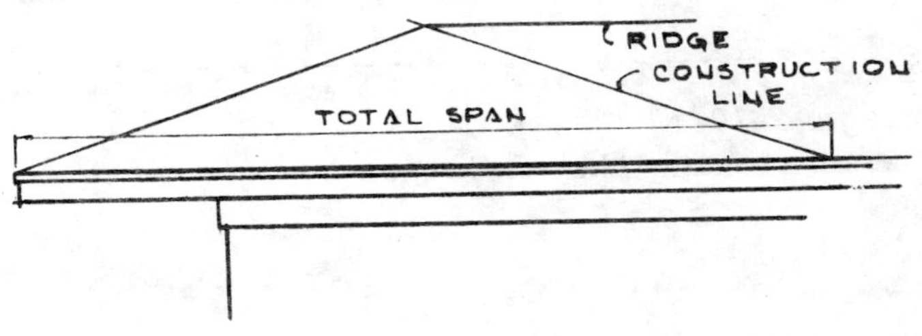

Figure 10-17
Hip roof, step 3.

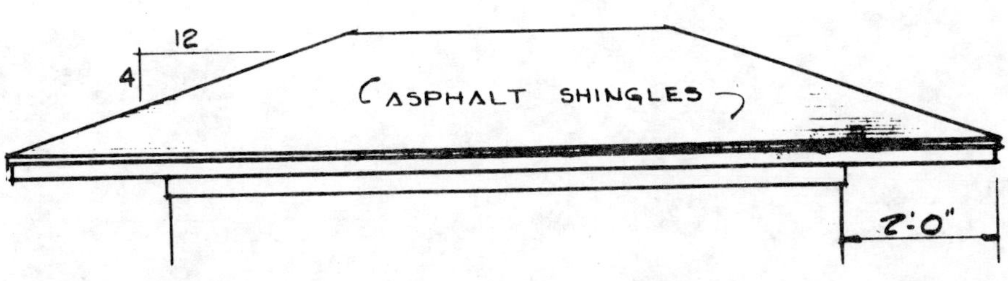

Figure 10-18
Hip roof, step 4.

NOTES AND DIMENSIONS

Once the details have been added to the elevations, notes and dimensions are added (Figure 10-19). In most cases, the dimensions are vertical, showing the distance from finished floor to finished ceiling, the thickness of the footing, and the distance of the footing to grade line. The only horizontal dimension that is usually given is the roof overhang.

Notes include: the type of roof covering; the material used as exterior siding; location of flashing; and any other special feature that needs notation.

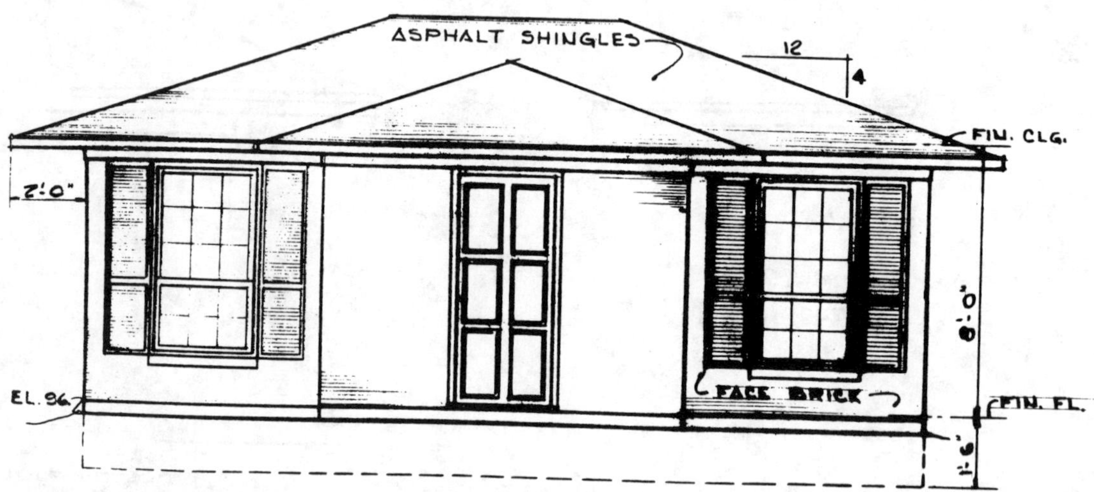

Figure 10-19
Dimensioning the elevation.

Assignment: Draw an elevation of a 3'-0" x 6'-0" double-hung window.

Assignment: Draw an elevation of a 3'-0" x 3'-0" double-hung window.

Assignment: Draw a 2'-0" x 3'-0" casement window.

Assignment: Draw a 5'-0" x 3'-0" sliding glass window.

Assignment: Draw an elevation of an exterior door.

Assignment: Draw an elevation of a sliding door.

Assignment: Complete the elevation.

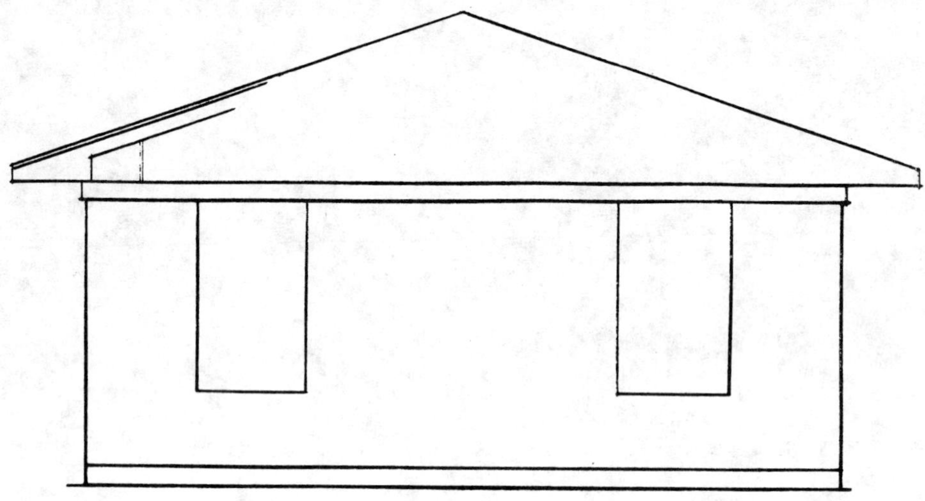

Assignment: Complete the elevation.

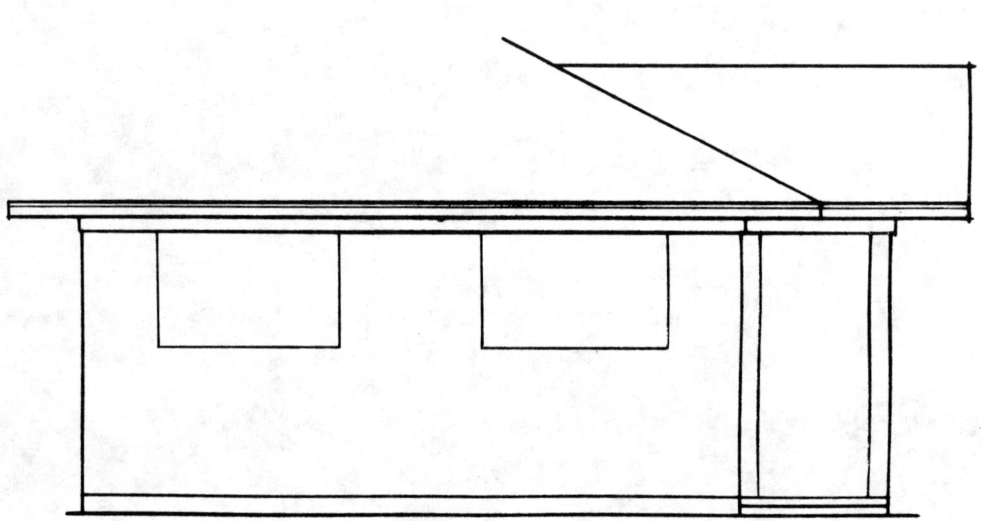

Assignment: Complete the hip roof (total span: 32 feet).

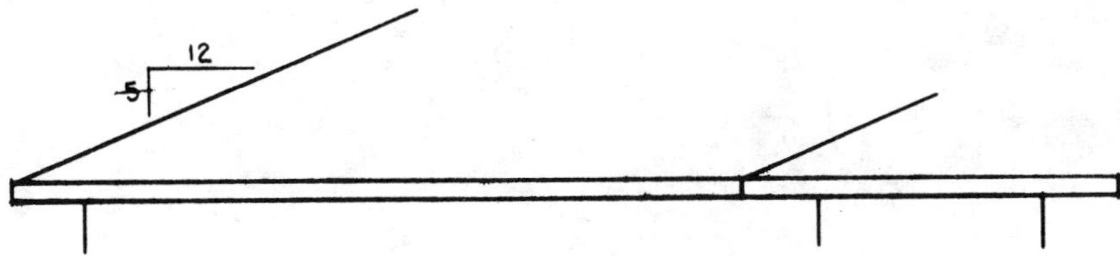

Assignment: Add the necessary notes and dimensions to the elevation.

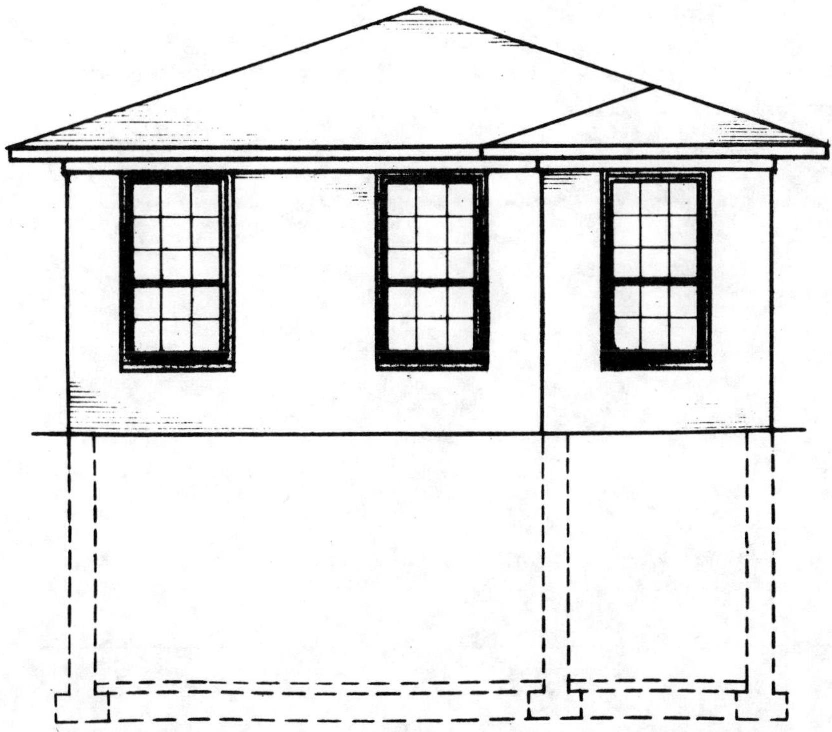

UNIT END TEST

1. The width of most exterior doors is ____________ or ____________.

2. Door casings are usually __________ inches in width.

3. A 12-foot ____________ is sometimes placed in the gable end and is used for ventilation.

4. The slope of a roof can be determined by using a ____________ or ____________.

5. Most of the dimensions on elevations are ____________.

6. Some of the notes on elevations include ____________, ____________, and ____________.

7. The height of most exterior doors is ____________.

8. The purpose of an elevation is to ____________.

9. Some of the most prominent features of an elevation are ____________, ____________, ____________, and ____________.

10. Rail and stile sashes are usually ____________ inches in width.

Unit End Assignment:

Draw the elevations for the developed floor plan from Chapter 7. Use an 18 x 24 inch sheet of tracing paper. Be sure to include a border and a title block.

Chapter 11
FRAMING PLANS

A framing plan is used to describe the shape of the building, show the location of the individual framing members, and indicate how the members are joined.

There are several types of framing plans, but the two most common are the roof framing plan and the floor framing plan. Although these plans are not always included in a set of plans, they should be. If there is any question pertaining to how the roof or floor is framed, the framing plans can be used as a reference.

THE ROOF FRAMING PLAN

The roof framing plan is used to describe the roof. There are many different types of roofs, but the two most common types are the hip and gable. The gable roof is sloped on two sides and is an economical roof (Figure 11-1). The hip roof is sloped on four sides and is more expensive to construct than the gable (Figure 11-2).

Some of the framing members of the roof are: the ridge, common rafters, hip rafters, valley rafters, hip jack rafters, valley jack rafters, and cripple jack rafters (Figure 11-3).

Note: 1. The hip and valley rafters are drawn at a 45-degree angle.

2. The structural members are usually not identified on the framing plan.

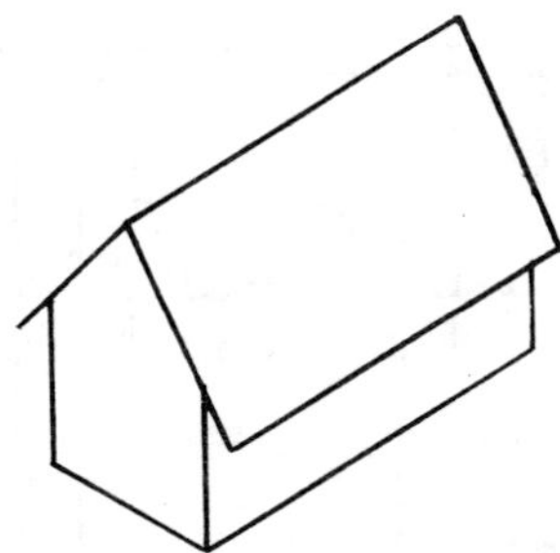

Figure 11-1
Gable roof.

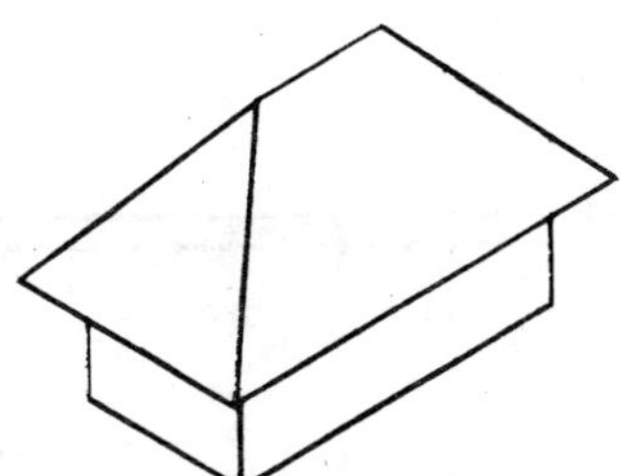

Figure 11-2
Hip roof.

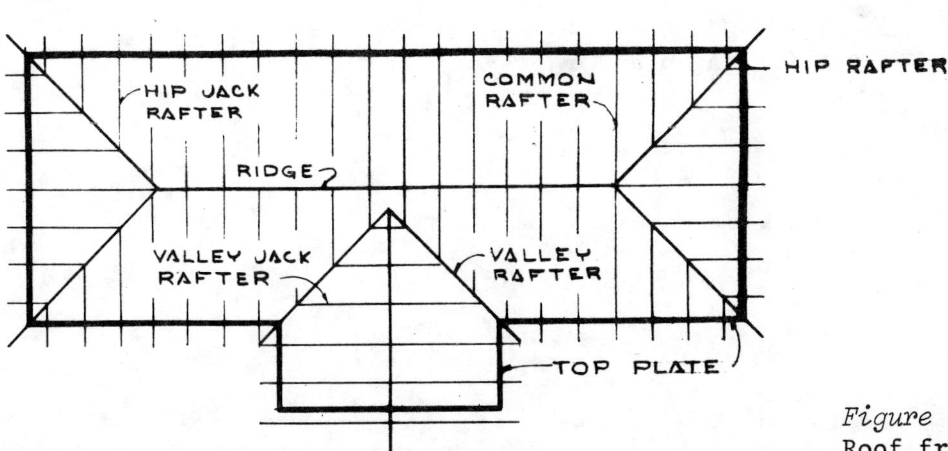

Figure 11-3
Roof framing plan.

THE FLOOR FRAMING PLAN

The floor framing plan is very similar to the roof framing plan, in that it shows the top view of the floor frame (Figure 11-4). In some cases the foundation plan and the first floor plan are one and the same, but usually the floor framing plan is a separate plan.

The floor framing plan indicates the direction and size of the joist, location and size of beams, and the location of columns or piers.

Note:

1. Double joists should be placed under all load-bearing partitions.
2. Joists are indicated by a center line.
3. Headers and trimmers are indicated by a solid line.

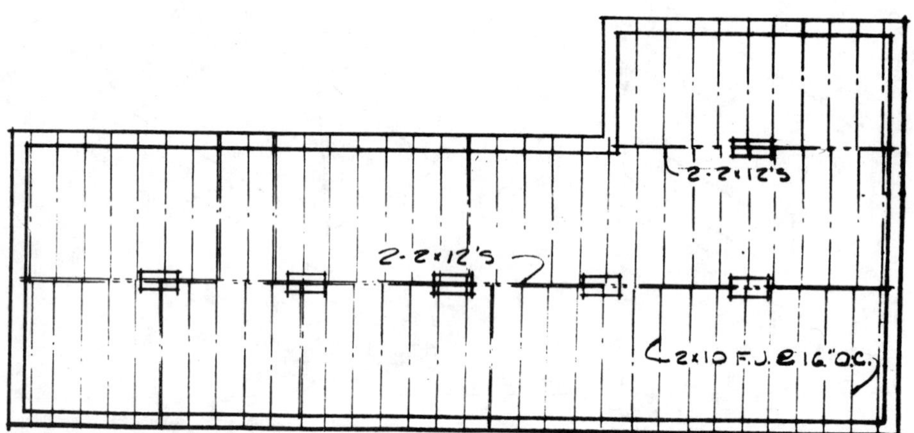

Figure 11-4
Floor framing plan.

Assignment: Complete the roof framing plan.

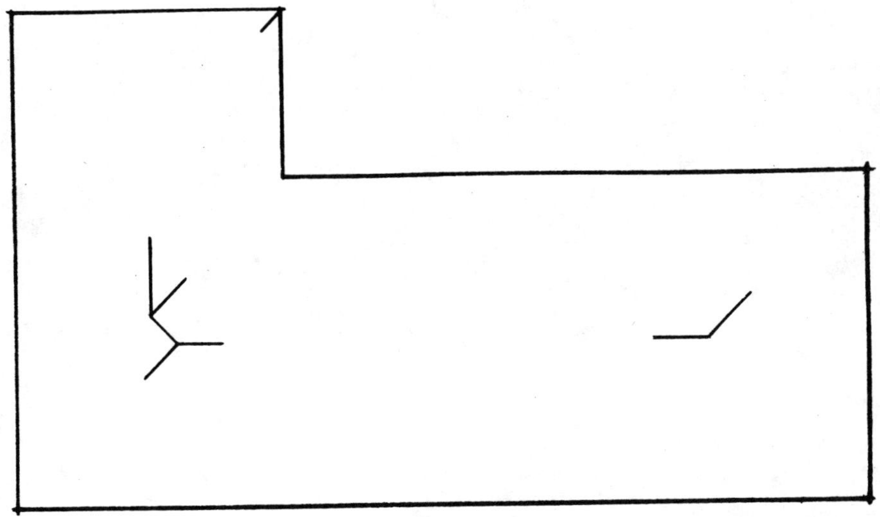

Assignment: Complete the floor framing plan.

UNIT END TEST

1. The two most common framing plans are the ___________ and ___________.

2. The hip rafter is drawn at an angle of ___________.

3. The ___________ rafter spans from the ridge to the wall frame.

4. The two most common types of roofs are the ___________ and ___________.

5. The ___________ is the uppermost structural member of the roof.

6. Double joists should be placed under ___________.

7. Headers are indicated by a ___________ line.

8. Joists are indicated by a ___________.

9. The hip roof is sloped on ___________ sides.

10. A ___________ rafter spans from the ridge to the valley.

Unit End Assignment:

Draw a roof framing plan, using the developed floor plan from Chapter 7. Use an 18 x 24 inch sheet of tracing paper. Be sure to include a border line and a title block.

Chapter 12
THE PLOT PLAN

A plot plan is a top view of the lot and building. It should: locate the building on the lot; show any natural features that exist; indicate the lot size and shape; show necessary elevations and contours; show roads and setbacks; include dimensions of front, rear, and side yards; show the location of walks, driveways, steps, patios, and porches; indicate the elevation of the first floor and the finish-grade at each primary corner; show any trees that need to be removed; and show the location and identification of utility service lines.

CONTOUR LINES

The plot plan is drawn to scale using the civil engineer's scale and is usually drawn to a scale of 1" = 20'. The first step in the drawing of the plot plan is to draw the lot and the contour lines (Figure 12-1). A contour line is an imaginary line that represents a particular elevation, which is used to indicate the amount of slope in a certain area. Contour lines are dimensioned by giving their elevation above sea level or a referance datum plan.

Note: 1. Contour lines that are close together indicate there is a steep rise in elevation; if they are far apart, the land is relatively flat.

2. Contour lines are usually spaced on intervals of 2, 4, or 6 feet, but other intervals can be used.

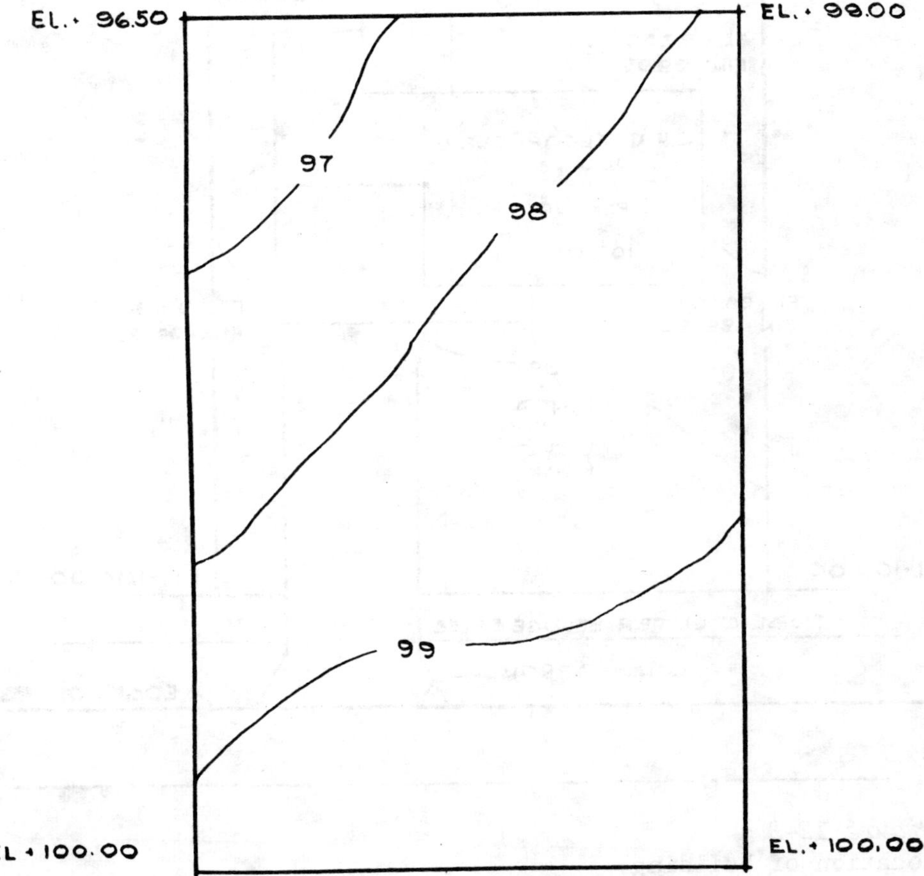

Figure 12-1
Contour lines.

LOCATION OF BUILDING

Once the lot and contour lines are drawn, the building should be located on the lot (Figure 12-2). Any walks, driveways, steps, patios, and porches should also be included. The elevation of the first floor and the finish-grade at each primary corner is also given.

The center line of the street is located, and the utility service lines are added. If there are any trees that need to be removed, they should be located.

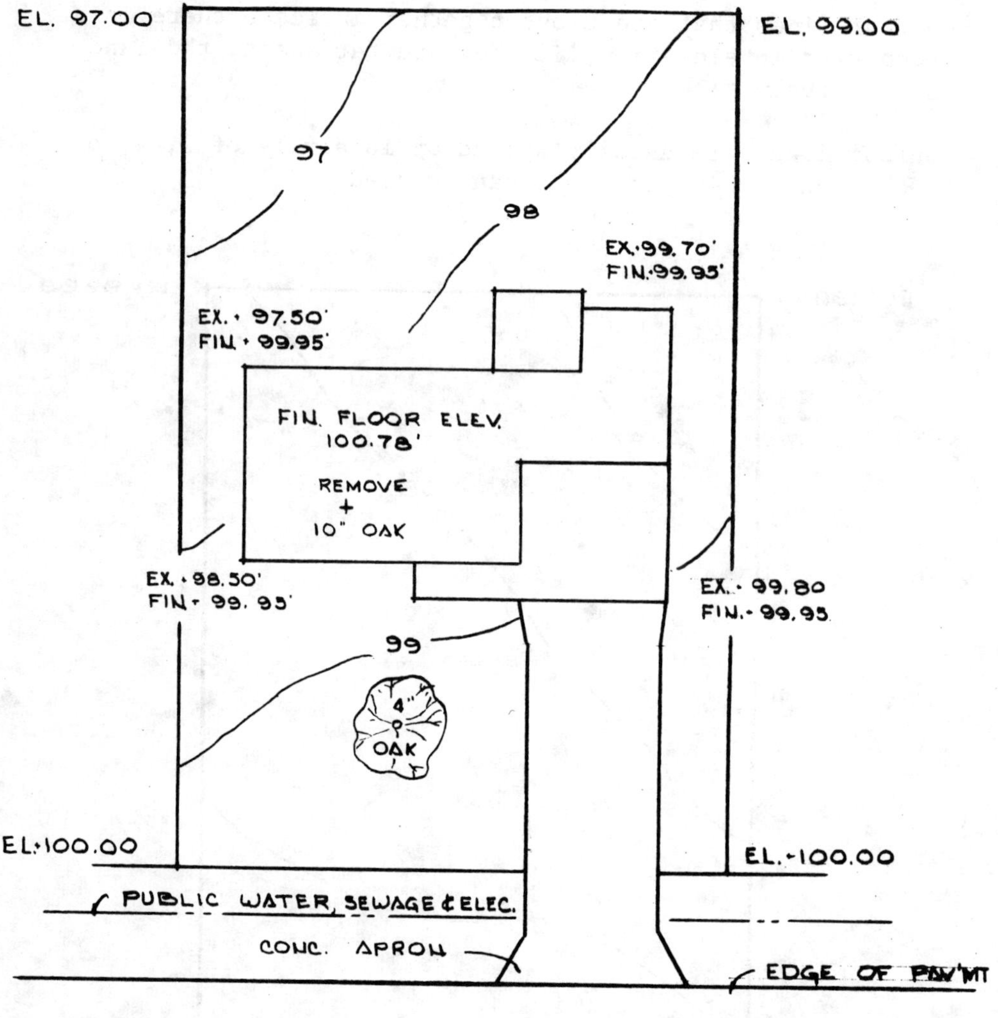

Figure 12-2
Location of building.

DIMENSIONING THE PLOT PLAN

To complete the plot plan, necessary notes and dimensions are added (Figure 12-3). The sides of the property and the setbacks should be dimensioned. Notes include such items as: lot number, subdivision, city, location of trees, location of utilities, name of any streets or roads, and the title and scale.

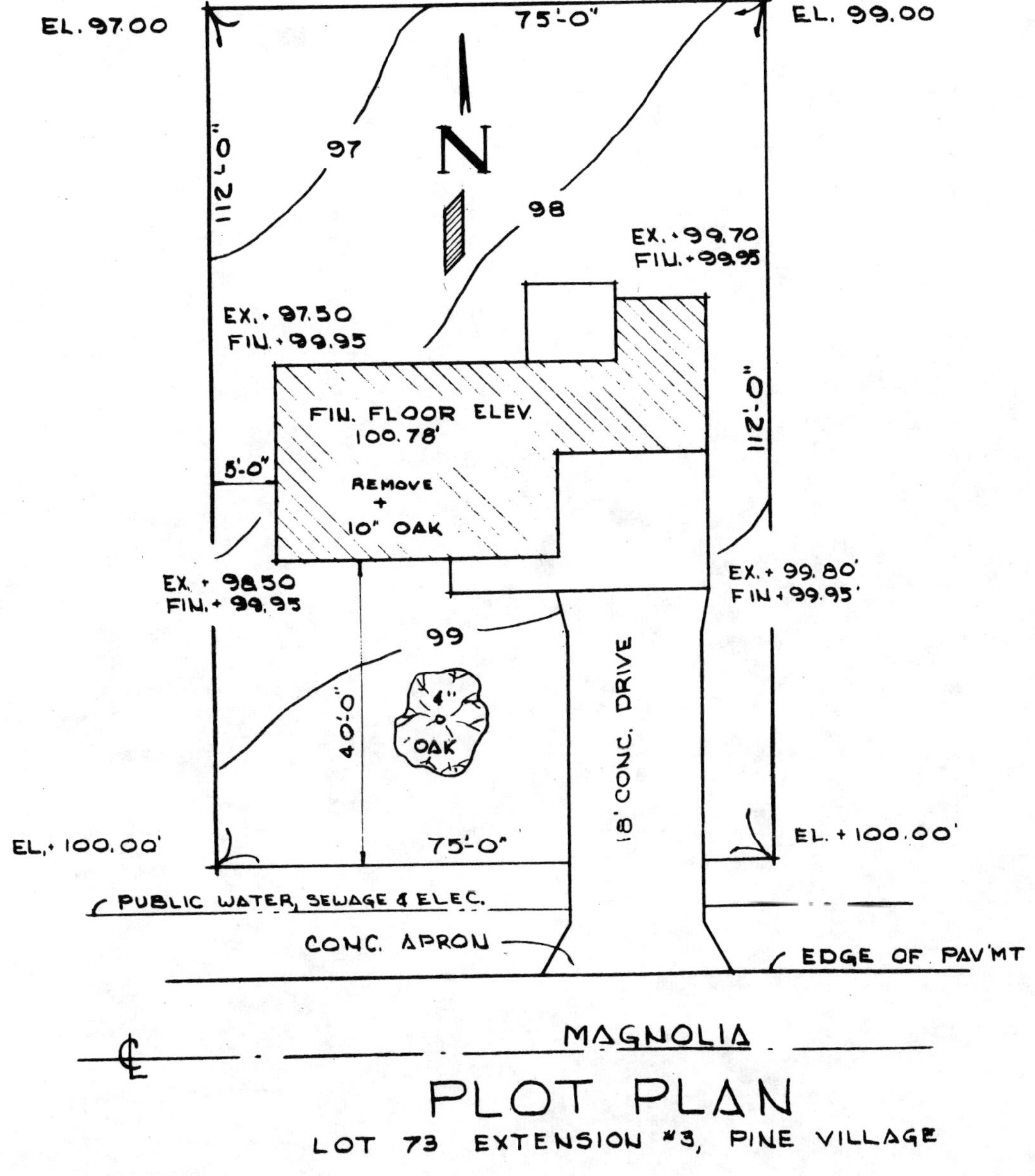

Figure 12-3
Dimensioning.

Assignment: Complete the addition of the contour lines.

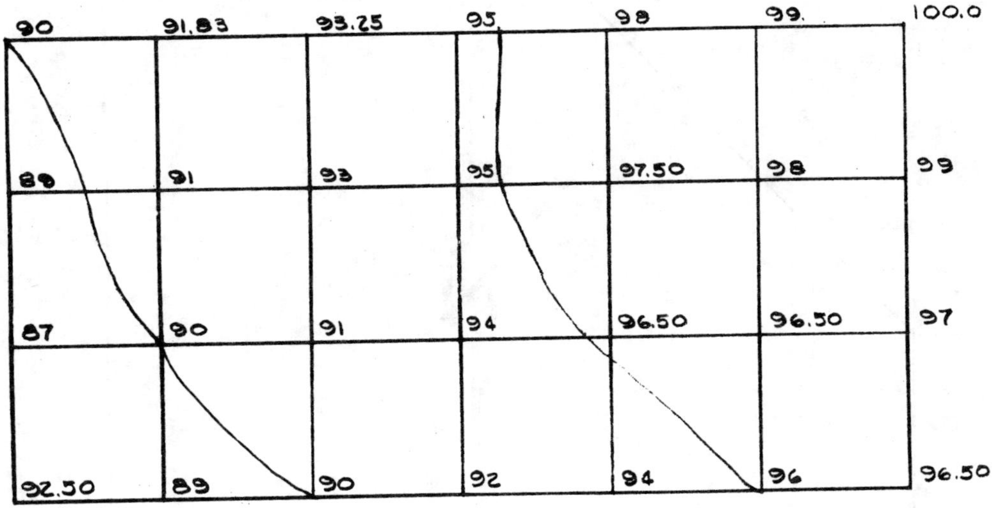

Assignment: Placed the developed floor plan from Chapter 7 on the lot. Place the necessary elevations and contour lines.

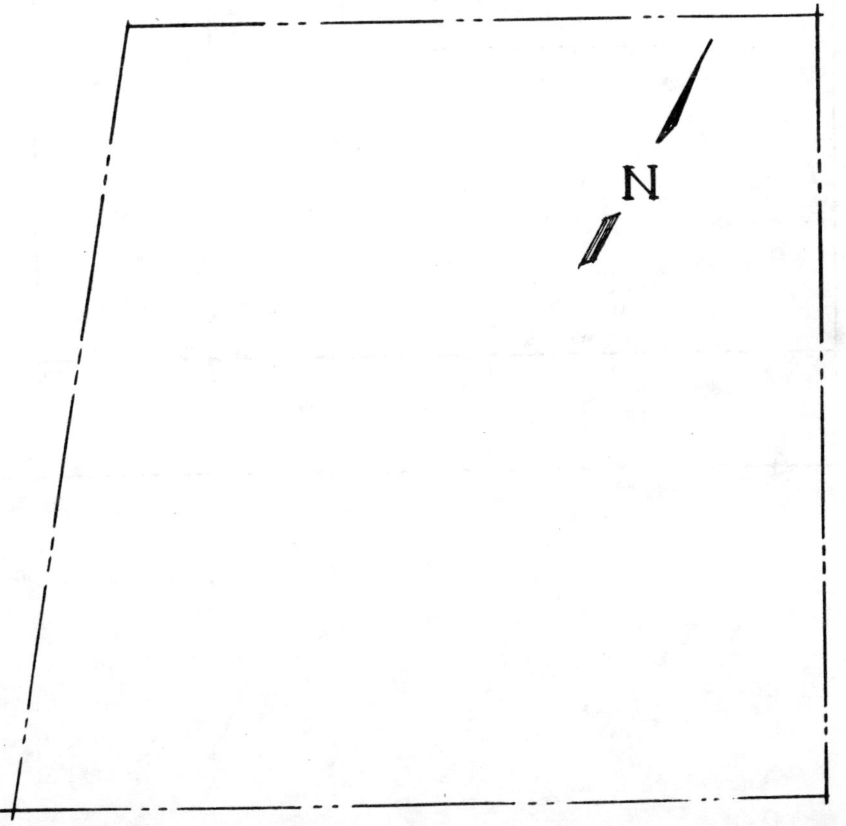

Assignment: Complete the plot plan.

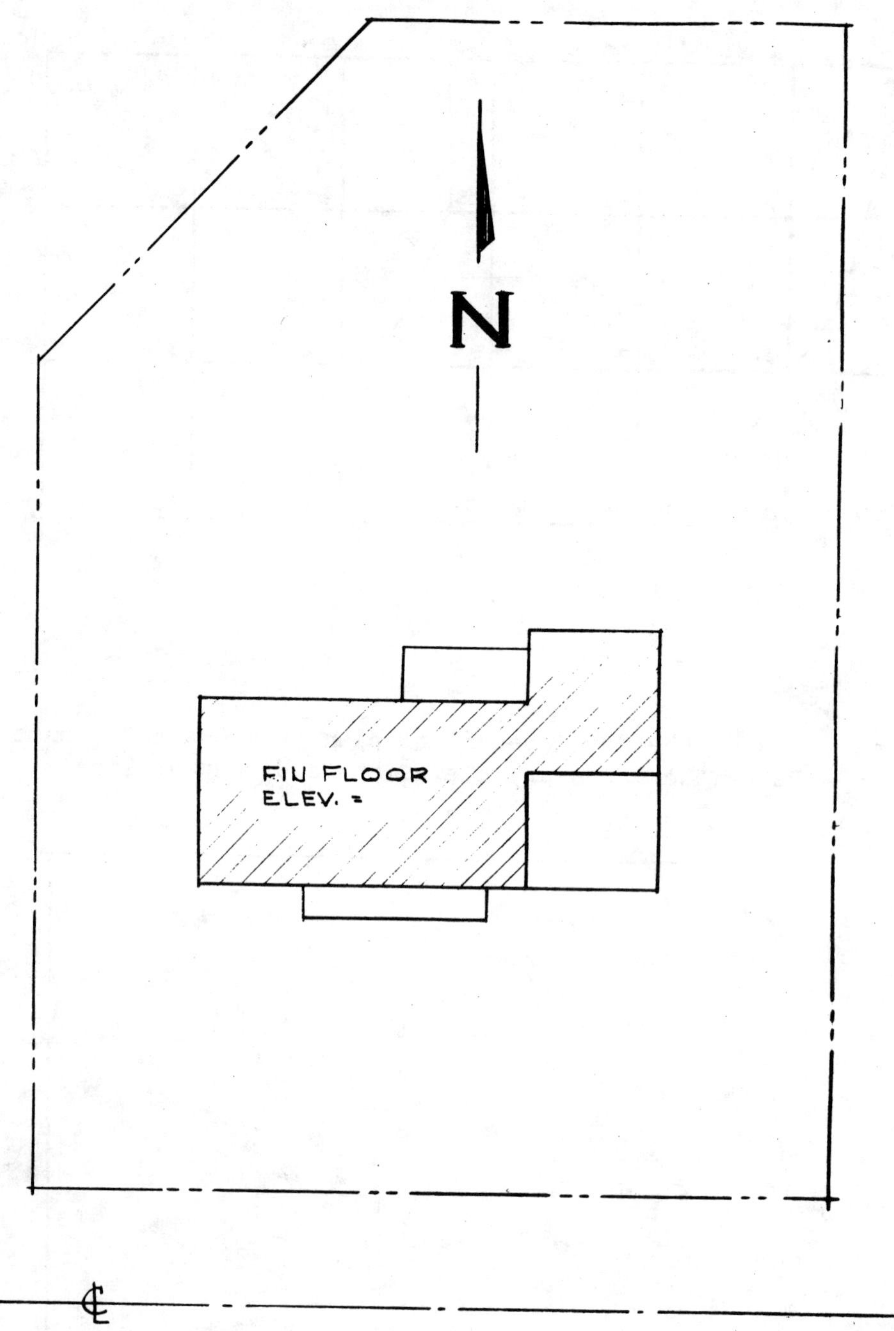

UNIT END TEST

1. List five things that should be included on a plot plan.

   a. ____________

   b. ____________

   c. ____________

   d. ____________

   e. ____________

2. The plot plan is usually drawn to a scale of ____________.

3. Contour lines are dimensioned by giving their ____________.

4. Contour lines close together indicate ____________.

5. Contour lines are usually spaced at intervals of ____________, ____________, or ____________ feet.

6. List the notes that should be included on a plot plan.

   a. ____________

   b. ____________

   c. ____________

   d. ____________

   e. ____________

Unit End Assignment:

Draw a plot plan, using the developed floor plan from Chapter 7.

Chapter 13
THE PLUMBING PLAN

The plumbing plan is used to show the location of all water lines, plumbing fixtures, drains, soil pipes, and waste pipes. Also, the plumbing plan usually has isometric details to describe the important features better.

The complete plumbing system (and the plumbing code that complements it) is quite complicated. In this chapter only the basic fundamentals will be covered.

WATER SUPPLY LINES

There are two basic types of water supply lines, hot and cold water lines (Figure 13-1). There are several different types of materials that can be used for a supply line, but a 3/4-inch copper line (type L) is the most common. The line should be as direct as possible and have a shutoff valve near the entry of the house. When the line enters the house, it branches to various locations. To reduce friction, the bends and turns should be kept to a minimum. One branch runs to the hot water heater; a hot water supply line is then available (Figure 13-2). To prevent heat transfer, the hot and cold lines should be separated by a minimum of 6 inches.

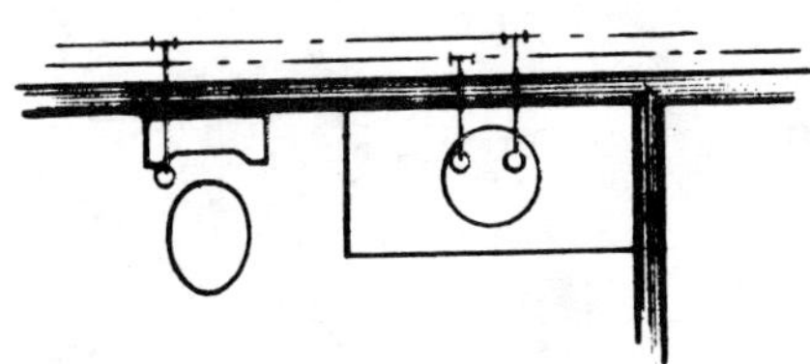

Figure 13-1
Hot and cold water lines.

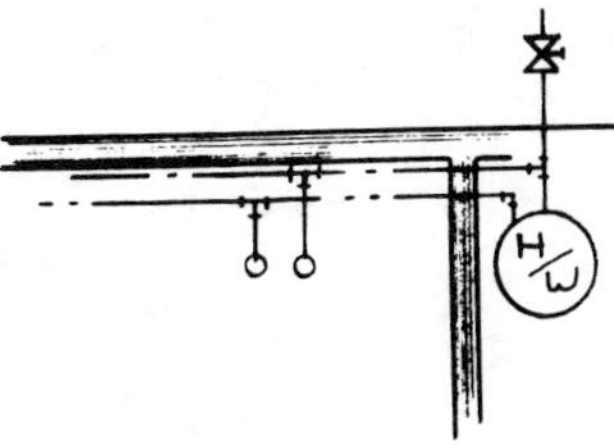

Figure 13-2
Hot water line.

THE WASTE DISPOSAL SYSTEM

A typical waste disposal system is composed of a house drain, soil stack, waste stacks, vents, and horizontal branches (Figure 13-3). The house drain is usually 4 inches and is sloped 1/8 to 1/2 inch per foot and receives the discharge from soil and waste stacks. The soil stack is usually 4 inches and is a vertical pipe that carries the discharge from water closets. It can also carry the waste water from tubs and lavatories, but to be classified as a soil stack the water closet must empty into it. The waste stack receives the discharge only from tubs, lavatories, sinks, and washers. Vents are used to reduce the possibility of siphonage and to reduce foul odors.

Note: 1. Provide an adequate number of clean-outs.

2. Never use a tee to make a 90-degree turn.

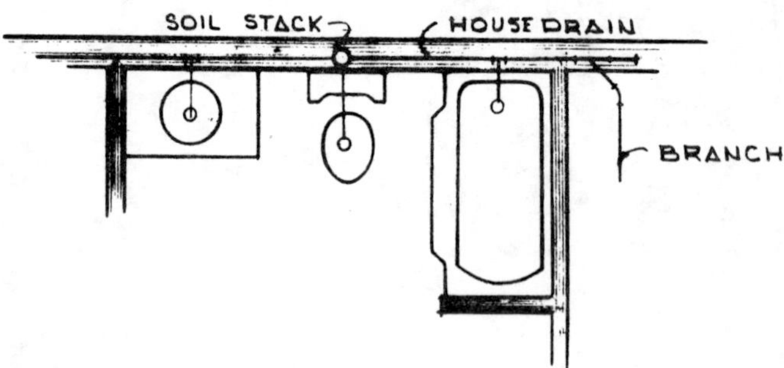

Figure 13-3
Typical waste disposal system.

RISER DETAILS

To describe the plumbing plan better, schematics are often drawn (Figure 13-4). They are drawn in isometric and not to any particular scale. There are two types of lines used in the schematic, solid and dashed lines. The solid lines represent the waste or soil lines, and the dashed lines represent the vents. If the building is only one story, the vents may be "looped" back into the stack vent.

Note: 1. Slope the loop vent to drain back to the fixture.

2. Make sloping turns.

3. Use the correct symbols.

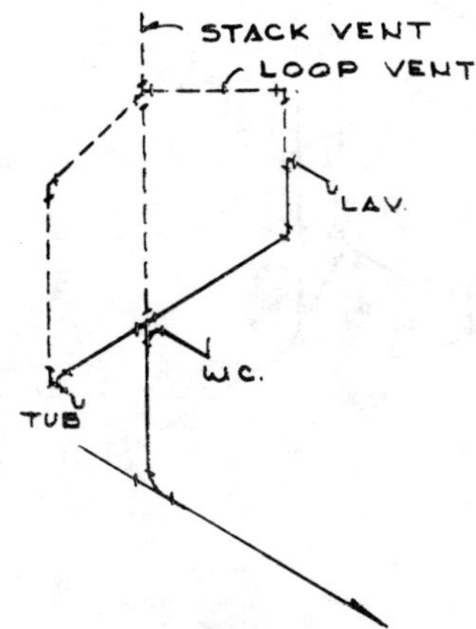

Figure 13-4
Loop vent.

If the building is more than one story and plumbing fixtures fall directly over each other, a different venting system must be used. Rather than looping the vent back into the stack vent, the loop vent must be "tied" into the vent stack (Figure 13-5). The vent stack is a vertical vent pipe that runs parallel to the soil or waste stack.

Note: 1. The vent stack is connected below the last fixture.

2. This technique provides adequate circulation and prevents the possibility of self-siphonage.

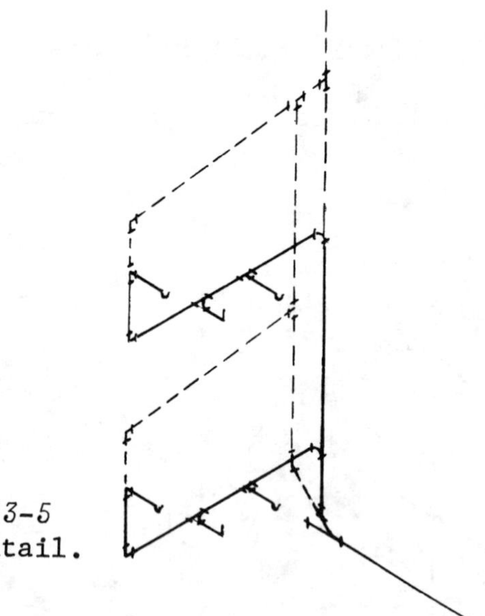

Figure 13-5
Riser detail.

Assignment: Place the hot and cold water lines on the floor plan.

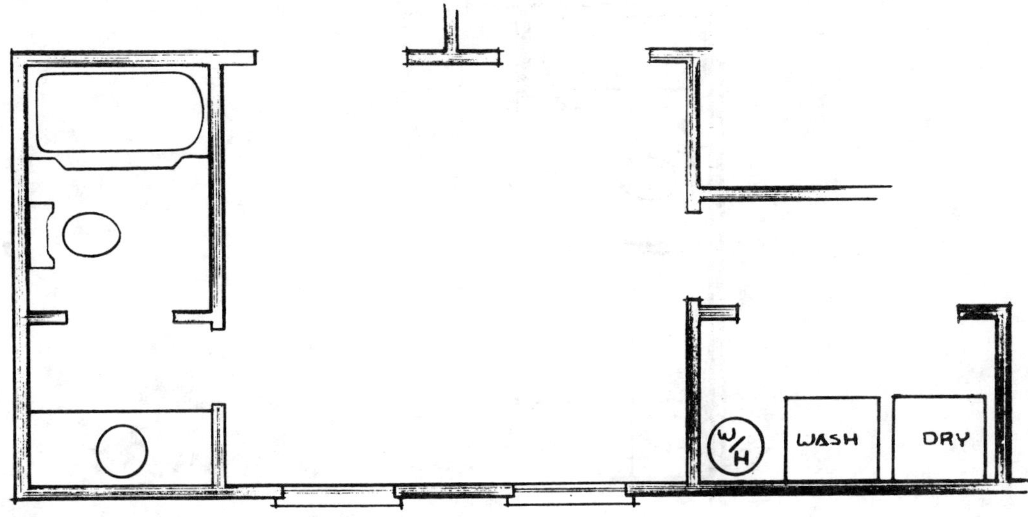

Assignment: Design the waste disposal system for the floor plan.

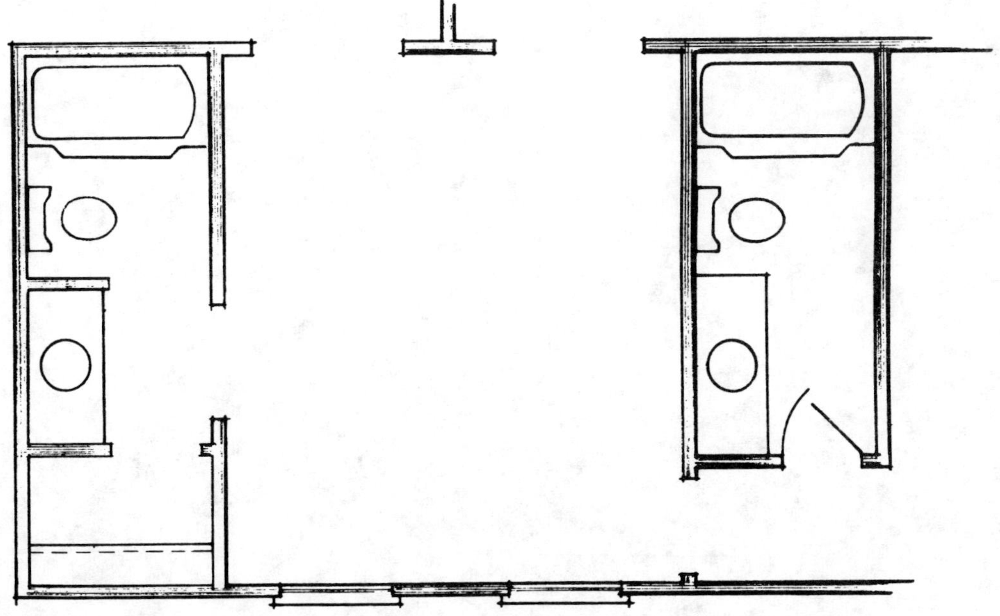

Assignment: Draw an isometric of the waste disposal and vent system.

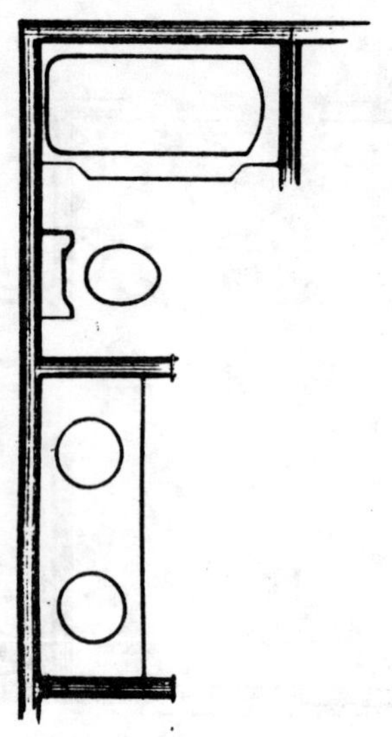

Assignment: Draw an isometric of the waste disposal and vent system. (Two-story apartment with identical baths; the second-story bath is placed directly over the first-story bath.)

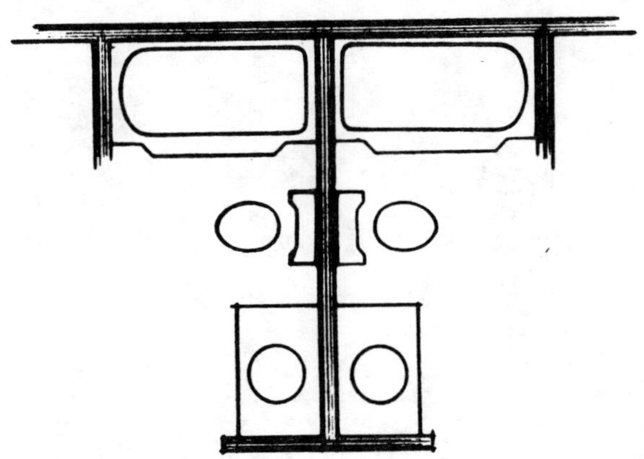

UNIT END TEST

1. The two types of water supply lines are ___________ and ___________.

2. A ___________ line is usually used as a water supply line.

3. Hot and cold water lines should be separated by a minimum of ___________ inches.

4. The house drain is usually sloped ___________ inches per foot.

5. A ___________ stack carries the discharge from water closets.

6. A ___________ stack receives the discharge only from tubs, lavatories, sinks, and washers.

7. The vent stack is connected below the ___________.

8. The ___________ is a vertical vent pipe that runs parallel to the soil or waste stack.

9. To describe the plumbing plan better, ___________ are often used.

10. A typical waste disposal system is composed of: ___________, ___________, ___________, ___________, and ___________.

Unit End Assignment:

Draw a plumbing plan, using the developed floor plan from Chapter 7. Use an 18 x 24 inch sheet of tracing paper. Be sure to include a border line and a title block.

Chapter 14
THE HEATING AND AIR CONDITIONING PLAN

The heating and air-conditioning plan is basically a floor plan with piping, heating ducts, furnaces, and other climate control equipment. The plan shows the location and sixes of the ducts, location of thermostats, plenum, and registers.

There are several ways to heat and cool a building, but the more common means are: electric heating systems, hot water systems, and forced air. If an air-conditioning system is used, it is usually combined with the heating system.

ELECTRIC HEATING SYSTEMS

An electric heating system has wires embedded in the ceiling or floor and uses electricity as an energy source. The system operates by reflecting heat rays from the different surfaces of the room. To control the temperature, a thermostat is placed in each room. The thermostat should be located 5 inches from the floor.

The electric cable should be placed 6 inches from the wall and 8 inches from any ceiling outlet (Figure 14-1). If the ceiling joists are placed 16 inches on center, only 10 cables may be placed between the joists. There should be a minimum of 2-1/2 inches between the cables.

Note: The staple spacing should be 16 inches on center.

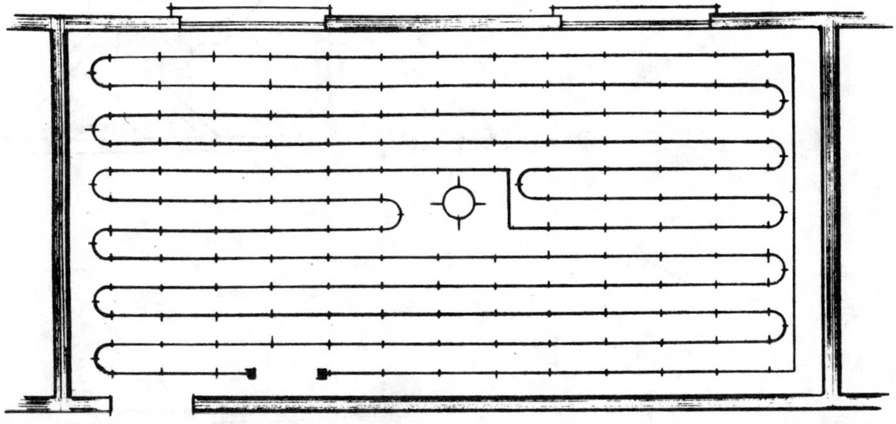

Figure 14-1
Electric heating system.

FORCED AIR SYSTEMS

A forced air system operates by heating air in a furnace and forcing it through ducts with a blower. Cool air is brought back into the furnace through a return air grill; the cool air is heated, and the cycle is repeated.

There are three basic types of duct systems; the perimeter system, the radial system, and the extended plenum system. The perimeter system has a duct that runs the perimeter of the building and is supplied by interconnecting ducts (Figure 14-2). The radial system has ducts extending from the plenum (Figure 14-3). The extended plenum is a system that has a long horizontal plenum and has ducts branching off from it (Figure 14-4).

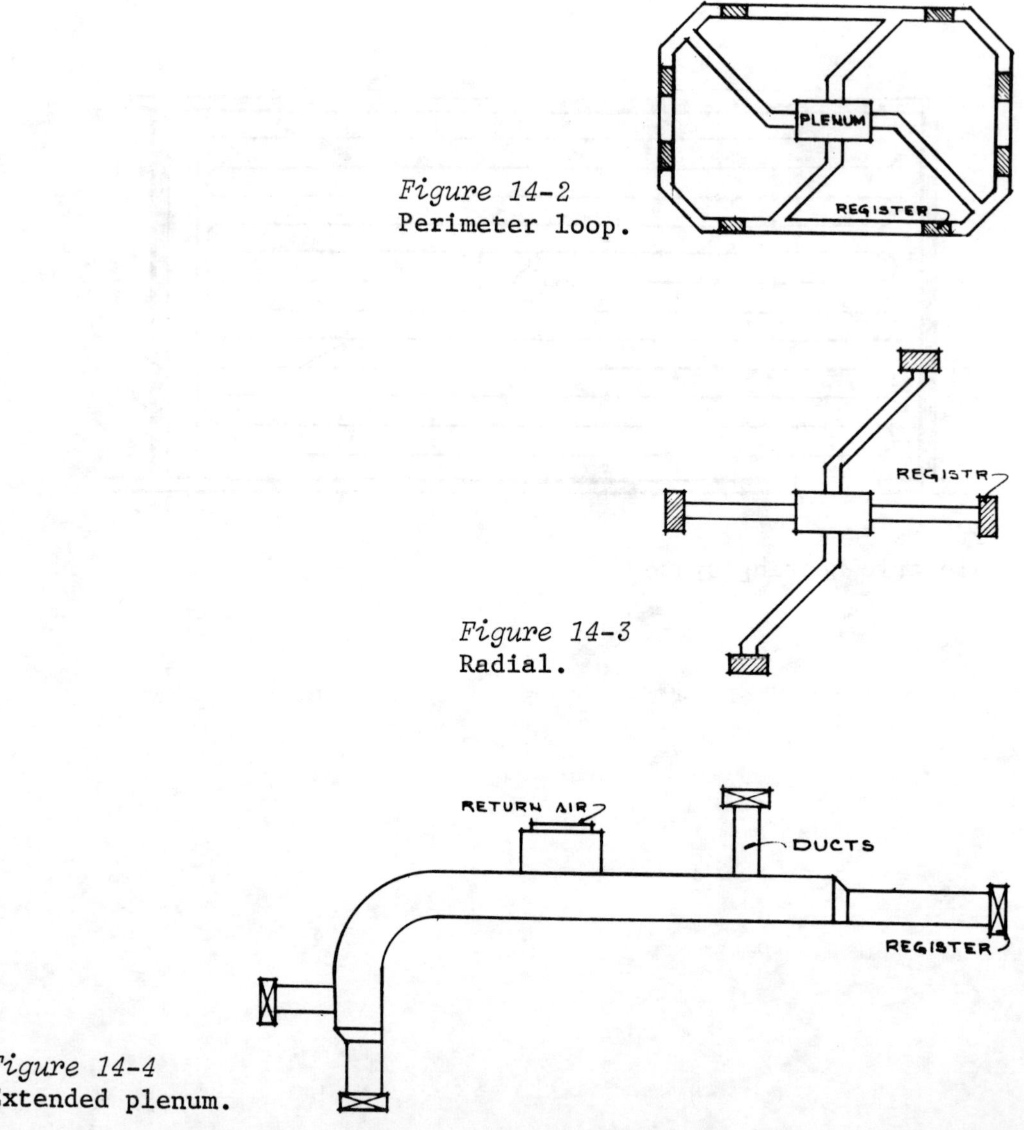

Figure 14-2
Perimeter loop.

Figure 14-3
Radial.

Figure 14-4
Extended plenum.

CENTRAL HEAT AND AIR

Most buildings are now equipped with central heating and cooling systems. This particular type of system can produce both cool and warm air. Cool air can be introduced by adding cooling coil, refrigerant compressor, and condenser. The compressor and condenser are located outside the building (Figure 14-5).

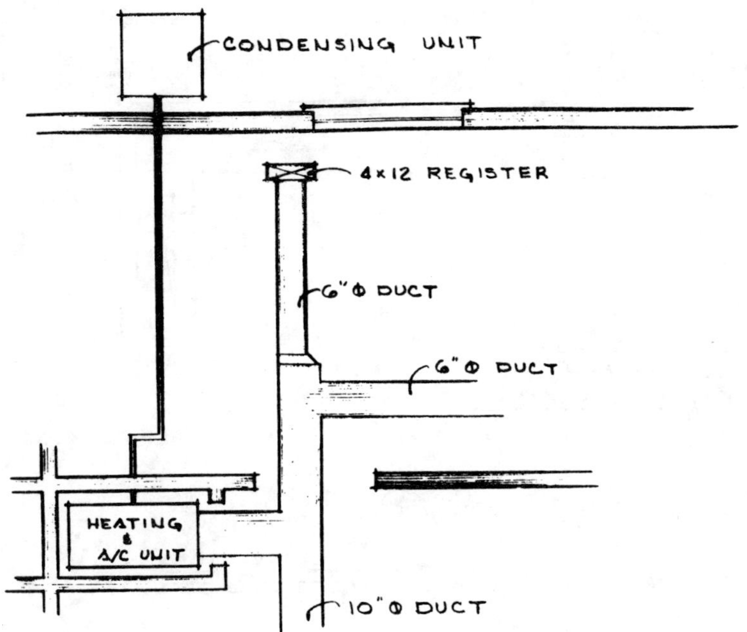

Figure 14-5
Forced heat and air.

HOT WATER SYSTEMS

In a hot water system a series of pipes carries heated water to convectors (Figure 14-6). The hot water is passed over convector fins, and the warm air is distributed over the room by means of convection.

The water is first heated in a boiler and is then circulated by means of a pump through the pipes and into the convectors (Figure 14-7). The water returns to the boiler, and the process is repeated.

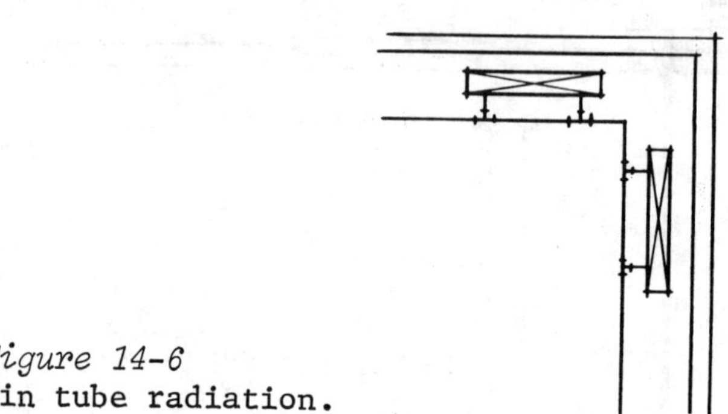

Figure 14-6
Fin tube radiation.

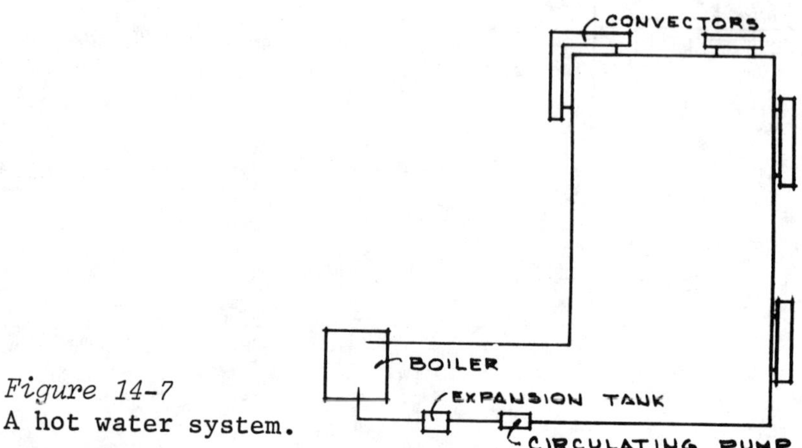

Figure 14-7
A hot water system.

Assignment: Using an electric heating system, design the system for the bedroom and den.

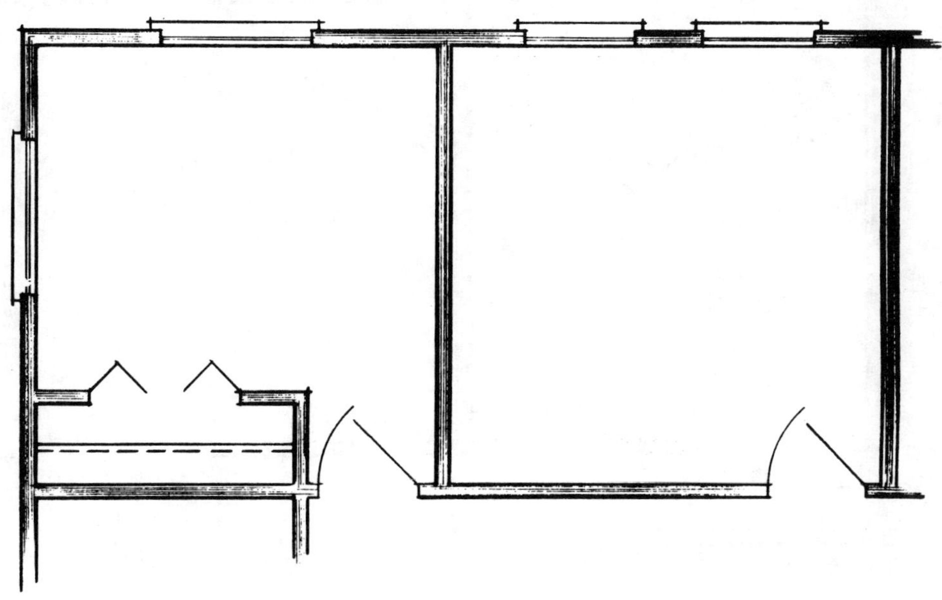

Assignment: Using a forced air system, design a system for the three bedrooms.

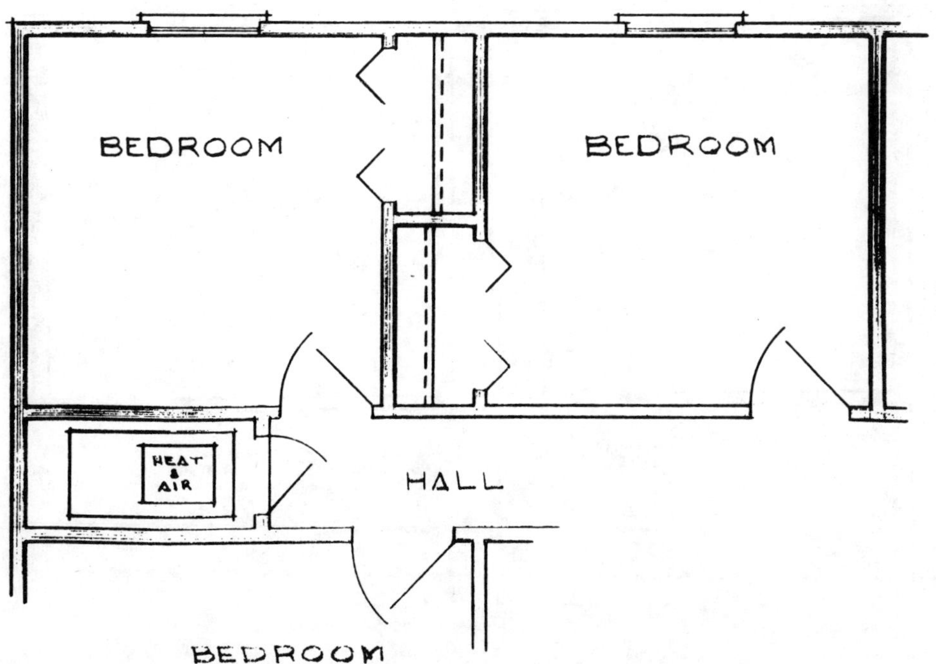

Assignment: Using a central heat and air system, design the system for the three bedrooms.

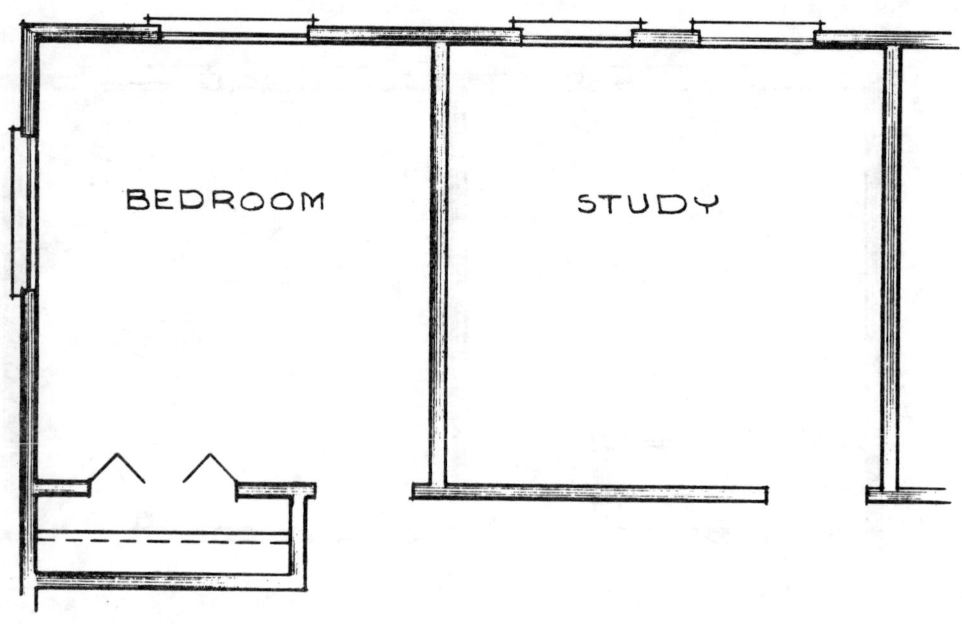

Assignment: Using a hot water system, design the system for the study and bedroom.

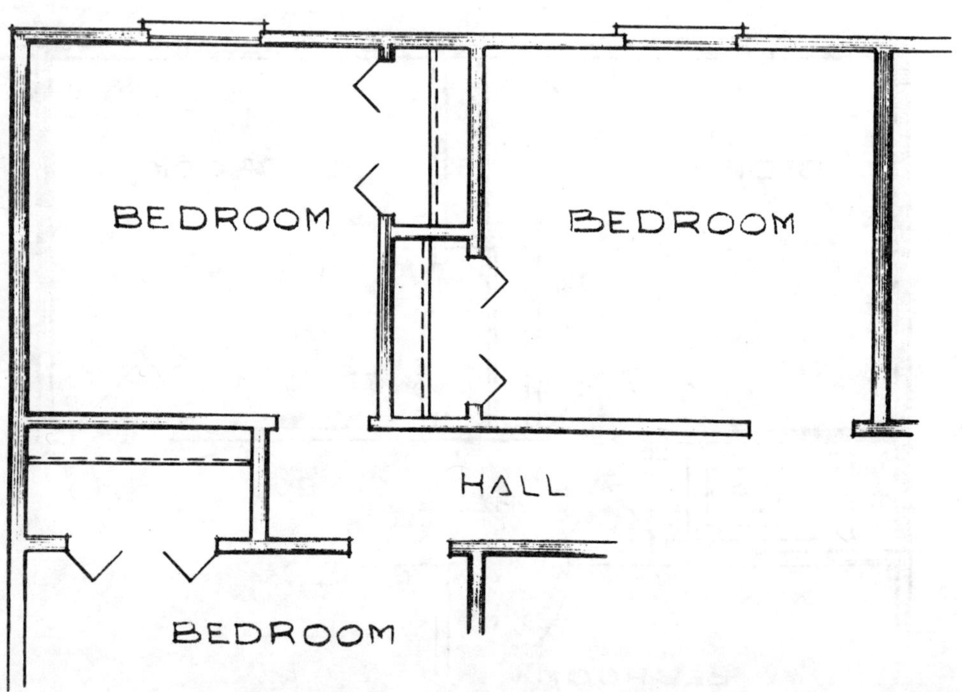

UNIT END TEST

1. Three ways to heat and cool a building are: ___________, ___________, and ___________.

2. The thermostat for an electric heating system should be located ___________ inches from the floor.

3. The electric cable should be placed ___________ inches from the wall and ___________ inches from any ceiling outlet.

4. Staple spacing for electric cables is ___________ inches on center.

5. Cool air is brought into the furnace through a ___________.

6. The two types of duct systems are ___________ and ___________.

7. The compressor and condenser are located ___________.

8. In a hot water system, the warm air is distributed by means of ___________.

9. Warm air is forced through ducts with a ___________.

10. The ___________ plenum is a system that has a long horizontal plenum with ducts branching off from it.

Unit End Assignment:

Draw a heating and air-conditioning plan, using the developed floor plan from Chapter 7. Use an 18 x 24 inch sheet of tracing paper. Be sure to include a border line and a title block.

Chapter 15
SCHEDULES

A schedule is a collection of organized notes and is placed in a convenient location on a set of plans. The notes could be included at various places on the plans, but they are usually included in a schedule.

The schedule is enclosed by a heavy border and has a title strip to identify it. There are three types of schedules that are usually found in a set of plans: the window schedule, the door schedule, and the room finish schedule.

THE WINDOW SCHEDULE

The window schedule includes the symbol, size, type of window, manufacturer, material, and remarks (Figure 15-1). The symbol used for windows is a letter. The size of a window is given in terms of its width and height. The width is given first, followed by the height. The type of window indicates whether it is a double-hung, casement, fixed, etc. The manufacturer or the manufacturer's number is given so that an order can be placed with a particular company. The material column indicates the type of material that the window is made of. The remarks column can be used for any further description of the window.

WINDOW SCHEDULE					
SYMBOL	SIZE	TYPE	MANUFACTURE	MATERIAL	REMARKS
A	3'-0"×5'-0"	D.H.	MANCO	WOOD	SEE DETAIL
B	3'-0×3'-0"	S.H.	MANCO	WOOD	DO

Figure 15-1
Window schedule.

DOOR SCHEDULES

A door schedule is very similar to a window schedule (Figure 15-2), but it may be presented in a pictorial or tabular form. The pictorial form shows the elevation of the door, the type of door, the symbol, the width and the height (Figure 15-3). The symbols used for doors are numbers. Each different number indicates a different type of door. The quantity is not always given on the door schedule, but it indicates how many doors of a certain type are used. The type of door indicates whether the door is a flush hollow core, panel, etc. The size of the door is first indicated by its width, and then its height is given (3'-0" x 6'-8"). The manufacturer's number represents a particular firm that manufactures doors. The material column indicates the type of material that the door is made of. The finish column is used to indicate the type of finish that will be used on the door (for example, varnish, shellac, or enamel paint). The remark column can be used for any further description.

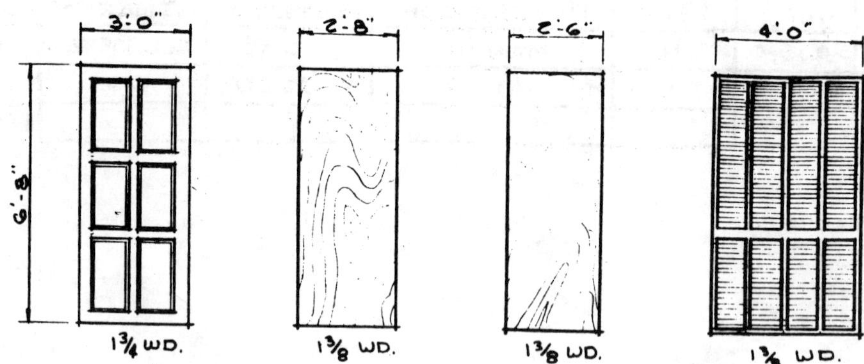

Figure 15-2
Door schedule.

DOOR SCHEDULE						
SYMBOL	QUANT.	TYPE	SIZE	MAFG. NO.	MATERIAL	REMARKS
1	1	PANEL	$3^{0} \times 6^{8}$	BF-M6	PINE	SEE DETAIL
2	3	FLUSH	$2^{8} \times 6^{8}$	BG-M3	BIRCH	
3	2	DO	$2^{6} \times 6^{8}$	BG-M4	DO	
4	5	BI-FOLD	$4^{0} \times 6^{8}$	BT-F1	PINE	

Figure 15-3
Door schedule.

ROOM FINISH SCHEDULE

A room finish schedule is used to describe the type of finishing materials used in a particular room (Figure 15-4). It includes items such as: name of the room, floor, base, walls, ceilings, and remarks. This type of schedule indicates whether the floor has carpet, hardwood flooring, quarry tile, etc., or whether the walls have gypsum, paneling, or paper.

ROOM FINISH SCHEDULE					
AREA	FLOOR	BASE	WALLS	CEILING	REMARKS
LIVING RM.	CARPET	WOOD	GYP. BD.	GYP. BD.	NONE
DINING RM.	CARPET	WOOD	GYP. BD.	GYP. BD.	NONE
BEDROOM	VINYL TILE	WOOD	PANELING	GYP. BD.	CLO. SIMILAR

Figure 15-4
Room finish schedule.

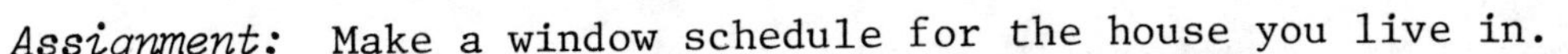

Assignment: Make a window schedule for the house you live in.

Assignment: Make a pictorial door schedule for the house you live in.

Assignment: Make a tabular door schedule for the house you live in.

Assignment: Make a room finish schedule for the house you live in.

UNIT END TEST

1. The three types of schedules usually found in a set of plans are: ___________, ___________, and ___________.

2. The size of a window is given in terms of its ___________ and ___________.

3. The symbol for a window is a ___________.

4. A door schedule can be either ___________ or ___________.

5. The size of a door is first indicated by its ___________.

6. The symbol for a door is a ___________.

7. A room finish schedule includes ___________, ___________, ___________, ___________, and ___________.

8. A schedule is located ___________.

9. A schedule is a ___________.

10. A window schedule includes ___________, ___________, ___________, and ___________.

Unit End Assignment:

Develop a window schedule, door schedule, and a room finish schedule. Use the developed floor plan from Chapter 7.

Chapter 16 STRUCTURAL MEMBERS

A building is constructed of many different items, each performing a particular function. Structural members are used to support dead and live loads. A dead load is defined as a stationary load, one that cannot move. A fireplace would be an example of a dead load. A live load is movable. Such things as wind, furniture, and people are classified as live loads.

Some structural members that are commonly used in construction are floor joist, ceiling joist, columns, rafters, and girders. Each one of these members must be properly designed to carry the imposed dead and live loads. In most cases charts and graphs have been designed to assist in the proper selection of structural members.

FLOOR JOIST

A floor joist is a member of the floor frame. It usually spans from the foundation wall to the girder. The span of a joist is considered to be clear span when it spans between the interfaces of the support. The factors that influence the maximum allowable span are: the species of the wood and the spacing of the joist (Table 16-1). To be compatible with the materials used for the subfloor, the joist should be placed 12, 16, or 24 inches on center.

To select the correct size joist, the span should first be determined. In addition to the span, the spacing of the joist, the live load, and the grade of the timber should be considered. The appropriate column and line is then used to determine the correct size joist.

Table 1

FLOOR JOIST

		Forty Pound Live Load			
Nominal size	Spacing	S.Y. Pine No. 1 1" Dim.	S.Y. Pine No. 2 2" Dim.	Douglas Fir	Redwood
2 x 6	12	10' - 6"	10' - 6"	10' - 6"	9' - 8"
	16	9' - 10"	9' - 8"	9' - 8"	8' - 8"
	24	8' - 4"	8' - 4"	8' - 4"	7' - 8"
2 x 8	12	14' - 4"	14' - 4"	14' - 4"	13' - 0"
	16	13' - 0"	13' - 0"	13' - 0"	11' - 10"
	24	11' - 6"	11' - 6"	11' - 6"	10' - 4"
2 x 10	12	17' - 4"	17' - 4"	17' - 4"	16' - 2"
	16	16' - 0"	16' - 2"	16' - 2"	15' - 0"
	24	14' - 6"	14' - 6"	14' - 6"	13' - 2"
2 x 12	12	20' - 0"	20' - 0"	20' - 0"	18' - 8"
	16	18' - 8"	18' - 8"	18' - 8"	17' - 4"
	24	16' - 10"	16' - 10"	16' - 10"	15' - 8"

CEILING JOIST

A ceiling joist spans from an exterior wall to a load-bearing interior partition, or it spans between two interior load-bearing partitions. When the attic will permit the development of a room, the joists are considered as floor joists.

Ceiling joist size can be determined in much the same way as floor joist. Table 16-2 is used to size the ceiling joist.

Table 2

CEILING JOIST

		No Attic Storage		Limited Attic Storage	
Nominal size	Spacing	S.Y. Pine No. 1 2" Dim.	S.Y. Pine No. 2 2" Dim.	S.Y. Pine No. 1 2" Dim.	S.Y. Pine No. 2 2" Dim.
2 x 6	12	11' - 10"	11' - 10"	9' - 6"	9' - 6"
	16	10' - 10"	10' - 10"	8' - 6"	8' - 6"
	24	9' - 6"	9' - 6"	7' - 6"	7' - 6"
2 x 8	12	17' - 2"	17' - 2"	14' - 4"	14' - 4"
	16	16' - 0"	16' - 4"	13' - 0"	13' - 0"
	14	14' - 4"	14' - 4"	11' - 0"	11' - 4"
2 x 10	12	21' - 8"	21' - 8"	18' - 4"	18' - 4"
	16	20' - 2"	20' - 2"	17' - 0"	17' - 0"
	24	18' - 4"	18' - 4"	15' - 4"	15' - 4"
12 x 12	12	24' - 0"	24' - 0"	21' - 10"	21' - 10"
	16	24' - 0"	24' - 0"	20' - 4"	20' - 4"
	24	21' - 10"	21' - 10"	18' - 4"	18' - 4"

GIRDERS

A girder is used to support the end of a floor joist or a wall. The width of most structures is so great that a joist cannot stretch from foundation wall to foundation wall. To support the end of the joist, a wooden girder is usually used. The girder is usually made of several pieces of 2-inch stock spiked together, or a laminated girder is used. Girder spans are given in Table 16-3. According to minimum property standards, columns used to support first-floor girders should be 6 inches x 6 inches.

Table 3

GIRDER SPANS

Width of Structure	Girder size (Solid or built-up)	Maximum Space: Supporting Bearing Partition		Supporting Non-bearing Partition	Intermediate Girders (other than main girders)
		1 story	1½ or 2 story		
1 to 26 feet wide	4 x 6	7' - 6"	6' - 0"	5' - 6"	7' - 6"
	4 x 8	9' -		5' - 6"	9' - 6"
	6 x 8	7' - 6"	6' - 0"	9' - 0"	12' - 0"
	6 x 10	9' - 0"	7' - 6"	11' - 6"	
	6 x 12	10' - 6"	9' - 0"	12' - 0"	
26 to 32 feet wide	4 x 6				6' - 6"
	4 x 8			7' - 0"	8' - 6"
	6 x 8	6' - 6"	5' - 6"	8' - 6"	10' - 6"
	6 x 10	8' - 0"	7' - 0"	10' - 6"	13' - 6"
	6 x 12	10' - 0"	8' - 0"	11' - 6"	

RAFTERS

Rafters span from the top of the wall frame to the ridge. They are used to support the roof sheathing and roof covering. To correctly size the rafters, the rafter span must be determined. Using the rafter span conversion diagram (Figure 16-1), the rafter span can be found. Once the span is determined Table 16-4 can be used to appropriately size the rafter.

Table 4

RAFTERS

		Light Roofing			
Nominal size	Spacing	S.Y. Pine No. 1 Dim.	S.Y. Pine No. 2 Dim.	Redwood	Cypress
2 X 4	12	11' - 6"	11' - 4"	10' - 6"	10' - 6"
	16	10' - 6"	9' - 10"	9' - 6"	9' - 6"
	24	8' - 10"	8' - 10"	8' - 4"	8' - 4"
2 x 6	12	16' - 10"	16' - 10"	15' - 8"	15' - 0"
	16	15' - 8"	15' - 0"	14' - 6"	14' - 6"
	24	18' - 4"	12' - 2"	12' - 8"	12' - 8"
2 x 8	12	21' - 2"	21' - 2"	19' - 10"	19' - 10"
	16	19' - 10"	19' - 10"	18' - 4"	18' - 4"
	24	17' - 10"	16' - 8"	16' - 8"	16' - 8"
2 x 10	12	24' - 2"	24' - 0"	23' - 8"	23' - 8"
	16	23' - 8"	23' - 8"	22' - 0"	22' - 0"
	24	21' - 4"	21' - 0"	19' - 10"	19' - 10"

RAFTER SPAN, CONVERSION DIAGRAM

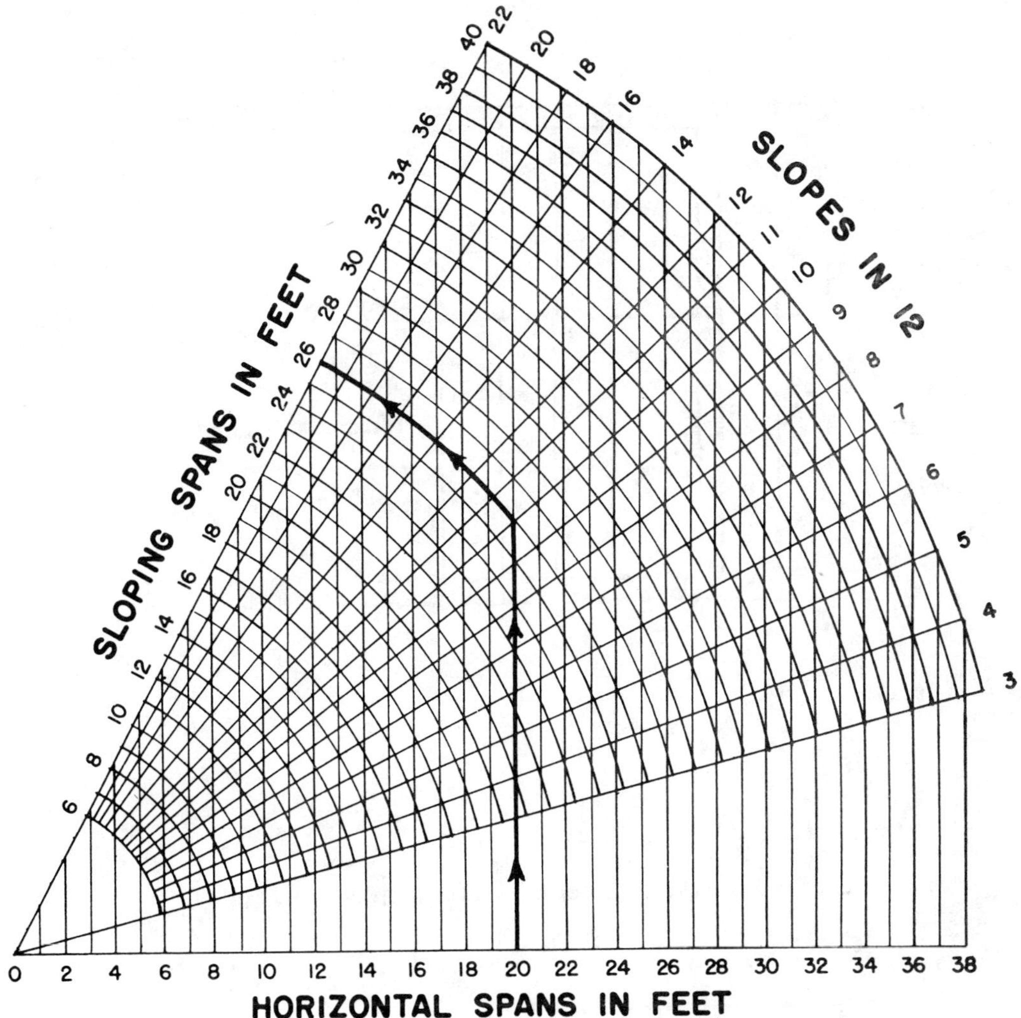

To find the rafter span when its horizontal span and slope are known, follow the vertical line from the horizontal span to its intersection with the radial line of the slope. From the intersection follow the curve line to the sloping span. The diagram also may be used to determine the horizontal span when the sloping span and slope are known, or to determine the slope when the sloping and horizontal spans are known.

Example: For a horizontal span of 20 feet and a slope of 10 in 12, the sloping span of the rafter is read directly from the diagram as 26 feet.

Figure 16-1
Rafter span conversion diagram.

Assignment: Determine the correct size of the joist.

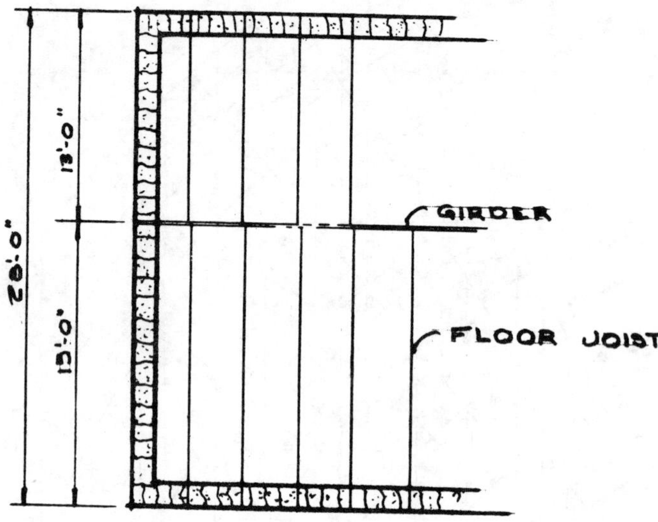

Assignment: Determine the correct ceiling joist size.

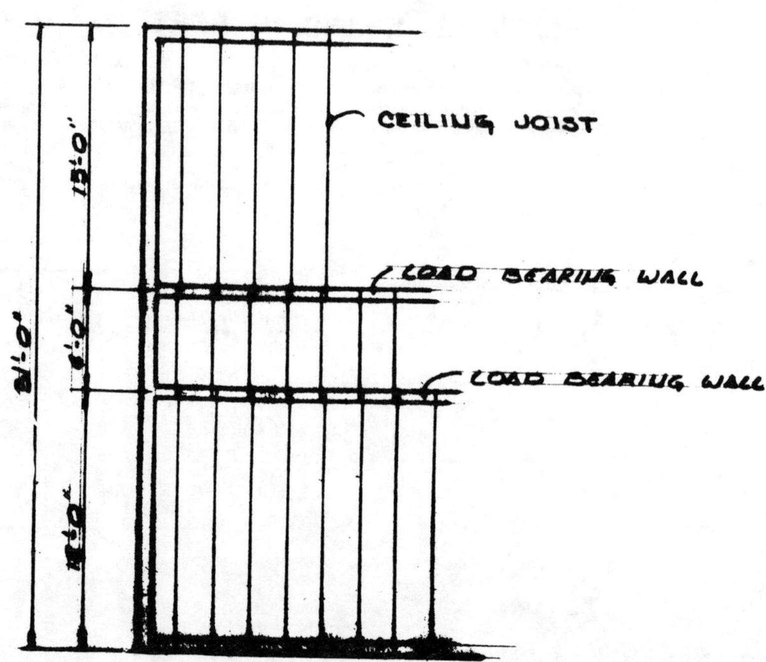

Assignment: Determine the size of the girder.

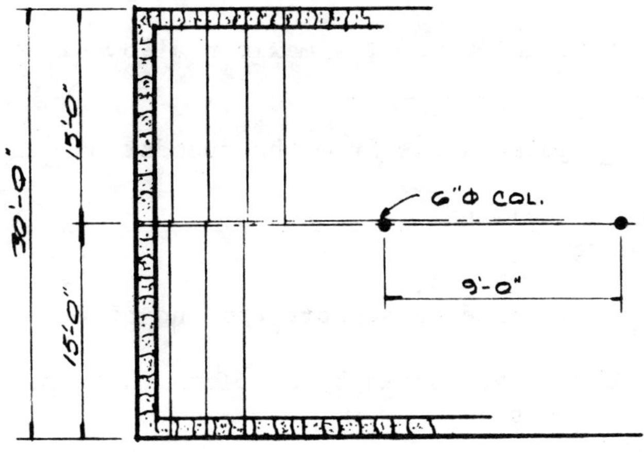

Assignment: Correctly size the rafters (slope: 4 in 12).

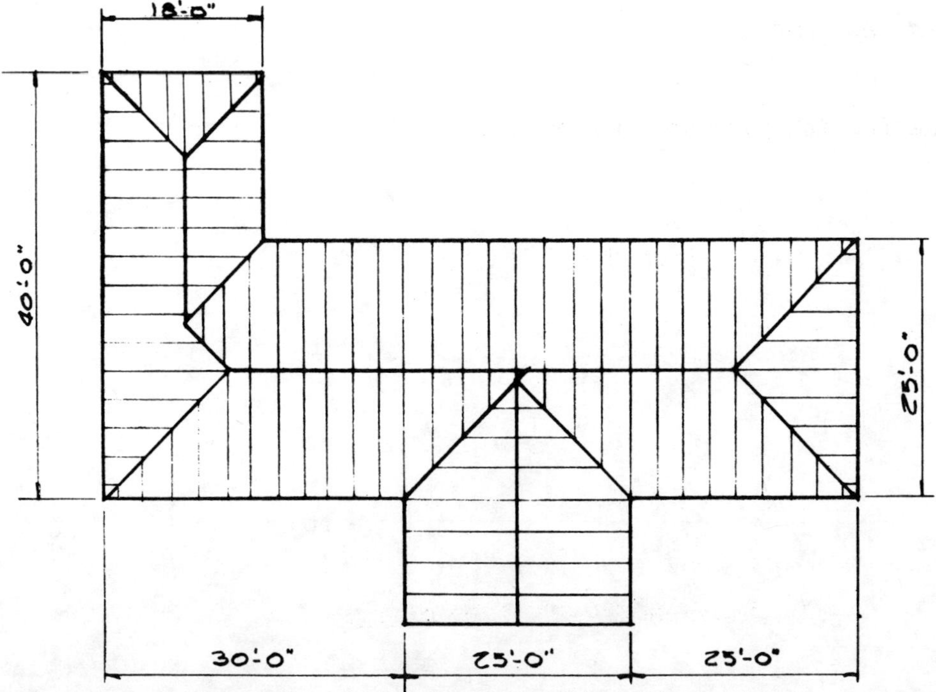

UNIT END TEST

1. Structural members are used to support ___________ and ___________ loads.

2. The factors that influence the maximum allowable span are ___________ and ___________.

3. A ___________ joist spans from the foundation wall to a girder.

4. Floor joists are placed ___________, ___________ or ___________ inches on center.

5. A ___________ is used to support the end of a floor joist.

6. A girder should be supported by a column that is ___________ x ___________ inches.

7. ___________ span from the top of the wall frame to the ridge.

8. A 2 x 8 Douglas fir floor joist spaced 16 inches on center can span ___________.

9. A 2 x 6 S. Y. Pine No. 1 ceiling joist (no attic storage) spaced 16 inches on center can span ___________.

10. A 2 x 6 redwood rafter spaced 24 inches on center (light roofing) can span ___________.

Unit End Assignment:

Size the framing plan in Chapter 11.

Chapter 17
PERSPECTIVES

A perspective is a pictorial drawing and is used to illustrate design principles and to illustrate the basic architectural design concept to a prospective client. It is used primarily to "sell" the client on a particular design.

There are two basic types of perspectives that are used in architectural drafting: a two-point perspective and a one-point perspective.

THE TWO-POINT PERSPECTIVE

Listed below are the necessary steps required in drawing a two-point perspective.

1. Draw the top view in the upper left-hand corner of the drawing paper. The right side view should then be drawn in the lower right-hand corner (Figure 17-1). The top view should be drawn at any convenient angle; usually it is placed at 30 degrees.

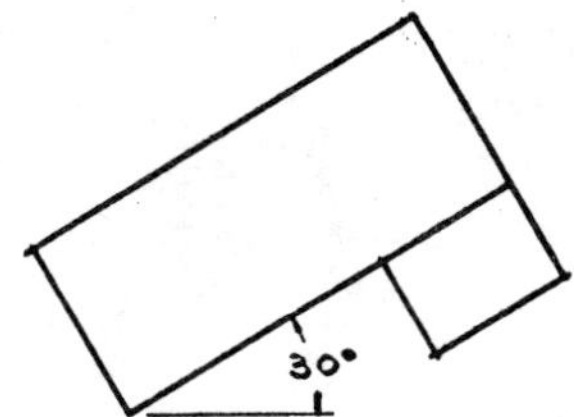

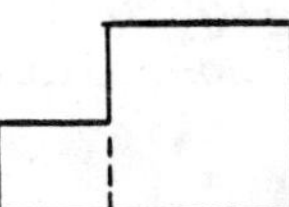

Figure 17-1
Two-point perspective, step 1.

2. Locate the picture plane line, horizon line, and station point. The horizon line is located at eye level from the ground line. A station point is located at least twice the length of the object from the picture plane (Figure 17-2).

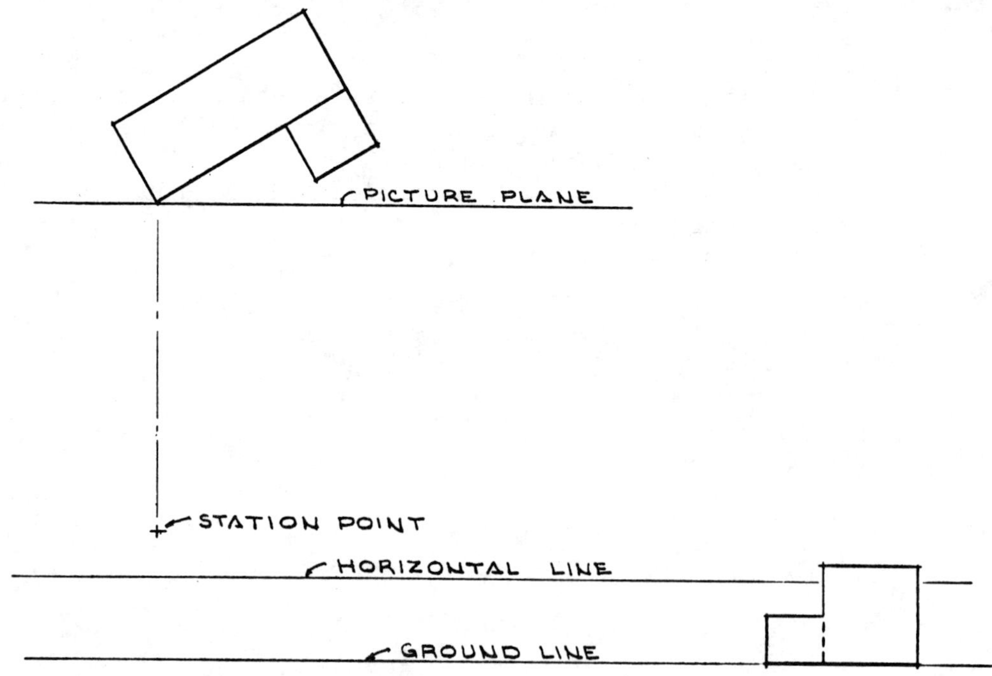

Figure 17-2
Two-point perspective, step 2.

3. Vanishing points are then located by drawing two lines parallel to the top view. The lines should be drawn from the station point, one line parallel to the front view and one line parallel to the side view. Where the two lines intersect the picture plane, a vertical line is dropped to the horizon. The vanishing points will be located at the intersection of the vertical lines and the horizon (Figure 17-3).

4. A true height-line is located by projecting a vertical line from the corner of the object that is touching the picture plane. Horizontal lines are then projected from the profile view. The intersection of the lines indicates true height (Figure 17-4).

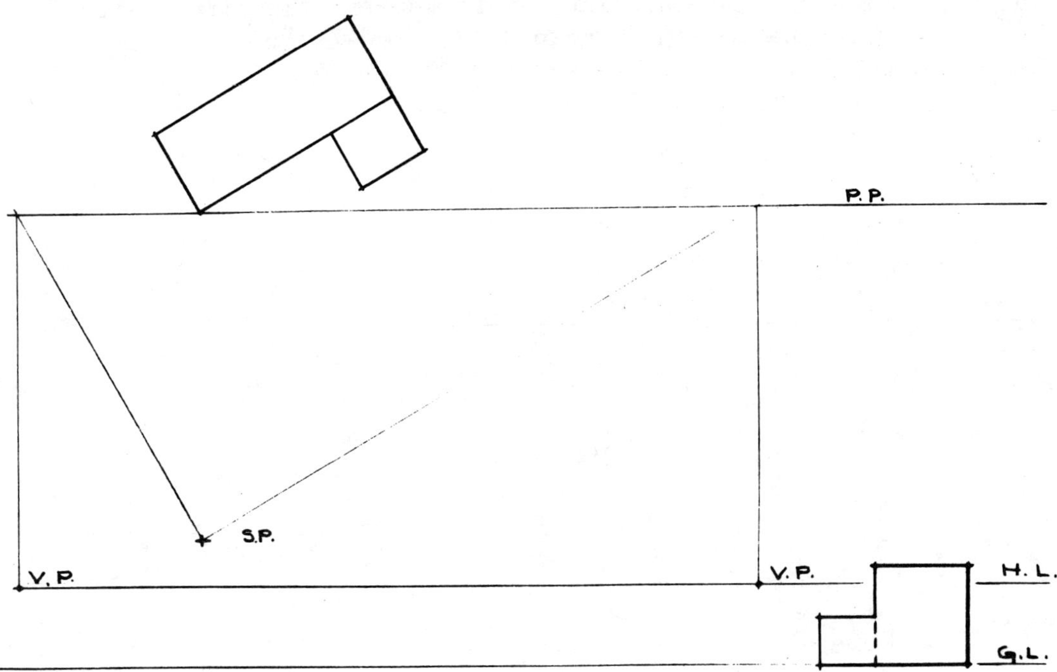

Figure 17-3
Two-point perspective, step 3.

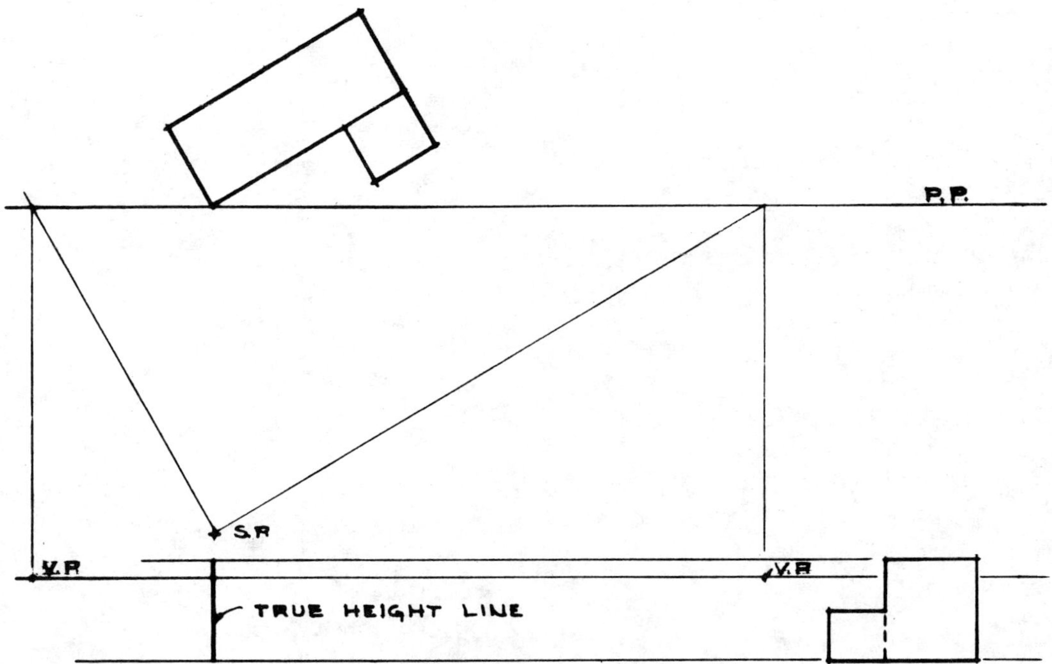

Figure 17-4
Two-point perspective, step 4.

5. From the true hieght-line, light construction lines are drawn to the vanishing points (Figure 17-5).

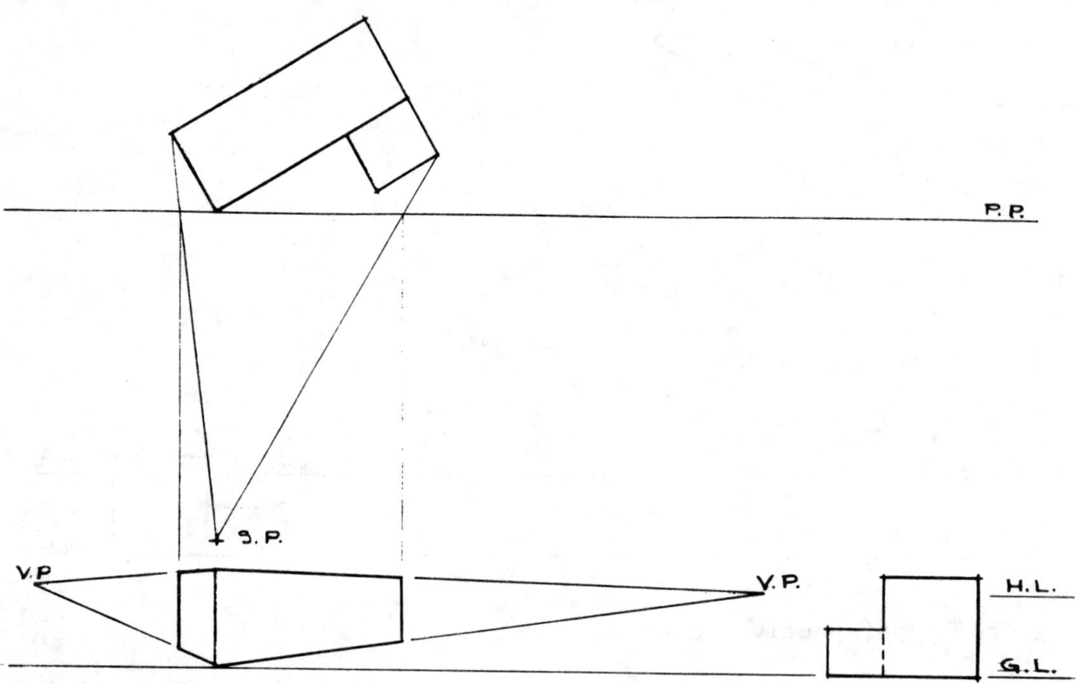

Figure 17-5
Two-point perspective, step 5.

6. Light construction lines are also drawn from the station point to the top view. Where the construction lines intersect the picture plane, vertical lines are projected to locate the corners of the perspective. Once the features are blocked in, the sight lines can be erased and the features darkened in (Figure 17-6).

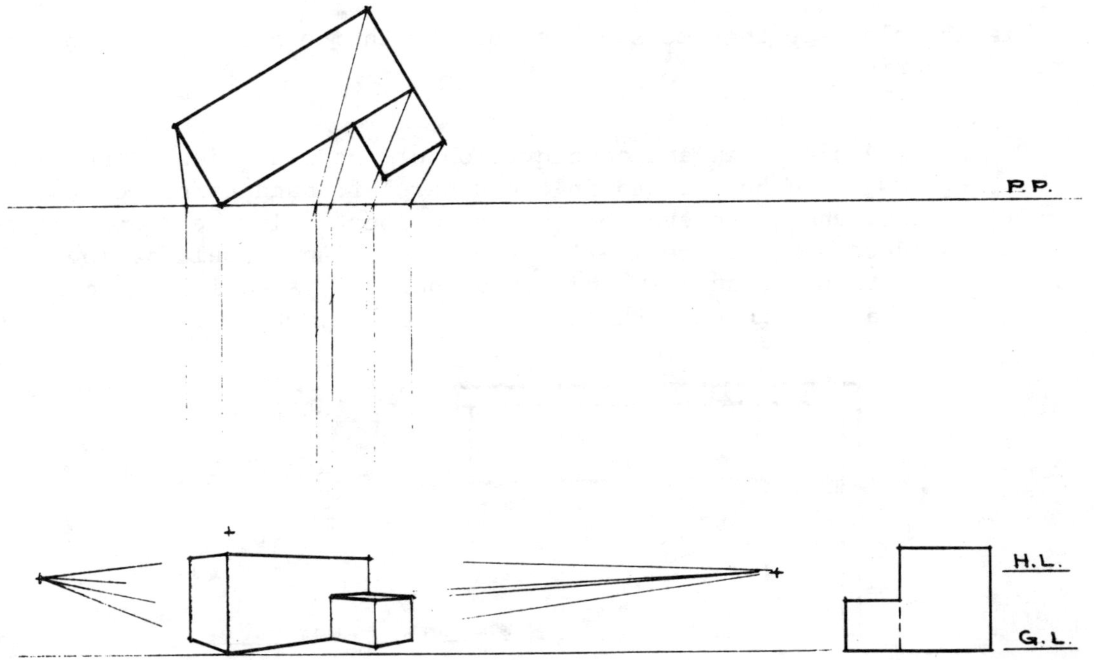

Figure 17-6
Two-point perspective, step 6.

ONE-POINT PERSPECTIVE

A one-point perspective is primarily used to show interior features. A one-point perspective is achieved when the picture plane is parallel to the face of the object.

Listed below are the necessary steps for the completion of a one-point perspective.

1. Draw a plan view and an elevation of the plan view. The plan view should be located in the upper left-hand corner of the paper, and the elevation should be located in the lower right-hand corner (Figure 17-7). A picture plane should be located on both the plan view and elevation. It is easier to work with a picture plan that falls directly on the view.

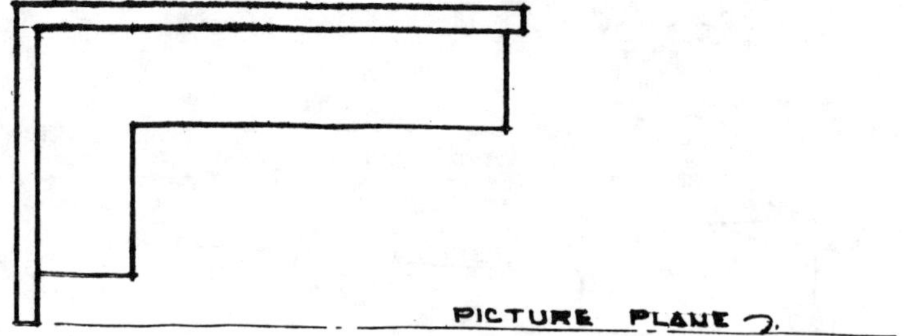

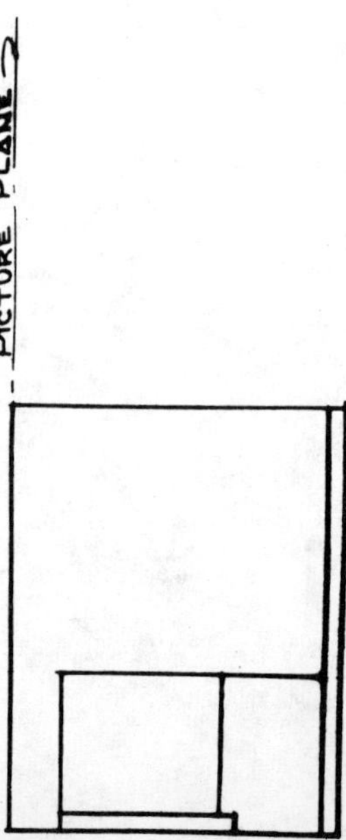

Figure 17-7
One-point perspective, step 1.

2. Once the plan view and elevation are drawn, station points are located (Figure 17-8). The station points will indicate where the observer is standing. The first station point should be labeled S.P.[1] and is located in front of the plan view. It can be placed in the center or to the right or left of center. It can be placed at any convenient distance from the picture plane. The second station point is then located and labled S.P.[2]. It should be located 5'-3" above the floor line, or it can be placed at viewing height. S.P.[2] should be the same distance from the picture plane as S.P.[1].

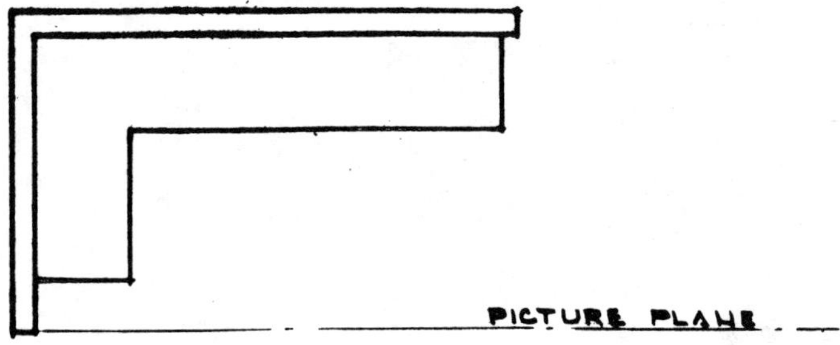

+ STATION POINT #1

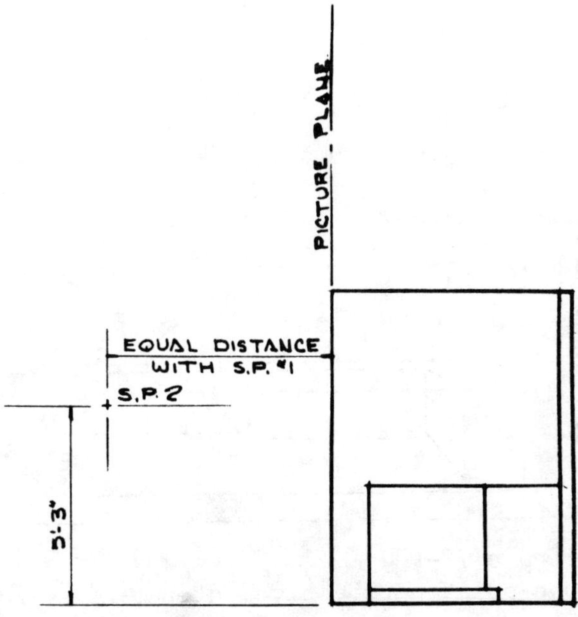

Figure 17-8
One-point perspective, step 2.

3. Points are then projected from the plan view to S.P.[1] and from the elevation to S.P.[2]. If a feature touches the picture plane, it will project in its true size. The dimension of depth is achieved by drawing vertical sight lines from the picture plane of the plan view and horizontal sight lines from the picture plane of the elevation. The intersection of the two sight lines indicates depth.

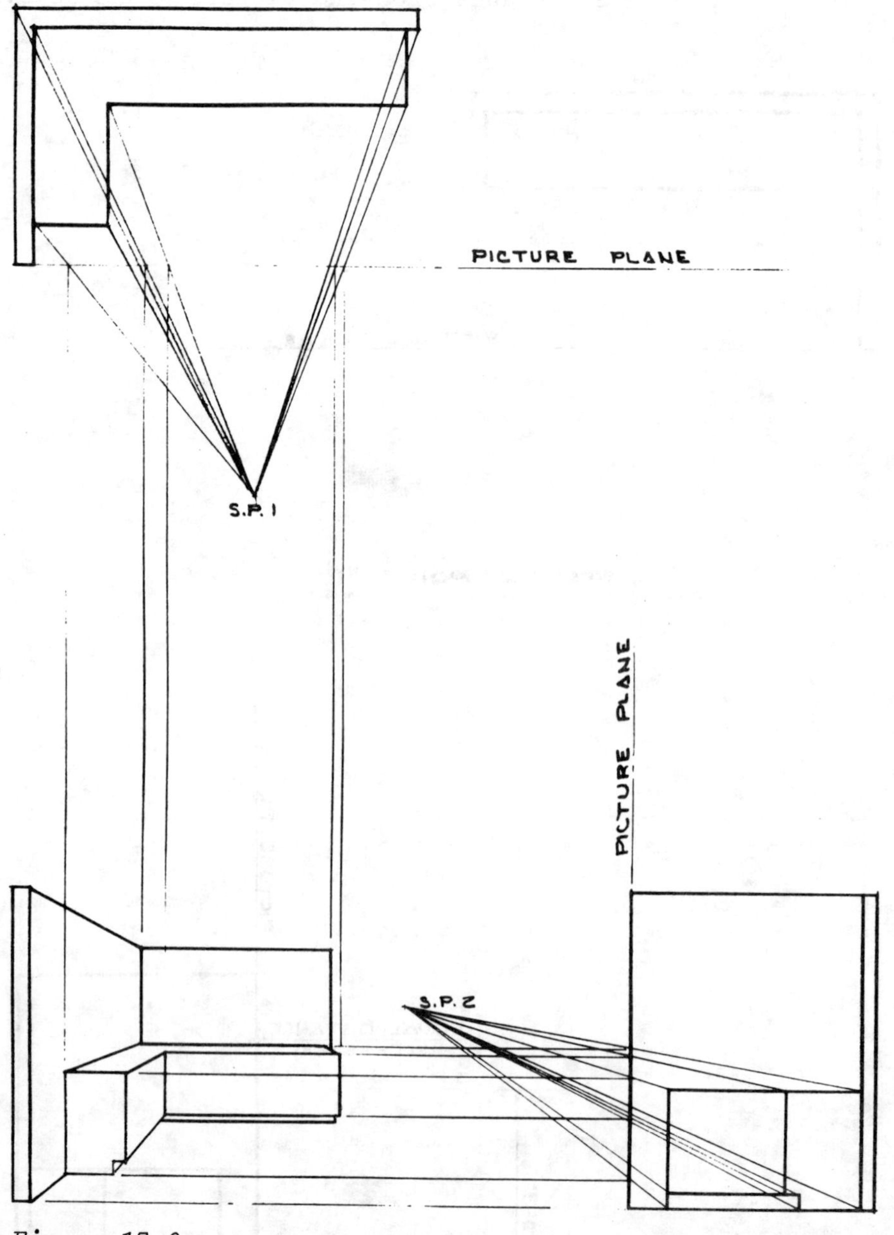

Figure 17-9
One-point perspective, step 3.

4. Once the features are blocked in, the sight lines can be erased and the features darkened in (Figure 17-10).

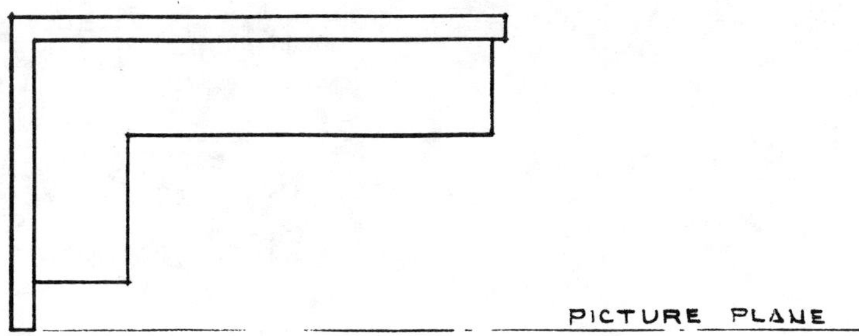

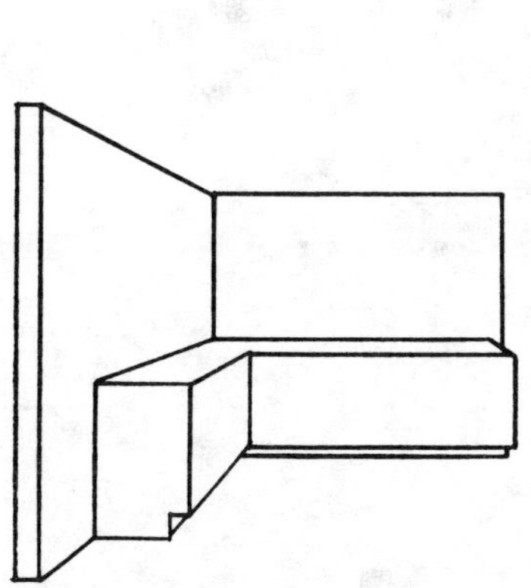

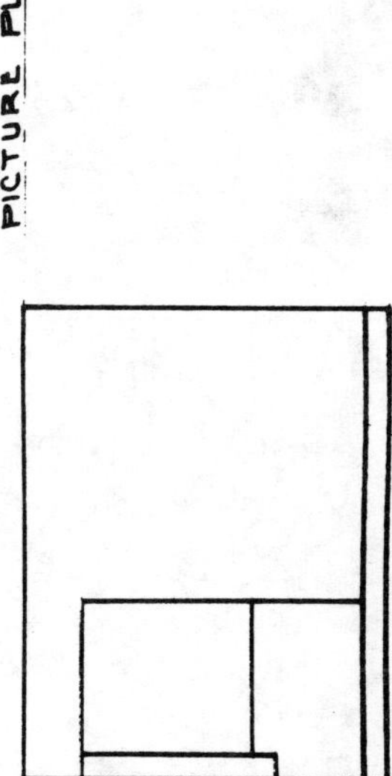

Figure 17-10
One-point perspective, step 4.

Assignment: **Draw a two-point perspective of the building.**

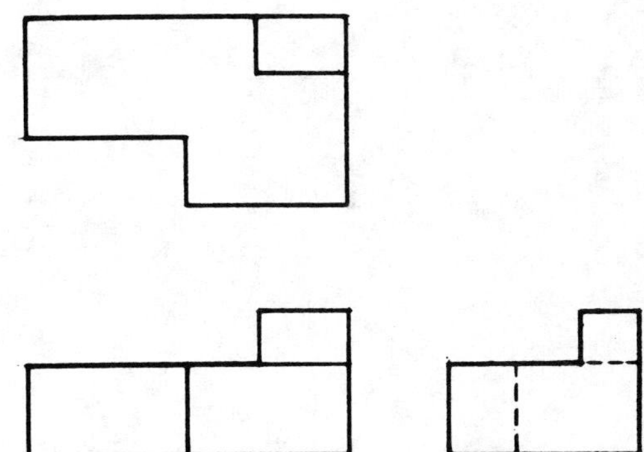

Assignment: Draw a one-point perspective of the kitchen.

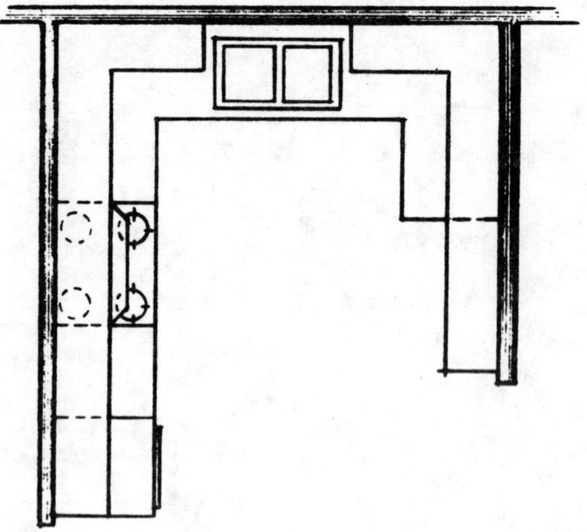

UNIT END TEST

1. Two types of perspectives used in architectural drawing are ____________ and ____________.

2. In drawing a two-point perspective, the top view is placed at an angle of ____________ degrees.

3. The horizon line is located at ____________ from the ground line.

4. A station point should be at least ____________ the length of the object from the picture plane.

5. A one-point perspective is used to ____________.

6. In a one-point perspective, the picture plane is ____________ to the face of the object.

7. In a one-point perspective the second station point should be located ____________ above the floor.

8. Station points are labeled ____________.

Unit End Assignment:

Draw a one-point perspective of the kitchen from the floor plan developed in Chapter 7.

Chapter 18
SPECIFICATIONS

Specifications are a written set of instructions that are used to convey any information that cannot be easily placed on the working drawings. They function as a legal document, a basis for building, and a guide for construction, as well as giving technical descriptions.

The specifications indicate the quality and kind of materials, workmanship, colors, and finishes.

FHA AND VA FORM

There are many different types of forms used for specifications, but two of the most popular forms used for residential construction are the FHA form 2005 and the VA form 26-1852 (Figure 18-1). The specifications are divided into sections and are listed in sequence as they occur.

In the writing of the specifications, there are standard rules that should be followed. They are: (1) use simple direct language; (2) avoid repetition; (3) use standard items; (4) use accepted standards; (5) specify number and names; and (6) give a description of the material used.

U. S. DEPARTMENT OF HOUSING AND URBAN DEVELOPMENT
FEDERAL HOUSING ADMINISTRATION

FHA Form 2005
VA Form 26-1852
Rev. 4/73

For accurate register of carbon copies, form may be separated along above fold. Staple completed sheets together in original order.

Form Approved
OMB No. 63-RO055

☒ Proposed Construction

DESCRIPTION OF MATERIALS

No. ______ (To be inserted by FHA or VA)

☐ Under Construction

Property address 31 MAGNOLIA City MONROE State LA.

Mortgagor or Sponsor APPLE CONST. CO. (Name) P.O. BOX 41 (Address)

Contractor or Builder SAME (Name) SAME (Address)

INSTRUCTIONS

1. For additional information on how this form is to be submitted, number of copies, etc., see the instructions applicable to the FHA Application for Mortgage Insurance or VA Request for Determination of Reasonable Value, as the case may be.
2. Describe all materials and equipment to be used, whether or not shown on the drawings, by marking an X in each appropriate check-box and entering the information called for in each space. If space is inadequate, enter "See misc." and describe under item 27 or on an attached sheet. THE USE OF PAINT CONTAINING MORE THAN ONE PERCENT LEAD BY WEIGHT IS PROHIBITED.
3. Work not specifically described or shown will not be considered unless required, then the minimum acceptable will be assumed. Work exceeding minimum requirements cannot be considered unless specifically described.
4. Include no alternates, "or equal" phrases, or contradictory items. (Consideration of a request for acceptance of substitute materials or equipment is not thereby precluded.)
5. Include signatures required at the end of this form.
6. The construction shall be completed in compliance with the related drawings and specifications, as amended during processing. The specifications include this Description of Materials and the applicable Minimum Property Standards.

1. EXCAVATION:

Bearing soil, type CLAY LOAM (FOOTING SHALL EXTEND 6" INTO UNDISTURBED SOIL)

2. FOUNDATIONS:

Footings: concrete mix 5 SACK ; strength psi 2500 PSI Reinforcing 3 - 5/8" ϕ RODS
Foundation wall: material ______ Reinforcing ______
Interior foundation wall: material ______ Party foundation wall ______
Columns: material and sizes ______ Piers: material and reinforcing ______
Girders: material and sizes ______ Sills: material ______
Basement entrance areaway ______ Window areaways ______
Waterproofing 6 MILL POLYETHLENE Footing drains ______
Termite protection PRESSURE TREATED TOE PLATES
Basementless space: ground cover ______ ; insulation ______ ; foundation vents ______
Special foundations ______
Additional information: ______

3. CHIMNEYS:

Material ______ Prefabricated *(make and size)* ______
Flue lining: material ______ Heater flue size ______ Fireplace flue size ______
Vents *(material and size)*: gas or oil heater 5" METALBESTOS ; water heater 3" METALBESTOS
Additional information: ______

4. FIREPLACES:

Type: ☐ solid fuel; ☐ gas-burning; ☐ circulator *(make and size)* ______ Ash dump and clean-out ______
Fireplace: facing ______ ; lining ______ ; hearth ______ ; mantel ______
Additional information: ______

5. EXTERIOR WALLS:

Wood frame: wood grade, and species #2 CEDAR ☒ Corner bracing. Building paper or felt #15 FELT
Sheathing ______ ; thickness ______ ; width ______ ; ☐ solid; ☐ spaced ______ " o. c.; ☐ diagonal; ______
Siding ______ ; grade ______ ; type ______ ; size ______ ; exposure ______ "; fastening ______
Shingles ______ ; grade ______ ; type ______ ; size ______ ; exposure ______ "; fastening ______
Stucco ______ ; thickness ______ "; Lath ______ ; weight ______ lb.
Masonry veneer BRICK & ROM Sills BRICK Lintels NONE Base flashing POLYETHLENE
Masonry: ☐ solid ☐ faced ☐ stuccoed; total wall thickness ______ "; facing thickness ______ "; facing material ______
Backup material ______ ; thickness ______ "; bonding ______
Door sills CONC. Window sills BRICK Lintels NONE Base flashing POLYETHLENE
Interior surfaces: dampproofing, ______ coats of ______ ; furring ______
Additional information: ______
Exterior painting: material EXTERIOR LATEX ; number of coats 2
Gable wall construction: ☐ same as main walls; ☒ other construction HARDBOARD OVER 2x4 FRAMING

6. FLOOR FRAMING:

Joists: wood, grade, and species ______ ; other ______ ; bridging ______ ; anchors ______
Concrete slab: ☐ basement floor; ☒ first floor; ☒ ground supported; ☐ self-supporting; mix 5 SACK ; thickness 4 ";
reinforcing 6x6 #10GA. W.W.M. ; insulation ______ ; membrane 6 MILL POLY.
Fill under slab: material FILL & GRAVEL ; thickness 12 ". Additional information: 8" FILL & 4" BASE COURSE OF WASH GRAVEL PLACED UNDER SLAB

7. SUBFLOORING: *(Describe underflooring for special floors under item 21.)*

Material: grade and species ______ ; size ______ ; type ______
Laid: ☐ first floor; ☐ second floor; ☐ attic ______ sq. ft.; ☐ diagonal; ☐ right angles. Additional information: ______

8. FINISH FLOORING: *(Wood only. Describe other finish flooring under item 21.)*

LOCATION	ROOMS	GRADE	SPECIES	THICKNESS	WIDTH	BLDG. PAPER	FINISH
First floor							
Second floor							
Attic floor	sq. ft.						

Additional information: ______

DESCRIPTION OF MATERIALS

9. PARTITION FRAMING:
Studs: wood, grade, and species #2 CEDAR size and spacing 2×6 @ 16"O.C. Other
Additional information:

10. CEILING FRAMING:
Joists: wood, grade, and species Other Bridging
Additional information: 1X4 STRIPPING @ 16" O.C.

11. ROOF FRAMING:
Rafters: wood, grade, and species Roof trusses (see detail): grade and species #2 S.Y.P.
Additional information: TRUSSES @ 24" O.C.

12. ROOFING:
Sheathing: wood, grade, and species 1/2" EXTERIOR PLYWOOD; ☐ solid; ☐ spaced ___" o.c.
Roofing 240 ASPHALT; grade C; size; type
Underlay 1 PLY #15 FELT; weight or thickness 240; size 12X36; fastening GALV. NAIL
Built-up roofing; number of plies; surfacing material
Flashing: material G.I.; gage or weight 26 GA.; ☐ gravel stops; ☐ snow guards
Additional information:

13. GUTTERS AND DOWNSPOUTS:
Gutters: material; gage or weight; size; shape
Downspouts: material; gage or weight; size; shape; number
Downspouts connected to: ☐ Storm sewer; ☐ sanitary sewer; ☐ dry-well. ☐ Splash blocks: material and size
Additional information:

14. LATH AND PLASTER
Lath ☐ walls, ☐ ceilings: material; weight or thickness Plaster: coats; finish
Dry-wall ☒ walls, ☐ ceilings: material GYP. BD.; thickness 1/2"; finish TEXTURED;
Joint treatment PERFOTAPE; FLOAT; SAND & SIZE

15. DECORATING: *(Paint, wallpaper, etc.)*

Rooms	Wall Finish Material and Application	Ceiling Finish Material and Application
Kitchen & DEN	1/4" BIRCH PLYWOOD PANELING	1/2" GYP. BD.
Bath	1/2" GYP. BD	
Other	" "	

Additional information:

16. INTERIOR DOORS AND TRIM:
Doors: type FLUSH H.C.; material MAHOGANY; thickness 1 3/8"
Door trim: type SANITARY; material FIR Base: type SANITARY; material FIR; size 3 1/4"
Finish: doors ENAMEL; trim ENAMEL
Other trim *(item, type and location)*
Additional information:

17. WINDOWS:
Windows: type S.H.; make; material ALUM.; sash thickness
Glass: grade SSB; ☐ sash weights; ☒ balances, type SPIRAL; head flashing
Trim: type SANITARY; material FIR Paint ENAMEL; number coats 3
Weatherstripping: type FIBER; material FELT Storm sash, number
Screens: ☒ full; ☐ half; type EXTERIOR; number ALL; screen cloth material ALUM.
Basement windows: type; material; screens, number; Storm sash, number
Special windows
Additional information:

18. ENTRANCES AND EXTERIOR DETAIL:
Main entrance door: material MAHOGANY; width 36"; thickness 1 3/4". Frame: material FIR, thickness 1 3/4"
Other entrance doors: material MAHOGANY; width 32"; thickness 1 3/4". Frame: material FIR; thickness 1 3/4"
Head flashing Weatherstripping: type; saddles
Screen doors: thickness ___"; number; screen cloth material Storm doors: thickness ___"; number
Combination storm and screen doors: thickness ___"; number; screen cloth material
Shutters: ☐ hinged; ☒ fixed. Railings, Attic louvers
Exterior millwork: grade and species C & BETTER YP. Paint EXTERIOR; number coats 2
Additional information:

19. CABINETS AND INTERIOR DETAIL:
Kitchen cabinets, wall units: material 3/4" BIRCH PLYWOOD; lineal feet of shelves SEE PLAN; shelf width 12"
Base units: material 3/4" BIRCH PLYW.; counter top PLASTIC LAM.; edging PLASTIC LAM.
Back and end splash PLASTIC LAM. Finish of cabinets STAIN & VARNISH; number coats 3
Medicine cabinets: make; model
Other cabinets and built-in furniture SEE PLANS
Additional information: 30 X 36 MIRROR IN BATH

20. STAIRS:

Stair	Treads		Risers		Strings		Handrail		Balusters	
	Material	Thickness	Material	Thickness	Material	Size	Material	Size	Material	Size
Basement										
Main										
Attic										

Disappearing: make and model number
Additional information:

21. SPECIAL FLOORS AND WAINSCOT

Floors:

Location	Material, Color, Border, Sizes, Gage, Etc.	Threshold Material	Wall Base Material	Underfloor Material
Kitchen	RESILIENT FLOORING (TILE)	VINYL	WOOD	CONC.
Bath	CERAMIC TILE - BROWN	MARBLE	VINYL	CONC.

Wainscot:

Location	Material, Color, Border, Cap. Sizes, Gage, Etc.	Height	Height Over Tub	Height in Showers (From Floor)
Bath				

Bathroom accessories: ☒ Recessed; material CHINA; number 1; ☒ Attached; material CHINA; number 2

Additional information:

22. PLUMBING:

Fixture	Number	Location	Make	Mfr's Fixture Identification No.	Size	Color
Sink	1	KITCHEN	APPLE	# 2567	32 x 21	WHITE
Lavatory	1	BATH	"	K 76	18"	
Water closet	1	"	"	M 416		
Bathtub	1	"	"	K 765	14 x 60	
Shower over tub△	1	"				
Stall shower△						
Laundry trays						

△☒ Curtain rod △☐ Door ☐ Shower pan: material

Water supply: ☒ public; ☐ community system; ☐ individual (private) system.★

Sewage disposal: ☒ public; ☐ community system; ☐ individual (private) system.★

★Show and describe individual system in complete detail in separate drawings and specifications according to requirements.

House drain (inside): ☒ cast iron; ☐ tile; ☐ other — House sewer (outside): ☐ cast iron; ☐ tile; ☐ other

Water piping: ☐ galvanized steel; ☐ copper tubing; ☐ other — Sill cocks, number 2

Domestic water heater: type GAS; make and model APPLE; heating capacity 37.8 gph. 100° rise. Storage tank: material; capacity 30 gallons.

Gas service: ☐ utility company; ☐ liq. pet. gas; ☐ other — Gas piping: ☒ cooking; ☒ house heating.

Footing drains connected to: ☐ storm sewer; ☐ sanitary sewer; ☐ dry well. Sump pump; make and model; capacity; discharges into

23. HEATING:

☐ Hot water. ☐ Steam. ☐ Vapor. ☐ One-pipe system. ☐ Two-pipe system.

☐ Radiators. ☐ Convectors. ☐ Baseboard radiation. Make and model

Radiant panel: ☐ floor; ☐ wall; ☐ ceiling. Panel coil: material

☐ Circulator. ☐ Return pump. Make and model; capacity gpm.

Boiler: make and model; Output Btuh.; net rating Btuh.

Additional information:

Warm air: ☐ Gravity. ☒ Forced. Type of system CLOSET INSTALLED CENTRAL HEAT

Duct material: supply G.I.; return; Insulation F/GL, thickness 2"; ☐ Outside air intake.

Furnace: make and model APPLE VF600; Input 80,000 Btuh.; output 66,000 Btuh.

Additional information: ROUGH-IN FOR A/C

☐ Space heater; ☐ floor furnace; ☐ wall heater. Input Btuh.; output Btuh.; number units

Make, model; Additional information:

Controls: make and types APPLE CONTROLS

Additional information:

Fuel: ☐ Coal; ☐ oil; ☒ gas; ☐ liq. pet. gas; ☐ electric; ☐ other; storage capacity

Additional information:

Firing equipment furnished separately: ☐ Gas burner, conversion type. ☐ Stoker: hopper feed ☐; bin feed ☐

Oil burner: ☐ pressure atomizing; ☐ vaporizing

Make and model; Control

Additional information:

Electric heating system: type; Input watts; @ volts; output Btuh.

Additional information:

Ventilating equipment: attic fan, make and model APPLE 36"; capacity 10,250 cfm.

kitchen exhaust fan, make and model APPLE HD140 30" HOOD

Other heating, ventilating, or cooling equipment APPLE CLG. HTR.

24. ELECTRIC WIRING:

Service: ☒ overhead; ☐ underground. Panel: ☐ fuse box; ☒ circuit-breaker; make SQUARE D AMP's; No. circuits 12

Wiring: ☐ conduit; ☐ armored cable; ☐ nonmetallic cable; ☐ knob and tube; ☐ other

Special outlets: ☐ range; ☐ water heater; ☐ other

☐ Doorbell. ☒ Chimes. Push-button locations EXT DOORS; Additional information:

25. LIGHTING FIXTURES:

Total number of fixtures; Total allowance for fixtures, typical installation, $

Nontypical installation

Additional information:

DESCRIPTION OF MATERIALS

26. INSULATION:

Location	Thickness	Material, Type, and Method of Installation	Vapor Barrier
Roof			
Ceiling	6"	BLOWN MINERAL WOOL	NONE
Wall	3½"	BATT TYPE FIBERGLASS	YES
Floor			

HARDWARE: *(make, material, and finish.)*

SPECIAL EQUIPMENT: *(State material or make, model and quantity. Include only equipment and appliances which are acceptable by local law, custom and applicable FHA standards. Do not include items which, by established custom, are supplied by occupant and removed when he vacates premises or chattles prohibited by law from becoming realty.)*

AUTOMATIC WASHER - PLUMBING ONLY
KITCHEN RANGE - APPLE HD100

27. MISCELLANEOUS: *(Describe any main dwelling materials, equipment, or construction items not shown elsewhere; or use to provide additional information where the space provided was inadequate. Always reference by item number to correspond to numbering used on this form.)*

ROUGH IN FOR A/C
COIL CASE IN PLACE
REFRIGERANT LINES IN PLACE
DRAIN UNDER SLAB
220V DISCONNECT; STUBBED OUT

PORCHES: SEE GARAGES

TERRACES:
SEE GARAGES

GARAGES:
INTEGRALLY POURED REINF. CONC. FTG. AROUND PERIMETER OF 4" REINF. CONC. SLAB WITH MONOLYTHIC FINISH. ROOF CONST AND ROOFING TO BE SAME AS HOUSE.

WALKS AND DRIVEWAYS:
Driveway: width 18 ; base material GRAVEL ; thickness 4 "; surfacing material CONC. ; thickness 4 "
Front walk: width ____ ; material ____ ; thickness ____ ". Service walk: width ____ ; material ____ ; thickness ____ "
Steps: material ____ ; treads ____ "; risers ____ ". Cheek walls ____

OTHER ONSITE IMPROVEMENTS:
(Specify all exterior onsite improvements not described elsewhere, including items such as unusual grading, drainage structures, retaining walls, fence, railings, and accessory structures.)
GRADE YARD TO PROVIDE ADEQUATE DRAINAGE

LANDSCAPING, PLANTING, AND FINISH GRADING:
Topsoil ____ " thick: ☐ front yard; ☐ side yards; ☐ rear yard to ____ feet behind main building.
Lawns *(seeded, sodded, or sprigged)*: ☐ front yard ____ ; ☐ side yards ____ ; ☐ rear yard ____
Planting: ☐ as specified and shown on drawings; ☐ as follows:
____ Shade trees, deciduous, ____ " caliper.
____ Low flowering trees, deciduous, ____ ' to ____ '
____ High-growing shrubs, deciduous, ____ ' to ____ '
____ Medium-growing shrubs, deciduous, ____ ' to ____ '
____ Low-growing shrubs, deciduous, ____ ' to ____ '
____ Evergreen trees, ____ ' to ____ ', B & B.
____ Evergreen shrubs, ____ ' to ____ ', B & B.
____ Vines, 2-year ____

IDENTIFICATION.—This exhibit shall be identified by the signature of the builder, or sponsor, and/or the proposed mortgagor if the latter is known at the time of application.

Date JAN. 19 Signature J. P. Apple

Signature ____

FHA Form 2005
VA Form 26-1852

Unit End Assignment:

Using the plans you have developed, complete the specifications.

FHA Form 2005
VA Form 26-1852
Rev. 4/73

U. S. DEPARTMENT OF HOUSING AND URBAN DEVELOPMENT
FEDERAL HOUSING ADMINISTRATION
For accurate register of carbon copies, form may be separated along above fold. Staple completed sheets together in original order.

Form Approved
OMB No. 63–RO055

☐ Proposed Construction

DESCRIPTION OF MATERIALS

No. ______ (To be inserted by FHA or VA)

☐ Under Construction

Property address ______ City ______ State ______

Mortgagor or Sponsor ______ (Name) ______ (Address)

Contractor or Builder ______ (Name) ______ (Address)

INSTRUCTIONS

1. For additional information on how this form is to be submitted, number of copies, etc., see the instructions applicable to the FHA Application for Mortgage Insurance or VA Request for Determination of Reasonable Value, as the case may be.
2. Describe all materials and equipment to be used, whether or not shown on the drawings, by marking an X in each appropriate check-box and entering the information called for in each space. If space is inadequate, enter "See misc." and describe under item 27 or on an attached sheet. THE USE OF PAINT CONTAINING MORE THAN ONE PERCENT LEAD BY WEIGHT IS PROHIBITED.
3. Work not specifically described or shown will not be considered unless required, then the minimum acceptable will be assumed. Work exceeding minimum requirements cannot be considered unless specifically described.
4. Include no alternates, "or equal" phrases, or contradictory items. (Consideration of a request for acceptance of substitute materials or equipment is not thereby precluded.)
5. Include signatures required at the end of this form.
6. The construction shall be completed in compliance with the related drawings and specifications, as amended during processing. The specifications include this Description of Materials and the applicable Minimum Property Standards.

1. EXCAVATION:

Bearing soil, type ______

2. FOUNDATIONS:

Footings: concrete mix ______; strength psi ______ Reinforcing ______
Foundation wall: material ______ Reinforcing ______
Interior foundation wall: material ______ Party foundation wall ______
Columns: material and sizes ______ Piers: material and reinforcing ______
Girders: material and sizes ______ Sills: material ______
Basement entrance areaway ______ Window areaways ______
Waterproofing ______ Footing drains ______
Termite protection ______
Basementless space: ground cover ______; insulation ______; foundation vents ______
Special foundations ______
Additional information: ______

3. CHIMNEYS:

Material ______ Prefabricated *(make and size)* ______
Flue lining: material ______ Heater flue size ______ Fireplace flue size ______
Vents *(material and size)*: gas or oil heater ______; water heater ______
Additional information: ______

4. FIREPLACES:

Type: ☐ solid fuel; ☐ gas-burning; ☐ circulator *(make and size)* ______ Ash dump and clean-out ______
Fireplace: facing ______; lining ______; hearth ______; mantel ______
Additional information: ______

5. EXTERIOR WALLS:

Wood frame: wood grade, and species ______ ☐ Corner bracing. Building paper or felt ______
Sheathing ______; thickness ______; width ______; ☐ solid; ☐ spaced ______" o. c.; ☐ diagonal; ______
Siding ______; grade ______; type ______; size ______; exposure ______"; fastening ______
Shingles ______; grade ______; type ______; size ______; exposure ______"; fastening ______
Stucco ______; thickness ______"; Lath ______; weight ______ lb.
Masonry veneer ______ Sills ______ Lintels ______ Base flashing ______
Masonry: ☐ solid ☐ faced ☐ stuccoed; total wall thickness ______"; facing thickness ______"; facing material ______
Backup material ______; thickness ______"; bonding ______
Door sills ______ Window sills ______ Lintels ______ Base flashing ______
Interior surfaces: dampproofing, ______ coats of ______; furring ______
Additional information: ______
Exterior painting: material ______; number of coats ______
Gable wall construction: ☐ same as main walls; ☐ other construction ______

6. FLOOR FRAMING:

Joists: wood, grade, and species ______; other ______; bridging ______; anchors ______
Concrete slab: ☐ basement floor; ☐ first floor; ☐ ground supported; ☐ self-supporting; mix ______, thickness ______";
reinforcing ______; insulation ______; membrane ______
Fill under slab: material ______; thickness ______". Additional information: ______

7. SUBFLOORING: *(Describe underflooring for special floors under item 21.)*

Material: grade and species ______; size ______; type ______
Laid: ☐ first floor; ☐ second floor; ☐ attic ______ sq. ft.; ☐ diagonal; ☐ right angles. Additional information: ______

8. FINISH FLOORING: *(Wood only. Describe other finish flooring under item 21.)*

Location	Rooms	Grade	Species	Thickness	Width	Bldg. Paper	Finish
First floor							
Second floor							
Attic floor ______ sq. ft.							

Additional information: ______

DESCRIPTION OF MATERIALS

9. PARTITION FRAMING:
Studs: wood, grade, and species ______ size and spacing ______ Other ______
Additional information: ______

10. CEILING FRAMING:
Joists: wood, grade, and species ______ Other ______ Bridging ______
Additional information: ______

11. ROOF FRAMING:
Rafters: wood, grade, and species ______ Roof trusses (see detail): grade and species ______
Additional information: ______

12. ROOFING:
Sheathing: wood, grade, and species ______; ☐ solid; ☐ spaced ______" o.c.
Roofing ______; grade ______; size ______; type ______
Underlay ______; weight or thickness ______; size ______; fastening ______
Built-up roofing ______; number of plies ______; surfacing material ______
Flashing: material ______; gage or weight ______; ☐ gravel stops; ☐ snow guards
Additional information: ______

13. GUTTERS AND DOWNSPOUTS:
Gutters: material ______; gage or weight ______; size ______; shape ______
Downspouts: material ______; gage or weight ______; size ______; shape ______; number ______
Downspouts connected to: ☐ Storm sewer; ☐ sanitary sewer; ☐ dry-well. ☐ Splash blocks: material and size ______
Additional information: ______

14. LATH AND PLASTER
Lath ☐ walls, ☐ ceilings: material ______; weight or thickness ______ Plaster: coats ______; finish ______
Dry-wall ☐ walls, ☐ ceilings: material ______; thickness ______; finish ______;
Joint treatment ______

15. DECORATING: *(Paint, wallpaper, etc.)*

Rooms	Wall Finish Material and Application	Ceiling Finish Material and Application
Kitchen		
Bath		
Other		

Additional information: ______

16. INTERIOR DOORS AND TRIM:
Doors: type ______; material ______; thickness ______
Door trim: type ______; material ______ Base: type ______; material ______; size ______
Finish: doors ______; trim ______
Other trim *(item, type and location)* ______
Additional information: ______

17. WINDOWS:
Windows: type ______; make ______; material ______; sash thickness ______
Glass: grade ______; ☐ sash weights; ☐ balances, type ______; head flashing ______
Trim: type ______; material ______ Paint ______; number coats ______
Weatherstripping: type ______; material ______ Storm sash, number ______
Screens: ☐ full; ☐ half; type ______; number ______; screen cloth material ______
Basement windows: type ______; material ______; screens, number ______; Storm sash, number ______
Special windows ______
Additional information: ______

18. ENTRANCES AND EXTERIOR DETAIL:
Main entrance door: material ______; width ______; thickness ______". Frame: material ______, thickness ______"
Other entrance doors: material ______; width ______; thickness ______". Frame: material ______; thickness ______"
Head flashing ______ Weatherstripping: type ______; saddles ______
Screen doors: thickness ______"; number ______; screen cloth material ______ Storm doors: thickness ______"; number ______
Combination storm and screen doors: thickness ______"; number ______; screen cloth material ______
Shutters: ☐ hinged; ☐ fixed. Railings ______, Attic louvers ______
Exterior millwork: grade and species ______ Paint ______; number coats ______
Additional information: ______

19. CABINETS AND INTERIOR DETAIL:
Kitchen cabinets, wall units: material ______; lineal feet of shelves ______; shelf width ______
Base units: material ______; counter top ______; edging ______
Back and end splash ______ Finish of cabinets ______; number coats ______
Medicine cabinets: make ______; model ______
Other cabinets and built-in furniture ______
Addftional information: ______

20. STAIRS:

Stair	Treads		Risers		Strings		Handrail		Balusters	
	Material	Thickness	Material	Thickness	Material	Size	Material	Size	Material	Size
Basement										
Main										
Attic										

Dis-ppearing: make and model number ______
Additional information: ______

21. SPECIAL FLOORS AND WAINSCOT

	Location	Material, Color, Border, Sizes, Gage, Etc.	Threshold Material	Wall Base Material	Underfloor Material
Floors	Kitchen				
	Bath				

	Location	Material, Color, Border, Cap. Sizes, Gage, Etc.	Height	Height Over Tub	Height in Showers (From Floor)
Wainscot					
	Bath				

Bathroom accessories: ☐ Recessed; material ______; number ______; ☐ Attached; material ______; number ______

Additional information: ______

22. PLUMBING:

Fixture	Number	Location	Make	Mfr's Fixture Identification No.	Size	Color
Sink						
Lavatory						
Water closet						
Bathtub						
Shower over tub△						
Stall shower△						
Laundry trays						

△☐ Curtain rod △☐ Door ☐ Shower pan: material ______

Water supply: ☐ public; ☐ community system; ☐ individual (private) system.★

Sewage disposal: ☐ public; ☐ community system; ☐ individual (private) system.★

★*Show and describe individual system in complete detail in separate drawings and specifications according to requirements.*

House drain (inside): ☐ cast iron; ☐ tile; ☐ other ______ House sewer (outside): ☐ cast iron; ☐ tile; ☐ other ______

Water piping: ☐ galvanized steel; ☐ copper tubing; ☐ other ______ Sill cocks, number ______

Domestic water heater: type ______; make and model ______; heating capacity ______

______ gph. 100° rise. Storage tank: material ______; capacity ______ gallons.

Gas service: ☐ utility company; ☐ liq. pet. gas; ☐ other ______ Gas piping: ☐ cooking; ☐ house heating.

Footing drains connected to: ☐ storm sewer; ☐ sanitary sewer; ☐ dry well. Sump pump; make and model ______

______; capacity ______; discharges into ______

23. HEATING:

☐ Hot water. ☐ Steam. ☐ Vapor. ☐ One-pipe system. ☐ Two-pipe system.

☐ Radiators. ☐ Convectors. ☐ Baseboard radiation. Make and model ______

Radiant panel: ☐ floor; ☐ wall; ☐ ceiling. Panel coil: material ______

☐ Circulator. ☐ Return pump. Make and model ______; capacity ______ gpm.

Boiler: make and model ______ Output ______ Btuh.; net rating ______ Btuh.

Additional information: ______

Warm air: ☐ Gravity. ☐ Forced. Type of system ______

Duct material: supply ______; return ______ Insulation ______, thickness ______ ☐ Outside air intake.

Furnace: make and model ______ Input ______ Btuh.; output ______ Btuh.

Additional information: ______

☐ Space heater; ☐ floor furnace; ☐ wall heater. Input ______ Btuh.; output ______ Btuh.; number units ______

Make, model ______ Additional information: ______

Controls: make and types ______

Additional information: ______

Fuel: ☐ Coal; ☐ oil; ☐ gas; ☐ liq. pet. gas; ☐ electric; ☐ other ______; storage capacity ______

Additional information: ______

Firing equipment furnished separately: ☐ Gas burner, conversion type. ☐ Stoker: hopper feed ☐; bin feed ☐

Oil burner: ☐ pressure atomizing; ☐ vaporizing ______

Make and model ______ Control ______

Additional information: ______

Electric heating system: type ______ Input ______ watts; @ ______ volts; output ______ Btuh.

Additional information: ______

Ventilating equipment: attic fan, make and model ______; capacity ______ cfm.

kitchen exhaust fan, make and model ______

Other heating, ventilating, or cooling equipment ______

24. ELECTRIC WIRING:

Service: ☐ overhead; ☐ underground. Panel: ☐ fuse box; ☐ circuit-breaker; make ______ AMP's ______ No. circuits ______

Wiring: ☐ conduit; ☐ armored cable; ☐ nonmetallic cable; ☐ knob and tube; ☐ other ______

Special outlets: ☐ range; ☐ water heater; ☐ other ______

☐ Doorbell. ☐ Chimes. Push-button locations ______ Additional information: ______

25. LIGHTING FIXTURES:

Total number of fixtures ______ Total allowance for fixtures, typical installation, $ ______

Nontypical installation ______

Additional information: ______

DESCRIPTION OF MATERIALS

26. INSULATION:

Location	Thickness	Material, Type, and Method of Installation	Vapor Barrier
Roof			
Ceiling			
Wall			
Floor			

HARDWARE: *(make, material, and finish.)* ______

SPECIAL EQUIPMENT: *(State material or make, model and quantity. Include only equipment and appliances which are acceptable by local law, custom and applicable FHA standards. Do not include items which, by established custom, are supplied by occupant and removed when he vacates premises or chattles prohibited by law from becoming realty.)* ______

27. MISCELLANEOUS: *(Describe any main dwelling materials, equipment, or construction items not shown elsewhere; or use to provide additional information where the space provided was inadequate. Always reference by item number to correspond to numbering used on this form.)* ______

PORCHES:

TERRACES:

GARAGES:

WALKS AND DRIVEWAYS:

Driveway: width ______ ; base material ______ ; thickness ______"; surfacing material ______ ; thickness ______"
Front walk: width ______ ; material ______ ; thickness ______". Service walk: width ______ ; material ______ ; thickness ______"
Steps: material ______ ; treads ______"; risers ______". Cheek walls ______

OTHER ONSITE IMPROVEMENTS:

(Specify all exterior onsite improvements not described elsewhere, including items such as unusual grading, drainage structures, retaining walls, fence, railings, and accessory structures.)

LANDSCAPING, PLANTING, AND FINISH GRADING:

Topsoil ______" thick: ☐ front yard; ☐ side yards; ☐ rear yard to ______ feet behind main building.
Lawns *(seeded, sodded, or sprigged)*: ☐ front yard ______ ; ☐ side yards ______ ; ☐ rear yard ______
Planting: ☐ as specified and shown on drawings; ☐ as follows:

______ Shade trees, deciduous, ______" caliper.
______ Low flowering trees, deciduous, ______' to ______'
______ High-growing shrubs, deciduous, ______' to ______'
______ Medium-growing shrubs, deciduous, ______' to ______'
______ Low-growing shrubs, deciduous, ______' to ______'

______ Evergreen trees. ______' to ______', B & B.
______ Evergreen shrubs. ______' to ______', B & B.
______ Vines, 2-year ______

IDENTIFICATION.—This exhibit shall be identified by the signature of the builder, or sponsor, and/or the proposed mortgagor if the latter is known at the time of application.

Date ______ Signature ______

Signature ______

FHA Form 2005
VA Form 26–1852

Glossary

A

Access: A passageway; a corridor between rooms.

Accordian doors: Doors that fold and are supported by rollers inserted in a track.

Air space: A space between walls; or the space between the brick veneer and the wall frame.

Anchor bolt: A bolt that is used to secure the frame of a building against wind and vibration forces.

Apron: A piece of window trim that is placed under the stool and against the wall.

Asphalt shingles: Composition roof shingles that are made from asphalt-impregnated felt covered with mineral granules.

Attic: The space or area that is located directly below the roof.

B

Backfill: Earth or other material that is placed in an area that has been excavated.

Baluster: A thin column that is used to support a railing.

Base course: A layer of aggregate that is used to stop the capillary action of ground water.

Basement: A full story space that is located below grade.

Base shoe: A piece of interior trim that is placed adjacent to the baseboard.

Batt: A type of insulation that is placed between framing members.

Batten: A thin strip of wood that is used to cover the intersection of two panels.

Beams: A principal horizontal member of a building.

Bearing plate: A plate that is used to support structural members.

Birds-mouth: A portion of a structural member that has been cut out so the member may fit over a cross timber.

Brick veneer: An outer covering of brick tied to a wall frame.

Building paper: Paper that is placed between sheathing and outside wall covering.

Building sewer: The lowest portion of a drainage system that extends from the building drain to the street sewer.

C

Capillary action: The ability of water to move through space, regardless of gravity.

Carport: Shelter for an automobile that is not fully enclosed.

Carriage: A wooden support for the treads and risers.

Column: A vertical structural member used to support structure loads.

Contour lines: Imaginary lines on a plot plan that represent particular elevations.

Convector: An electric hot water or steam heating room unit.

Cornice: A part of the exterior trim that is located where the roof and side walls meet.

Cove: A piece of concave molding.

Crawl space: The space between the first floor and the surface ground.

Cripple: A stud that is cut less than full length.

D

Dead load: A stationary load imposed on a structure; a constant weight.

Deformed bar: A reinforcing bar that has a lub-like ridge around it to provide a tight bond with surrounding concrete.

Degree: One 360th part of a circumference of a circle.

Direct lighting: A lighting system where the majority of the light is directed downward.

Door casing: The trim that is placed around a door opening.

Door jamb: The vertical and horizontal piece of wood that is placed in the rough door opening.

Drain tile: A pipe that is used to carry ground water to a storm sewer or dry stream bed.

Drywall: A type of interior wall finish that is placed without the use of water.

Duct: A round or rectangular pipe used for distributing warm or cool air.

Duplex outlet: An electrical wall outlet that has two plug receptacles.

E

Eaves: A part of the roof that projects over the side wall.

Elbow: A plumbing fitting that is used to make a 90-degree turn.

Elevation: A modified orthographic drawing that shows one side of an object.

Excavate: To remove earth below grade level.

Expansion joint: A space between members that allows for possible expansion and contraction.

F

Fascia: A board that is placed at the lower end of the rafter tails; it can be used by itself or in combination with moldings.

Fill: Soil or loose rock that is used to raise a grade.

Fire resistance: The ability of a material to withstand fire or give protection from it.

Flashing: A particular type of material used to cover open joists to make them waterproof.

Flitch beam: A built-up beam constructed by placing a metal insert between two wooden members.

Footings: An enlarged portion of the foundation that spreads and transmits imposed loads.

Frieze: A horizontal band that is placed at or near the top of a wall.

Furr down: A drop in ceiling height, usually found over kitchen cabinets.

Furring: Thin strips of wood that are used to level a surface.

G

Gable: The triangular portion of a side wall that is located above the eave line.

Girder: A main supporting element of the floor frame.

Glazing: The placing of glass in an opening.

Grade: The slope, elevation, or face of the ground.

Grade beam: A horizontal foundation member.

Grout: A fluid mixture or portland cement, sand, and water that is used to fill joints or masonry and tile.

Gypsum: Commonly known as plaster of paris; a mineral, hydrous sulphate of calcium.

Gypsum wallboard: A sheet of wallboard that has a core of gypsum sandwiched between covers of paper.

H

Header: A wooden structural member that is placed at right angles to joist.

Headlap: A portion of a shingle that is covered by another shingle.

Hip: The angle that is formed by the intersection of two sloping roofs.

Hip jack rafter: A short rafter that extends from the plate to the hip rafter.

Hip rafter: A rafter that is used to form the hip of a roof.

Hip roof: A roof that is inclined from all four sides.

House drain: The main lower horizontal pipe that receives the discharge of soil and waste stacks.

I

Insulation: A material used for the reduction of heat gain and heat loss.

J

Jamb: The exposed interior lining of an opening.

L

Lally column: A cylindrically shaped steel member that is used as a girder or beam; the steel member is sometimes filled with concrete.

Lath: A base for plastering, usually expanded metal.

Lookout: The supporting agency for the soffit.

Loop vent: A pipe that connects to the stack vent to prevent back siphonage.

Louver: An opening used for ventilating closed areas.

M

Masonry: A type of construction that is composed of shaped or molded units.

Mullion: The thin vertical bars that separate the individual lights in a window.

N

Nominal size: The size of lumber before it is planed.

Nosing: The projecting part of windowsill or stair tread.

O

On center: The distance from the center of one structural member to the center of another.

Outlet: A distribution source for electrical current.

Overhang: The projection of a roof beyond the supporting wall.

P

Patio: A surfaced area that is an extension of the residence; the area can be partially or entirely enclosed by the residence.

Perspective: A pictorial drawing that is used to illustrate design principles.

Pier: A support for beams and girders, usually constructed of concrete or masonry.

Pilaster: A columnar projection that is part of the foundation wall.

Pitch: The degree of inclination of a roof.

Plate: A flat horizontal member that is connected to the top and bottom of the studs.

Plenum: A chamber or area forming a part of an air-conditioning system.

Porch: A roofed structure placed at an entrance to a building.

Purlin: A horizontal member that is used to brace the rafters.

Q

Quarter round: A small piece of molding that has a quarter circle profile.

R

Rafter: A structural member that is used to support roof loads.

Register: The end of a duct, usually covered with grillework.

Reinforcement bar: Metal bars that are embedded in concrete.

Ridge: The uppermost horizontal board of a roof.

Riser: The vertical board of a stair that is placed under the nosing.

Rough opening: An unfinished opening.

Run: In roof construction, the horizontal distance between the ridge and the face of a wall. In stair construction, the horizontal distance covered by the stairs.

S

Saddle: A raised area behind the chimney that is used to support flashing and divert moisture away from the chimney.

Sash: The framework that holds glass in a window.

Schedule: A collection of organized notes.

Setback: An imaginary line established by law or deed restriction, fixing the distance from the property line to the face of a building.

Sheathing: Exterior wall or roof covering, usually plywood or nominal 1" x 6" boards.

Sill: A horizontal structural member that is placed on top of a foundation wall. In a door frame, the sill is a horizontal board that is placed at the bottom of the frame.

Soffit: A board attached to the underside of the rafter tail.

Soil stack: A vertical pipe that receives the discharge of a fixture that receives human excreta specifications.

Subfloor: A floor that is nailed directly to the floor joist, to which a finished floor is placed.

Symbol: A mark, character, or figure that represents the name of something.

T

Thermostat: An automatic device that is used to regulate the temperature of a room.

Trap: A device used to prevent sewer gases from escaping through a plumbing fixture.

Trimmer: A part of the floor frame that is placed around an opening in the floor.

Truss: An assemblage of structural members fastened together to form a supporting assembly for the roof sheathing.

V

Valley rafter: The diagonal rafter placed at the intersection of two sloping roofs.

Vapor barrier: A material that is used to stop the flow of vapor into a wall or floor.

Veneer: A thin layer of wood that is laminated to a support.

Veneered construction: A method of construction where face brick or other facing material is applied to a frame wall.

Vent stack: A vertical pipe that carries foul gases from a building and prevents back siphonage.

W

Wall tie: A small piece of metal that is used to bind brick veneer to the wall frame.

Water closet: A toilet that flushes.

Weep hole: Small openings left in masonry walls to permit drainage and reduce pressures.